International Multiparty Mediation and Conflict Management

T0271889

This volume aims to provide a detailed explanation of the effects of cooperation and coordination on international multiparty mediation in conflicts.

Contemporary scholarship stresses that the crucial ingredients for a successful multiparty mediation are 'consistency in interests' and 'cooperation and coordination' between mediators. This book seeks to supplement that understanding by investigating how much the 'consistency of interests' and 'cooperation and coordination' affect the overall process, and what happens to the mediation process when mediating parties do not share the same idea and interest in finding a common solution. At the same time, it explores the obstacles in achieving coordination and coherence between various mediators in such an environment and how to surmount the problems that multiple mediators face when operating without a 'common script' in attempting to mediate a negotiated settlement.

The study investigates three distinct mechanisms (both on the systemic and contextual level) that have the potential to deter defection from a (potential) member of the multiparty mediation coalition: geo-political shifts, changes in the conflict dynamics, and mediators' ability to bargain for a cooperative relationship. As the number of states and international actors that are involved in mediation increases, a careful assessment is necessary not only of their relative institutional strengths and weaknesses, but also of how to promote complementary efforts and how to synchronize the whole process when one actor is transferring the responsibilities for mediation to others.

This book will be of much interest to students of mediation, conflict management, war and conflict studies, security studies and IR.

Siniša Vuković is Assistant Professor at the School of Advanced International Studies (SAIS), Johns Hopkins University. He is also a visiting professor at the University of Amsterdam, Leiden University, Radboud University Nijmegen and the University for Peace. He has a PhD in international relations from Leiden University.

Series: Security and Conflict Management
Series Editors:
Fen Osler Hampson
Carleton University, Canada
Chester Crocker
Georgetown University, Washington DC
Pamela Aall
United States Institute of Peace, Washington DC

This series will publish the best work in the field of security studies and conflict management. In particular, it will promote leading-edge work that straddles the divides between conflict management and security studies, between academics and practitioners, and between disciplines.

Aid, Insurgencies and Conflict Transformation
When greed is good
Rob Kevlihan

Human Security in Turkey
Challenges for the 21st century
Edited by Alpaslan Özerdem and Füsun Özerdem

Understanding Complex Military Operations
A case study approach
Edited by Volker Franke, Karen Guttieri and Melanne A. Civic

Regional Organisations and Peacemaking
Challengers to the UN
Edited by Peter Wallensteen and Anders Bjurner

International Mediation Bias and Peacemaking
Taking sides in civil wars
Isak Svensson

Conflict Management in International Missions
A field guide
Olav Ofstad

International Multiparty Mediation and Conflict Management
Challenges of cooperation and coordination
Siniša Vuković

International Multiparty Mediation and Conflict Management

Challenges of cooperation and coordination

Siniša Vuković

Routledge
Taylor & Francis Group

LONDON AND NEW YORK

First published 2016
by Routledge

2 Park Square, Milton Park, Abingdon, Oxon OX14 4RN
711 Third Avenue, New York, NY 10017, USA

Routledge is an imprint of the Taylor & Francis Group, an informa business

First issued in paperback 2017

British Library Cataloguing-in-Publication Data
A catalogue record for this book is available from the British Library

Library of Congress Cataloging-in-Publication Data
Vukovic, Siniša, 1973–
International multiparty mediation and conflict management : challenges
of cooperation and coordination / Siniša Vukovic.
   pages cm. – (Security and conflict management)
   Includes bibliographical references and index.
   1. Mediation, International. 2. Mediation, International–Case studies.
   3. Conflict management. 4. Conflict management–Case studies. I. Title.
   JZ6045.V85 2016
   341.5'2–dc23   2015016775

ISBN: 978-1-138-80958-1 (hbk)
ISBN: 978-1-138-08789-7 (pbk)

Typeset in Times New Roman
by Wearset Ltd, Boldon, Tyne and Wear

Contents

Illustrations

Figures

Tables

Acknowledgments

The present volume is a result of a post-doctoral research project "Modeling and Analyzing Multiparty Mediation Processes" supported by the Netherlands Organization for Scientific Research under the *Rubicon* research grant (file number 446–12–004). I am thankful to the Conflict Management Program of the Johns Hopkins University's School of Advanced International Studies (SAIS) for hosting this research, and providing an exceptional working environment. I would like to express my most sincere gratitude to I. William Zartman and P. Terrence Hopmann for their continuous encouragement, patient guidance and useful critiques of my research, and to Madeleine O. Hosli and Paul Meerts for their generous advice and assistance in broadening the scope of my research and disseminating it at various research institutes around the world. I would like to extend my gratitude to Maria Groenveld-Savisaar for her outstanding work on the Sri Lankan case, to Jessica Kroezen in editing this volume, Isak Svesson for his valuable comments, and Ben Allen for his help in developing the game theoretical model during our research experience at the International Institute for Applied Systems Analysis (IIASA). The early empirical findings of this research were defended as a doctoral thesis at Leiden University's Institute of Political Science. Last but not least, I thank my family for their unconditional support and encouragement to pursue my interests and follow my dreams. Any potential error of fact or interpretation in this manuscript is my sole responsibility.

Introduction

In an international system devoid of any central authority, mediation has often been advocated as being the most appropriate tactic in the realm of third-party conflict management. Traditional academic literature on international mediation derived most of its insights from labor-management disputes (Zartman 2008). These insights largely relied on the assumption that mediation is conducted by a single trustworthy third party that is does not have a stake in the conflict or its outcome. Over the past three decades, this traditional conceptualization of international mediation has experienced important advancements and change. For instance, as will be illustrated later in this book, over time, the issue of impartiality has been challenged and several theories specified conditions under which a third party's bias might not be a liability to the peace-process. Similarly, mediation is no longer viewed as a mere dynamic of facilitating communication between conflicting parties, where third parties have very limited (if any) control over the conflict management process. Rather, mediators' involvement is increasingly viewed to be pivotal in altering parties' perceptions and preferences, and they do this not only by facilitating communication, but also by formulating viable solutions and incentivizing the parties to accept the terms that were initially unthinkable. As such, mediation is today defined simply as a process in which a third party helps conflicting sides to find a solution to their conflict that they cannot find themselves (Touval and Zartman 2006). Nevertheless, despite these important theoretical developments, the core assumption that mediation is conducted by a *single* third party still limits the practical applicability of various academic studies of international mediation.

As numerous cases around the world have shown, international conflicts are increasingly being managed by more than one third party. Mediation increasingly involves more than one third party, and the growing prevalence of this model makes it imperative that we understand the costs and benefits of this multiparty intervention. While much has been written about the damaging effects of uncooperative multiparty mediation have on a peace process, this book explores another perspective – the benefits both to the peace processes and to the third parties themselves of cooperative action. It bases its conclusion on insights from game theory and an in-depth review of five cases of mediation. Given the increasing pervasiveness of this model it is crucial to understand its practical and theoretical ramifications. Although some studies have devoted their attention in unveiling the effects of uncooperative relations between multiple mediators, this book takes on a different focus: it looks at the potential benefits that cooperative behavior may generate both for the peace process and for the third parties themselves. The conclusions are drawn from insights developed through a game theoretical model and an in-depth analysis of five cases of mediation.

Take this case, for example. Following the dissolution of the Soviet Union, in the early 1990s the United Nations Secretary General (UNSG) entered a peacemaking process aimed at mediating an escalating conflict between Georgia and the breakaway republic of Abkhazia. Alongside the UNSG was Russia, formally entrusted with the role of 'facilitator.' Russian interest in managing the conflict was a direct consequence of its desire to maintain its strong influence in its 'near abroad.' Furthermore, a group of Western states – the United States of America (US), the United Kingdom (UK), Germany and France – joined the UNSCG as 'Friends of Georgia.' As the number of interested external actors increased, so did the complexity of the peacemaking process. The process was complex not only because of the long duration of the conflict's destructive phase. In fact, the 13 months of violence were suspended with a cease-fire agreement facilitated by Russia under the auspices of the UN. Russian influence in the region was soon reflected in the choice of peacekeeping troops that were dispatched to the war-affected areas: instead of UN troops, the peacekeeping operation was entrusted to Russian forces, formally under the mandate of the Commonwealth of Independent States (CIS). The cease-fire agreement was never superseded by a comprehensive peace settlement. According to Whitefield there were two fundamental problems with the peacemaking process:

> The first was the enduring importance to Russia of Georgia and the significance of Abkhazia in relations between the two. The second was that differences between the principal external actors widened. To Russia's evident frustration, the "western Friends" (long perceived as partial by the Abkhaz for their robust defence of Georgia's territorial sovereignty) encouraged Georgia in aspirations that included one day joining NATO. No confidence in a negotiated solution could be built and a complex spiral of events descended downwards towards the open conflict seen between Georgia and Russia in August 2008.
>
> (Whitefield 2010, 15)

Evidently, in the Georgia-Abkhazia conflict, incompatibility of interests between various external actors prevented the mediation process from resulting in a peaceful solution. A similar trend was also seen during the dissolution of the former Yugoslavia in the early 1990s when a variety of international actors tried to reduce the differences between the conflicting parties and bring them to a mutually acceptable agreement. The principal mediators came from the governments of the member states of the European Union (EU), the US and Russia, as well from various international organizations such as the United Nations and the

EU. The sheer number of international actors that took part in the peacemaking processes meant that most peacemaking activities were conducted collectively, either via formal frameworks of international organizations or in ad hoc formats such as the Contact Groups. Touval notes that:

> [t]he collective endeavours pursued through the EC/EU, the UN and the Contact Group were encumbered with significant disadvantages. The participating states often disagreed about the policy to be pursued, causing the disputants to doubt the credibility of the international organizations' and Contact Group's promises and threats. These weaknesses of the collective mediation efforts detracted significantly from their effectiveness.
>
> (Touval 2002, 8)

The concept of international mediation generally refers to mediation activities conducted by various international actors with the aim of managing international conflicts on interstate (between countries) and intrastate (between governments and groups challenging their power) levels. Just as disputants in such conflicts can be both state and non-state actors, third-parties that might have an interest to mediate these conflicts can be just as diverse, and include: representatives of states (neighboring ones, global powers, states of medium and small relative size); representatives of global and regional international organizations; representatives of global NGOs (which could include religious organizations, interest groups with an international agenda, etc.); and, finally, even individuals (such as Jimmy Carter, Desmond Tutu, Maarti Ahtisaari, etc.) who have an established international reputation in managing international conflicts and are able to act as mediators without a formal mandate from a particular state or international organization. Contemporary scholarship defines the processes in which a conflict is managed (i.e., mediated) by more than one third party as *multiparty mediation* (Crocker *et al.* 1999; Crocker *et al.* 2001). Existing literature on international mediation has often emphasized the benefits of having multiple mediators working in concert. As put by Zartman, "if a number of conciliators are available to the parties themselves and if a number of friends of the conflicting parties can coordinate their good offices and pressure, the chances of success are improved" (1989, 276). At present, several studies have outlined the potential benefits and liabilities associated with having multiple mediators (Crocker *et al.* 1999, 2001; Diehl and Lepgold 2003), the relationship between the size of the mediating coalition and its effectiveness (Böhmelt 2011) and the need to have a cooperative endeavor by multiple mediators in order to achieve success in the mediation process (Whitefield 2007; Böhmelt 2011; Hampson and Zartman 2011). There are a number of benefits that collective activities bring to the mediation process. When mediators decide to work together they can pool in their resources and create incentives that would otherwise be unavailable to a single party. At the same time, they can share the costs and burdens associated with the peacemaking process. Furthermore, depending on their capabilities, they can enter the process at a particular stage, when their leverage can be put to use most effectively and by means of a coordinated effort, induce the conflicting parties to accept a negotiated agreement. However, all these benefits become elusive if the mediators do not have a shared understanding of how the conflict should be managed and what kind of outcome should be pursued. In such circumstances, the mediators may start sending mixed signals to the conflicting parties, start working at cross purposes and seriously jeopardize the effectiveness of the peacemaking process.

With this in mind, contemporary studies of multiparty mediation are unanimous in their claim that *cooperation* is the key ingredient for successful multiparty mediation. However, apart from having empirically confirmed that cooperation exerts a positive influence on multiparty mediation effectiveness (Böhmelt 2011, 874), the complexities of cooperation as a concept have not yet been scrutinized. As such, the studies mentioned above fall short in some areas. First of all, the concept of cooperation has often been seen as being synonymous with the concept of coordination, which has limited the analytical depth of some studies. Secondly, in each study, cooperation has been treated as a static phenomenon, on that does not change over time, but is observed in a binary manner: as present or not, throughout the entire process. Therefore, what these studies fail to integrate is the impact of a potential change in mediator attitudes that might occur over the course of the process. In other words, while in the beginning one mediator might show a clear intention to cooperate with the rest of the mediating coalition and thus contribute to the potential overall effectiveness of the process, along the way, as the mediating process unfolds, due to different circumstances, this attitude might change completely. Similarly, an initially non-cooperative mediator might eventually alter its preferences and decide to cooperate with the rest of the mediators. The fact that a mediator's attitude might change from favoring cooperative to non-cooperative behavior and *vice versa* throughout the process will inevitably have an effect on the effectiveness of the mediating coalition.

Although considerable progress has been made in studying multiparty mediation, the process still poses several unanswered questions. Following the logic of earlier studies that challenged the traditional literature on the impartiality of mediators, contemporary research on multiparty mediation still lacks a clear emphasis on the particular self-interests that drive various mediators to get involved in managing the conflict. Third parties often publically invoke humanitarian concerns as their sole motivation to act as mediators. However, given the considerable costs that mediation entails, it is reasonable to presume that mediators are at least as motivated by self-interest as by humanitarian impulses (Touval and Zartman 1985, 8). Mediation represents a useful foreign policy tool that helps international actors promote specific self-interests (Touval 1992). As such, the investment of substantial material and non-material resources should not be seen as only being aimed at resolving a dispute; this investment is also made so that mediators might gain something from managing the dispute (Greig 2005). Thus, just as a mediator's involvement needs to be compatible with its self-interest, its choice to cooperate once it has committed to mediation also needs to be perceived as useful for the promotion of its self-interest.

International conflicts usually draw all sorts of outside actors into the mediation process that are "just as numerous and frequently as diverse in their interests as the warring parties themselves" (Hampson and Zartman 2012, 133). Since each mediator will try to promote their own self-interest, the greater the number of participants in a multiplayer mediation effort, the greater the probability of conflicting interests and positions existing and the more complex the relationship between the parties will be (Crocker *et al.* 1999). Potential conflict of mediator interests will have a direct impact on the likelihood of achieving cooperation. In other words, compatibility or convergence of interests between mediators is a necessary precondition for the achievement of cooperation. The intention of this volume is to confer a special focus on the impact of 'drop-outs' – mediators that, due to various circumstances, believe that non-cooperative behavior is in their self-interest and as such choose not to cooperate with the rest of the mediating coalition – and potential factors that might change their general strategy/attitude from defection to cooperation. As a result, this book will emphasize the importance of three basic factors – exogenous geo-political shifts, changes in conflict dynamics and bargaining for cooperation – that might induce mediators to alter their attitude from non-cooperative to cooperative.

These factors have not been chosen randomly. Even though mediators enter the peacemaking process with the aim of affecting and altering the conflictual relations between the parties to a dispute, a potential incompatibility of interests in the mediating coalition generates a novel conflict between mediators that needs to be overcome. A conflict becomes ripe for resolution when the parties perceive that their unilateral and non-cooperative strategies are no longer yielding the expected results. As the parties become aware of the fact that they are stuck in a painful and unbearable stalemate, they may seek a way out of this predicament by pursuing a cooperative endeavor like engaging in negotiations (Zartman 2001). The aforementioned three factors are directly related to the process of ripening the conflict between mediators for resolution. Exogenous geo-political shifts, caused by pivotal political, social, economic and/or natural events, might strongly affect an actor's strategic priorities and encourage it to re-evaluate the guiding principles of its foreign policies. These may include the escalation of a parallel conflict, the occurrence of a disastrous natural or man-made event or a change in control at the level of political elites that present a novel formulation of foreign policy priorities for the mediators. Changes in conflict dynamics are directly related to the possibility that some external actors might be directly involved in supporting the belligerent activities of one or more conflicting parties. As the costs of fighting increase, external supporters may start perceiving the continuation of confrontational strategies as being unsustainable. The perception of a 'hurting stalemate' may induce them to explore cooperation as an alternative means of achieving their goals. Finally, external actors may decide to incentivize non-cooperative third parties to assume a stance that is more favorable to compromise, by forming a 'team of rivals' through which mediators may negotiate the terms of their cooperation.

Once external actors achieve the necessary convergence of interests, the mediating coalition will then have to overcome the challenge of *coordinating* different mediators' actions. While in earlier studies, the conceptual difference between coordination and cooperation was blurry at best, the research presented here will aim to avoid the analytical limitations associated with this lack of conceptual clarity. When joining a mediating coalition, each mediator enters with a specific set of resources that could be used to leverage the disputants towards a mutually acceptable solution. The theory of international mediation defines these resources as power or leverage, which is 'the ability to move a party in an intended direction' (Touval and Zartman 2006, 436). This ability derives from the very fact that disputing sides need the mediators' assistance to find a solution to their problems (Touval and Zartman 1985; Touval 1992). Earlier studies have shown that one of the most important comparative advantages of multiparty mediation efforts is in the dynamic created by various mediators pooling their resources, which allows for the creation of the necessary incentives for resolution that would have otherwise been unavailable from a single mediator (Crocker *et al.* 1999). The harmonious employment of various sources of leverage can be instrumental to the effectiveness of the mediation process – "where direct leverage is limited it may be borrowed from others" (Crocker *et al.* 1999, 40). *Coordination* is defined here as the method of synchronized usage of different sources of leverage and resources each mediator has at its disposal in the process in order to create incentives that are instrumental to successfully resolving the conflict. Since power/leverage is never employed aimlessly, the decision to use a particular type of leverage (depending on the mediator's relative capacities) will be directly linked to the self-interest that the mediator aims to promote in the process.

In essence, the aim of this volume is to explain in more detail the effects of cooperation and coordination on multiparty mediation. As previous studies have shown, the crucial challenges that must be overcome in multiparty mediation processes are (1) the achievement of adequate *cooperation* between the mediators and (2) consequent *coordination* of their activities in the mediation process. While the two concepts share the common presumption that actors involved in the mediating coalition need to be in agreement as to how to resolve the conflict, there is still a clear difference between the two: a necessary prerequisite for a successful cooperation is that all parties recognize the mutual benefits of working together; once the parties perceive the benefits of working together, cooperation may lead to a coordinated endeavor which implies a more mechanical process of dividing labor effectively and clarifying who needs to do what, when and how.

With all this in mind, the crucial ingredients for successful multiparty mediation seem to be '*consistency of interests*' and '*cooperation and coordination*' between mediators. The aim of this book is to further expand the existing body of knowledge on multiparty mediation by answering a number of questions. First of all, how much do 'consistency of interests' and 'cooperation and coordination' affect the overall process? Given the dynamic nature of cooperation and the likelihood that a party will change its behavior from cooperative to non-cooperative in the process of multiparty mediation, it is important to know whether or not the efforts that do not enjoy cooperation inevitably end in failure. Similarly, what happens to the mediation process when mediating parties do not share the same idea of and interests in a common solution? At the same time, the obstacles to achieving coordination and coherence between various mediators in such an environment will be explored and the question of how the problems that multiple mediators face can be surmounted when they operate without a 'common script' in attempting to mediate a negotiated settlement. In other words, this study will investigate which mechanisms (both at the systemic and contextual level) have the potential to deter the defection of a (potential) member of the multiparty mediation coalition? Finally, as the number of states and international actors that are involved in mediation increases, a careful assessment is necessary not only of their relative institutional strengths and weaknesses, but also of how best to promote complementary efforts and how to synchronize the whole process when one actor transfers the responsibility for mediation to others. This book seeks to point out the importance of the self-interest that motivates third parties to get involved and to unveil the link between coordination and self-interest (also described as strategic interests) and the impact of these interactions on the overall effectiveness of the mediation process.

Multiparty mediation is not a new theory of mediation, rather it is an advancement of existing knowledge. Therefore, this volume will start by laying out a theoretical framework of mediation in Chapter 1. Existing literature will reflect the multi-causal nature of the mediation process, in which the interplay of a variety of factors (systemic and behavioral) directly affects the effectiveness of the process. The chapter will first provide an operational definition of international mediation and will highlight its most fundamental characteristics. Special attention is paid to the elusive notion of a mediator's impartiality, followed by a more nuanced discussion of two types of biases that mediators may bring to the process: bias of actor and bias of outcome. Furthermore, the chapter reflects on the various motives that induce the conflicting parties to accept mediation and the interests that drive mediators to get involved. The discussion also addresses different types of third parties that may have an interest in getting involved in managing the conflict, the relevant leverage they possess and strategies that they can employ in the process. The chapter also reflects on the intractable nature of conflicts that elicit mediation by external actors because the disputing sides are either unable or unwilling to find a solution on their own. Finally, the chapter concludes with an explanation of the various degrees of success in international mediation.

Once the fundamental theoretical framework of international mediation has been described, the discussion will move on to the state of the art of multiparty mediation in Chapter 2. The chapter will start by discussing the potential benefits and liabilities associated with multiparty mediation initiatives, the comparative advantages of multiparty mediation processes in light of their composition and the stage of the conflict cycle. The chapter will then address the most challenging task that any multiparty mediation endeavor is faced with:

the achievement of the necessary level of cooperation between multiple mediators and subsequent coordination of their mediating activities. Given the limitations of the literature with regard to cooperation and coordination, the core arguments will be expanded and illustrated with the help of a game theoretical model, developed in order to observe a general pattern of mediator behavior in multiparty mediation. Reflecting on the insights from the model and existing multiparty mediation literature, the chapter will offer an argument that cooperation and coordination are not only instrumental to the peacemaking process, but are highly significant to mediators themselves and that such dynamics generate greater benefits than any strategy of defection.

Furthermore, this chapter will explore potential mechanisms that can induce cooperation between the third-parties. As each mediator enters the process with a specific set of interests, preferences and alliances, in the case their interests become incompatible, the peacemaking process becomes further complicated by an emerging conflict between mediators. Expanding on the existing notions of ripeness theory (Zartman 1989a, 2001), this chapter will propose three distinct mechanisms that can ripen the conflict between mediators for resolution and promote cooperative behavior in the mediating coalition: exogenous geopolitical shifts, changes in conflict dynamics, and bargaining for cooperation. Subsequently, the chapter will illustrate various mechanisms intended to facilitate coordination between mediators, and emphasize the relevance of leadership in multiparty mediation efforts.

The insights from the proposed theoretical framework in Chapter 2 will be applied to the contexts of five cases of contemporary multiparty mediation (Chapters 3–7). While three cases that were selected had a successful outcome (Tajikistan, Namibia and Cambodia) and two of them failed (Sri Lanka and Kosovo), all the cases provide a comprehensive, structured and focused analysis (George and Bennett 2005; Beach and Pedersen 2012) of the effects of cooperation and coordination on the multiparty mediation process. The cases offer an abundance of empirical evidence of the various dynamics that have contributed to the achievement of cooperation between mediators and of the effects of coordinated activities on the peacemaking process. The cases also show the dynamic nature of cooperation, as the parties may have altered their priorities throughout the process. As a consequence, these changes – either related to various exogenous geo-political shifts, the conflict dynamics on the ground or the fact that the external actors managed to negotiate their cooperation – had a significant impact on the conflicting parties and their behavior in the peacemaking process. The last chapter (Chapter 8) offers a summary of the core findings of this research project and outlines the potential relevance of these findings in terms of policy making. It provides a discussion of various factors that could induce a change in mediator attitudes and promote cooperative behavior within the mediating coalition, which in turn has the capacity to improve the chances of successfully managing the conflict.

1 Theory of international mediation[1]

Conflict management repertoire

Conflicts are interactions in which two or more actors see their goals as being mutually incompatible. Despite the fact that, within the vast spectrum of all social processes, conflicts are seen as the most insidious and costly, they are not always violent and destructive. Rather, they may be waged according to the rules and procedures that parties have agreed to in advance. According to Kriesberg, these 'constructive' conflicts are especially common at the domestic level, where they tend to be regulated and channeled through existing political and judicial institutions and, as such, represent an essential feature of democracy (Kriesberg 2003). Nevertheless, many conflicts are not managed in the context of preexisting institutional arrangements. And this is particularly true for conflicts that occur at the international level, which may last for a long period of time during which the parties resort to destructive measures in order to advance their interests. In their fundamental form, destructive conflicts imply a methodical employment of various forms of violence, ranging from physical to cultural and structural[2] (Galtung 1969, 1990; Crocker *et al.* 2005). Numerous studies have shown that human causalities and material damage, produced in such conflicts, are generally regarded as the most salient type of political costs a society can incur (Mueller 1973; Gartner and Segura 1998, 2000; Gartner *et al.* 2004). Not surprisingly, there is an increasing demand to manage conflicts coming from the same (political) actors that are involved in them, accompanied by pressures from both local and global civil society.

Conflicts often produce high levels of distrust, resulting in a significant (if not complete) breakdown of communication. In these conditions, parties are frequently either unable or unwilling to reach a mutually acceptable solution on their own. For this reason, conflicting parties might find it useful to delegate conflict management activities to a distinct third party. Broadly speaking, third-party intervention varies from joining the dispute (i.e., taking the side of one of the disputants) to managing one. Conflict management efforts may assume different forms and encompass a wide range of activities, the use of which depends on the extent of the third party's commitment to managing the dispute. Frazier and Dixon have developed a useful taxonomy of conflict management activities and identify five main forms: verbal actions, diplomatic approaches, judicial processes, administrative assistance and the use of military force.

Verbal actions represent the most passive form of conflict management and can be observed in various statements issued by third parties in which they urge the belligerents to end violence and resort to peaceful means in order to settle their dispute. Given the low cost of such efforts, in the period between 1946 and 2000, verbal actions represented the bulk (nearly 44%) of all third-party activities (Frazier and Dixon 2006, 395). Nevertheless, as Frazier and Dixon argue, third parties activity was 'not all talk,' as diplomatic efforts (namely mediation) accounted for just over 40% of third-party activities (Frazier and Dixon 2006, 395). The last three types – judicial processes (for example arbitration or the use of war crime tribunals), administrative assistance (such as humanitarian aid, election supervision and monitoring) and military intervention (such as military observation, peacekeeping and demobilization monitoring) – comprised a rather small fraction of third-party activities. As they imply increased levels of commitment (in terms of financial costs or providing personnel and necessary logistic support), the last three forms together amounted close to 16% of all conflict management activities.

In practice, various methods of conflict management show a strong degree of interdependence. This is especially true of verbal actions and mediation efforts. Mediation efforts often follow up other conflict management activities, including previous mediation attempts. However, since verbal expressions also include third parties' offers to mediate the dispute, mediation and verbal strategies complement each other most often (Greig and Diehl 2012). According to Oswiak, third parties are most inclined to reuse less costly methods: while in more than 50% of cases mediation efforts were followed by verbal action through which violence was denounced and parties were called to reach a cease-fire, mediators were more reluctant to resort to more costly strategies such as economic sanctions or military intervention (Oswiak 2014).

In line with its popularity in practice, mediation has also been deemed the most efficient method of managing conflicts through peaceful means in the academic literature.[3] The growing academic interest in mediation was also fueled by the acknowledgment that a large number of internationalized conflicts were not as often and as easily handled by other modes of conflict management, such as legal tribunals, arbitration or the use of force. In fact, compared to other forms, mediation represents a relatively low-cost alternative to the options of doing nothing and a conducting a large-scale military intervention.

What is mediation?

Definitional characteristics

The popularity of mediation as a method of conflict management can be traced back to its definitional characteristics. Mediation represents a form of 'assisted negotiation,' in which an external actor enters the peacemaking process in order to influence and alter the character of previous relations between the conflicting sides (Bercovitch and Jackson 2009). It is a voluntary, non-coercive and legally non-binding activity that is particularly practical given the intricate dynamics of international relations that are dominated by the principles of the preservation of actors' independence and autonomy (Bercovitch 2005). Given its low degree of intrusiveness and ad-hoc nature, mediation allows the parties to maintain their autonomy throughout the decision-making process (Frazier and Dixon 2006; Greig and Diehl 2012). To use the argument put forward by Touval and Zartman, mediation should be understood as a "political process with no advance commitment from the parties to accept mediator's ideas" (Touval and Zartman 2001, 427).

Elusive nature of mediator's impartiality

While over time scholars have managed to reach an overwhelming consensus on the necessary characteristics that a mediator should possess in order to successfully assist the parties in reaching a solution, one issue has remained controversial: mediator impartiality. Early studies that followed the logic of domestic mediation, considered impartiality to be a fundamental and even definitional characteristic of a mediator, as without it, one cannot even speak of mediation (Jackson 1952; Assefa 1987; Burton and Dukes 1990; Miall 1992; Hume 1994). According to these studies, there was a clear causal link between impartiality and mediation effectiveness: a mediator's impartiality was essential to instilling confidence on the part of the conflicting sides, which was necessary to a mediator's being accepted. This in turn, was fundamental to producing a successful outcome of the mediation. By relying purely on persuasion, mediators were supposed to facilitate the impaired communication between the disputants and formulate potential solutions based on the newly provided information. For instance, Raymond and Kegley (1985) defined mediation as an activity in which a third party helps the disputants to reach a voluntary agreement using facilitative methods such as agenda setting, simplification of communication, clarification of respective positions, issue 'reconceptualization,' bargaining facilitation and support for agreement. Similarly, for Moore (1986), mediation should be seen as an extension of the negotiation process, in which an 'acceptable, impartial and neutral' third party, holding no 'authoritative' power, assists the conflicting parties in reaching a mutually acceptable settlement.

Insights derived from domestic mediation are still fundamental to our understanding of international mediation and there is a great deal of overlap in the theoretical understanding of both dynamics. The particular differences that can be found between the two processes are a direct result of the context in which they are conducted. In an international system that is devoid of a central authority, various international actors conduct mediation activities in conditions that differ greatly from those found at the domestic level. Although there are still strong similarities between the processes of international and domestic mediation, lack of a clear structure at the international level, where actors seek to preserve their independence at all costs, has made international mediation efforts more susceptible to the particular self-interests that drive various international actors to get involved in mediating a particular international conflict. While in certain domestic settings mediation is per definition conducted by a single, trustworthy third party that has no stake in the dispute, international conflicts usually attract and bring into the mediation process different types of outside actors that are "just as numerous and frequently as diverse in their interests as the warring parties themselves" (Hampson and Zartman 2012, 133). As pointed out by Bercovitch and Jackson:

> Mediators bring with them consciously or otherwise, ideas, knowledge, resources and interests, of their own or of the group they represent. Mediators often have their own assumptions and agendas about the conflict in question.
>
> (Bercovitch and Jackson 2009, 35)

Types of bias

Preferences that mediators bring with them to the process are reflected in two types of bias. The first type of bias can be traced back to the interests that drive mediators to enter the process. The assumptions and agendas that the mediators have about the conflict may shape their preferences for the type of outcome that is being pursued through mediation. The *bias of outcome* might be seen as a serious source of problems in terms of bargaining dynamics, as it reduces the range of possible outcomes for the disputing sides. Nevertheless, this bias engenders a higher degree of predictability for the process and a sense of direction for the parties. When Richard Holbrooke brought together representatives of the three warring factions in the Bosnian civil war to the Dayton air-force base, he immediately laid down his plan for the future of Bosnia – a unified country, within its existing borders, composed of two parts (entities) – which was used as a foundation for the subsequent negotiations between the parties (Holbrooke 1998). His preferences eliminated the possibility of exploring options such as partition, integration of particular parts into the neighboring countries or a complete redrawing of borders based on the principle of ethnicity (Touval 2002). Another illustrative case of bias of outcome is the Soviet mediation of the Indo-Pakistani dispute over Kashmir in 1966. While the Soviet Union had often been perceived as being biased toward India during the Krushchev administration, following his removal from power in 1965, the new Kosygin regime took a more balanced stance vis-à-vis the parties (Thornton 1985). During the talks in Tashkent in 1966, the Soviet Union had a strong strategic interest in ending the hostilities between India and Pakistan; however this interest had less to do with the actual conflict in Kashmir, and more to do with an increasing Chinese influence in the region. As pointed out by Beber, "Kosygin was biased toward Chinese influence in South Asia, but not biased toward either of the disputants negotiating at Tashkent" (Beber 2012, 417). Soviet commitment to mediate a cease-fire agreement and the withdrawal of troops to pre-war lines of control was a direct result of its intention to limit the Chinese strategic standing and potential strengthening of ties between Beijing and Islamabad (Dixit 2002; Beber 2012). Lastly, bias of outcome is also reflected in the mediator's mandates. The mandates dictate the manner in which a third party enters the dispute. They give guidance as to how the process should be conducted and, most importantly, what a mediator is expected to achieve. Insights from Jan Eliasson's experience as a mediator show how practitioners and academics have somewhat different expectations in terms of what the purpose of mediation is. In their analysis of Eliasson's mediation efforts, Svensson and Wallensteen note that "mediation does not always result in complete and durable peace agreements between the parties, [as] such an outcome may not even be the purpose of mediation" (Svensson and Wallensteen 2010, 109). In fact, Eliasson's objectives generally included goals such as improvement and maintenance of communication channels between conflicting sides, alleviation of humanitarian crises and exploration of elements that could be used for a final agreement in possible future mediation activities.

Mediators might also have close personal, political or economic relations with one of the disputants. Although this type of bias was outright rejected in the traditional literature as being a definitional incongruity, several studies have shown the potential benefits of having a mediator with close ties to one of the parties (Touval 1975; Zartman and Touval 1985; Carnevale and Arad 1996; Kydd 2003; Svensson 2014). A mediator's *bias of actor* may be instrumental in cases characterized by power asymmetry between the disputants. As argued by Kleiboer, biased mediators "might empower weaker parties in their interest of an equitable settlement to end human misery" (Kleiboer 1996, 370). Similarly, a biased mediator might be acceptable to a disfavored party because that specific third party may be the only one capable of mustering the necessary resources to produce the incentives that could make a difference to the process. In other words, when a mediator has closer relations with the side that has a greater say over the outcome of the conflict, the less powerful conflicting side might expect that the mediator will use partiality to influence the other side and move it toward an agreement that would be unattainable through non-mediated negotiations. For instance, despite an unequivocal US bias in the Arab–Israeli conflict, the Arabs accepted US mediation efforts believing that such relations could be used to extract concessions from Israel (Touval 1975). In essence, disfavored sides accept biased mediators because they may be able to pressure their partners toward accepting a solution that would otherwise be unattainable. During the 1979 hostage crisis, the US accepted Algerian mediation not because of its impartiality, but because it had an open access to the inner circle of Khomeini's regime and was thus able to promise help in releasing the hostages (Touval and Zartman 2006, 433; Sick 1985). Similarly, without Venezuelan assistance the Colombian government would be unable to bring the Fuerzas Armadas Revolucionarias de Colombia (FARC) to the peace process held in Havana. Venezuelan willingness to put its bias toward FARC to promote the peace talks was also conducive for a parallel and gradual warming up or relations between the governments in Caracas and Bogota. In other words, mediation may be used to improve relations between the disfavored party and the mediator. When the UK and the US mediated the dispute over the city of Triste between Italy and Yugo-slavia in 1954, the process was largely conditioned by the Cold War, partisan attitude of the Western countries toward their allies in Italy (Campbell 1976). While the Yugoslav officials publicly protested the Anglo-American intention to give the northern part of Trieste to Italy, outside of the scrutiny of the public eye, the UK and the US used this process to improve their relations with Tito's Yugo-slavia in the aftermath of Yugoslav split from the Soviet sphere in 1948 (Zartman and Berman 1982, 68; Favretto 2009, 256).

Credibility

The evident ambiguity of impartiality as a concept induced some scholars to shift their analytical focus from perceived impartiality to a more specific notion of *perceived credibility* of a mediator. According to this approach, while medi-ators may preserve their biased attitude in the process and with it contribute to the eventual effectiveness of the process, they still need to be perceived as cred-ible in order to be acceptable to the disputants. For Maoz and Terris, mediator credibility is the

> extent to which disputants think that (1) the mediator's offer is believable (i.e., the mediator is not bluffing and/or is not being deceived by the opponent) and (2) the mediator can deliver the offer (i.e., mediator can make the offer stick).
>
> (Maoz and Terris 2009, 69)

According to their study, when mediation takes place, a mediator's credibility is a feature that increases the likelihood of a partial or full settlement (Maoz and Terris 2009, 88). In order to be credible, a guarantor must fulfill at least three basic conditions: it must have a specific self-interest in upholding a promise; it must be willing to use force if necessary (and capable of punishing whoever vio-lates the agreement); and to be able to signal resolve (Walter 1997). Hence, a direct interest that leads to a more unyielding presence by the third party makes the agreement more relevant to the conflicting parties, who would then be induced further to obey the contract (Bercovitch 2002).

Mediator credibility is directly linked to mediator bias. If we look at conflicts as a result of incomplete information between the disputants, mediators' ability to convey the necessary information about the parties' preferences, capabilities and resolve becomes instrumental in managing the conflict (Fearon 1995, Powell 2002). According to Kydd (2003), in order for this information to be believable, mediators must be biased toward one of the actors. His analysis shows that an unbiased mediator is seldom trusted in sending messages that might increase and decrease the likelihood of conflict. If the mediator only has a preference for ending hostilities, it will advise both sides to exercise restraint. Since the parties might anticipate the mediator's preferences, they will not find their statements to be credible. Mediators who are interested in persuading one of the parties to make a concession because the other side has strong resolve must be biased toward the side that is receiving the information in order to be successful (Kydd 2003, 607). During the last months of war in Bosnia, the success of the US initiative to halt the Bosniak and Croat offensives in the aftermath of NATO campaign against Serb military, was largely due to the misinformation about Serb regrouping and consolidating that the US officials provided to their Bosniak and Croat partners. This information was instrumental to inducing the parties to explore negotiations as a viable alternative to fighting (Holbrooke 1998, Touval 2002).

Definition

It should be noted that although mediators seem to be acceptable despite their evident bias, some studies still remain suspicious of the generalizability of utility generated by the presence of a biased mediator. According to these studies, the conclusions about their effectiveness are still based on a limited number of cases and it is still the mediator's technique (i.e., strategy) rather than his or her characteristics (i.e., bias) that condition the final outcome of the process (Gent and Shannon 2011; Beber 2012). Nevertheless, and in summary, since mediator impartiality and neutrality do not represent the necessary prerequisites of a mediator acceptance or of a successful outcome, mediation is best understood as a voluntary and legally non-binding negotiation process conducted in an ad-hoc manner through which an external actor assists the parties in reaching a solution that they are unable or unwilling to find themselves.[4]

Demand for mediation: when and why do disputants accept mediation?

Mediators are often initially faced with rejection by the disputing parties. Thus, as Zartman and Touval point out, "their first diplomatic effort must be to convince the parties of the value of their services before mediation can get started" (Zartman and Touval 1996, 446). Rejection is a product of the suspicion and mutual mistrust that characterize many conflicts (Svensson and Wallensteen 2010). Parties will engage with only those mediators they deem trustworthy and expect that the actors involved will reciprocate and not exploit one's willingness to cooperate (Kydd 2006).

Making the parties amenable to mediation is not an easy task. In order for mediation to take place, parties need to perceive it as a reasonably attractive alternative to the continuation of belligerent activities. More specifically, disputants will accept a mediator's offer to the extent that the expected utility of an agreement exceeds the expected utility of continued conflict (Maoz and Terris 2006). On the one hand, parties will accept mediation if they perceive it to be a process that may produce a better outcome than the one they can achieve by fighting. On the other hand, they would also expect that mediation might generate a better outcome than any solution that could be reached through direct negotiations.

Ripening the conflict

The decision to manage a conflict is not unilateral, but rather a result of a careful analysis by all sides of whether or not a conflict has become "ripe" for resolution (Zartman 1989a, 2001). According to Zartman's ripeness theory, the parties first need to perceive that they are locked in a 'mutually hurting stalemate,' which is an unbearable, painful and costly impasse experienced by both parties in which neither party is able to escalate the conflict unilaterally to achieve victory and in which both parties can expect an impending catastrophe if confrontational strategies continue. Under such conditions, the parties begin to perceive negotiations as a preferable alternative to the continuation of belligerent activities and see them as a 'way out' of the impasse (Zartman 2001, 8). Both conditions – 'mutually hurting stalemate' and 'way out' – are based on the conflicting parties' subjective perceptions: they have to recognize that they are at a painful impasse (no matter what the 'evidence' on the ground says and/or how the situation is perceived by other actors) and develop a sense of seeing a negotiated solution as an alternative to continued fighting. It should be noted, that the word 'mutually' does not imply symmetry; it only refers to the environment in which both parties feel the pain from the stalemate (Zartman and de Soto 2010, 13). Since ripeness is a perceptual condition, in order to foster subjective awareness of the present situation as ripe for resolution, parties might look for objective indicators of the rising costs of the conflict. These include information such as: the number and the makeup of causalities, number of refugees and internally displaced persons, increasing financial costs of sustaining the current strategies, material damage caused by the conflict, etc. At the same time, parties need to develop subjective perceptions of ripeness, which are often a reaction to objective events. Generally, subjective indicators can be deduced from parties' statements, both official and unofficial. Parties may emphasize their exhaustion as a result of the ongoing conflict, recognition that confrontational activities are not yielding expected results, intention to re-evaluate positions and interests in the conflict and voice their concern that the ongoing conflict might further tarnish their international reputation and hurt their economies (Zartman and de Soto 2010, 15–18).

Given the costs that conflicts generate, the absence of ripeness does not preclude action by third parties. As Zartman and de Soto emphasize, outside actors "can develop a policy of ripening, cultivating both objective and subjective elements of ripeness if these elements do not appear on their own" (Zartman and de Soto 2010, 7). In order to ripen the stalemate and a provide a way out, third parties might employ various measures – diplomatic, economic and/or military – that may help to reframe the conflict and accentuate the attractiveness of mediation as an alternative to fighting. These measures help parties perceive and understand how unbearable their stalemate is and, more importantly, that negotiations are the only way in which they can obtain certain benefits. Once the parties recognize negotiations as a way out, keeping them in the process is influenced by the mediators' ability to foster the perception that negotiations generate 'mutually enticing opportunities' that would be unavailable outside of the process (Zartman 2001, 14).

Costs of accepting mediation and devious objectives

Accepting mediation also generates costs (both domestic and international, tangible and intangible in nature) for the conflicting parties. First of all, the parties may be apprehensive that their willingness to negotiate with 'the enemy' might be perceived as a sign of weakness and even be labelled as treason by their constituencies. Secondly, the disputants can be enticed into making unexpected concessions, by giving up a certain level of control over the process, which increases the overall level of uncertainty regarding a desired outcome. As a result they could end up accepting less than what was initially planned for a mutually acceptable outcome or face the degradation of having to establish political and economic ties with the mediator (Bercovitch and Gartner 2006).

Thus, accepting mediation and even conducting the process should not be immediately conflated with the parties' intentions to reach a peaceful solution. Even when mediation is under way, parties do not automatically abandon belligerent activities. As noted by Sisk, violence often proves to be a useful off the table tactic, which the parties use to improve their bargaining position at the negotiating table by affecting the situation on the ground (Sisk 2009). The Colombian President Juan Manuel Santos, while strongly promoting the idea of a peace process with FARC also objected to sign a cease-fire agreement as a prelude to the peace talks in Havana. He explains this decision:

> I made the decision not to accept a cease-fire before signing a peace contract. If we agreed to a cease-fire there would be a reason for FARC to prolong negotiations eternally. And if by any chance those talks fail, I don't want to be seen by history as another president who was naive and stupid and gave the guerrillas all the opportunity to gain strength and keep fighting. I know that a lot of people don't understand how we can be talking in Havana while simultaneously fighting in Colombia. But in that respect, I follow the words of former Israeli Prime Minister Yitzhak Rabin: I fight terrorism as if there was no peace process, and I negotiate the peace process as if there was no terrorism.
>
> (Spiegel 2014)

Evidently, the parties might use mediation for various 'devious reasons' that are unrelated to the achievement of a peace deal. According to Richmond, parties may use mediation as a stalling tactic that buys them time to regroup and reorganize on the ground: by buying time they may postpone making costly concessions; they may also see mediation as a platform through which their goals may gain international traction; mediation can serve as a mechanism through which they could gain more international allies; and the process could confer a higher degree of legitimacy for their claims and bargaining positions (Richmond 1998). For instance, the government of Rwanda's acceptance of mediation in 1991 had nothing to do with accepting direct negotiations with RPF or reaching a compromise settlement, rather the government wanted to attract sympathy from the international community and induce regional leaders to label RPF's incursions as an act of Ugandan aggression that impinged upon Rwandan sovereignty (Maundi *et al.* 2006, 52).

Advantages of accepting mediation

Mediation also yields a number of advantages for the parties. First of all, parties could use mediation as a convenient political cover for making unpopular decisions, such as making necessary concessions to the other side that would be unimaginable in the absence of a third party. Mediators provide the necessary information to help the parties gain a more complete picture of the situation and better understand their opponents' preferences, capabilities and resolve in the dispute. More importantly, mediators' presence fosters the expectation that the utility of the agreement attainable through mediation exceeds the utility of an agreement that the parties could reach if they negotiated directly. Mediators can use their tangible and intangible resources in order to increase the costs of ongoing conflict, improve the attractiveness of a negotiated settlement and incentivize the parties to be more amenable to compromise. At the same time, third parties could deliver guarantees of overseeing the implementation of the agreement and provide assistance in the post-agreement phase. According to Beardsley, while these incentives might prove useful in terminating violence and reaching a peaceful agreement, if the third party does not maintain its commitment in the long-run, these incentives might prove to be highly artificial and, as such, will foster re-escalation of violence (Beardsley 2011). For example, in the case of East Timor, the civil strife that inflamed the country in 2006 is directly linked to the fact that the UN Mission in Support of East Timor (UNMSET) was given a fixed mandate of three years and had to terminate its presence in 2005 (Hood 2006).

Supply side of mediation: who and why mediates

Mediators are also subjected to certain costs. Mediators often provide logistical support for the peacemaking process: arranging a suitable location, accommodation for the parties, and other technical aspects pertinent to the talks. At the same time, along with material costs, mediators also invest their non-material capital in the peace process. As such, they may face strong reputational risks and criticism in media (Princen 1992). Norwegian attempts to mediate the conflict in Sri Lanka were often criticized by pro-Sinhala groups that were concerned by the Norwegian empowerment and legitimization of the LTTE, which, in the eyes of the protesters, were largely a terrorist group. Despite the fact that their government was also involved in the talks with the LTTE, the criticism was directed primarily at Norway (BBC 2004; IPS News 2006). On a similar note, mediators might face high domestic political costs for endorsing an unpopular settlement. As the case of Cambodia will illustrate, the US State Department was severely criticized by the American public and Congress once it was revealed that the official US stance to support Prince Sihanouk and oppose the pro-Vietnamese Hun Sen faction, was indirectly empowering and legitimizing the controversial Khmer Rouge led by Pol Pot (Solomon 2000). Finally, the mediation process also requires considerable investments in personnel and logistics, which could prove to be burdensome as the peacemaking process becomes more protracted. Thus, an effective mediation process is strongly dependent upon the mediators' motivations to get involved and a perception that the expected benefits exceed the potential costs of engaging in the process (Bercovitch and Schneider 2000).

A mediator's entry into the process is a result of a synchronized effort by the disputants and the third party. Mediators may be invited by the conflicting parties; they may offer their services themselves; or mediation may be based on a previously established arrangement between the disputants and specific external actors. Whatever the mechanism through which the third parties become involved, they never do it aimlessly.

Humanitarian reasons and mediators' self-interests

Publically, third parties often justify their involvement on humanitarian grounds. In situations in which escalation of a conflict could generate gross violations of human rights, mediators might face strong public pressure and develop a sense of moral imperative to intervene. Fear of genocide, forced displacement of populations and other severe human rights violations in Darfur propelled public opinion in the US and other Western countries to see external involvement in the conflict as a moral priority (Seymour 2014). It is not unusual that in such circumstances mediators become actors who are more interested in the fate of the civilian population than that of the conflicting parties themselves (Crocker *et al.* 2004, 28). Although promoting peace and alleviating human suffering might not yield direct benefits and in some instances, actors mediating such conflicts do not have a strong strategic interest in the region, these actors may expect to benefit from improved international reputation and a strengthened role in international affairs. The Norwegian interest in mediating a variety of conflicts[5] have boosted the country's image of being an important international actor and a peacemaker whose influence exceeds that which its power position would predict (Greig and Diehl 2012, 82). As the following discussion will show, humanitarian concerns are at the core of the motivation of various actors to intervene. In the first place, these are international organizations and NGOs whose *raison d'être* is the promotion of the principles of international peace and security. In fact, just as conflicts can involve both state and non-state actors, the third parties that might have an interest in mediating these conflicts can be just as diverse and may include: representatives of states (neighboring ones, global powers, states of medium and small relative size), representatives of global and regional international organizations, representatives of global NGOs (which could include religious organizations, interest groups with an international agenda, various epistemic communities, etc.), and finally even individuals (such as Jimmy Carter, Desmond Tutu, Maarti Ahtisaari, etc.) that have an established international reputation in managing international conflicts and are able to act as mediators without a formal mandate from a particular state or international organization.

Given the sheer variety of international actors, it would be implausible to expect that mediators only be driven by humanitarian concerns to intervene. Keeping in mind the considerable investment of resources that mediation calls for, it is reasonable to presume that mediators are no less motivated by self-interest than by humanitarian impulses (Touval and Zartman 1985, 8). Mediators play their role in negotiations and expend resources not only because they aim to resolve a dispute, but because they also seek to gain something from it (Greig 2005). For many actors, international mediation is a useful foreign policy instrument through which they can pursue some of their interests without creating too much opposition (Touval 1992). Essentially, a mediator's involvement is driven by cost-benefit calculations. Young notes that "it is perfectly possible for situations to arise in which there is a distinct role for an intermediary but in which no third party finds it worth his while to assume this role" (Young 1972b, 55). Thus, the fact that a mediator has an interest in managing a dispute is a direct indication that it also has something at stake in that dispute.

States

For states, self-interest is reflected in attempts to produce settlements that will "increase the prospects of stability, deny their rivals opportunities for intervention, earn them the gratitude of one or both parties, or enable them to continue to have a role in future relations" (Zartman and Touval 1996, 446). First of all, the fear of spillover effects of an escalating conflict may prompt neighboring countries to get involved as mediators. States that are affected by an internal conflict may have difficulties controlling their borders in an effective way, which paves the way for various sources of regional instability such as the rapid influx of refugees, suspicious cross-border activities and even incursions of rebel groups into the territory of neighboring countries. Secondly, from a foreign policy perspective, states may use mediation as a method of expanding their zone of influence or limiting the influence of rival states. Russian mediation in the zone of 'near-abroad' countries – such as in the context of conflicts between Georgia and breakaway regions of Abkhazia and South Ossetia, the Nagorno-Karabakh conflict between Armenia and Azerbaijan and the conflict between Moldova and secessionist region of Transdniestria[6] – is an indication of Moscow's demarcation of its zone of influence. The US involvement in managing the Bosnian war following the inability of the European Community to broker a peaceful solution was a way for the US to affirm its relevance in Europe (Touval 2002). Frequent British and French involvement in their conflict-afflicted ex-colonies can be explained by their interest in maintaining political and economic influence in those countries. By acting as mediators, states may expect to earn gratitude from the conflicting parties and assume a more relevant role in future regional dynamics. As the Norwegian and Algerian experiences show, this is especially significant for small and medium-sized states that have fewer foreign policy tools in their repertoire than global superpowers.

International and regional organizations

Undoubtedly, the motives behind the involvement of international organizations (excluding military alliances) are much more complex. Rarely does an international organization have the leverage and resources its individual member states possess. Lacking these capabilities, it has to rely on its status as a global/ regional organization (i.e., the United Nations and the European Union), the legitimacy it derives from this status, its credibility as an international actor, the cohesiveness of its members, and mediators' experience and persuasiveness (Fretter 2002, 98). In principle, the acceptability of international organizations as mediators is reflected in the possibility that conflicting sides can address their different opinions to all member states and potentially find support from within the organization. Many of the foundational charters and statutes of international organizations specify the promotion of peace and security (globally and/or regionally) as their primary focus. At the same time, these entities are also constrained by the particular interests of their member states. Despite the fact that the interests of member states might differ, the perceived legitimacy enjoyed by international organizations derives from two sources: the channeling and balancing process by which the diverging interests of member states are consolidated and the norms and values that are recognized as commonly shared and promoted by these same member-states.

The United Nations is unique in this regard. Though it lacks the coercive power and resources that its individual member states possess, ever since its establishment, the UN has gradually built a reputation of being an effective conflict manager (Holsti 1966; Butterworth 1978; Bercovitch 1996). Generally perceived as a "bastion of international morality" (Fretter 2002, 100), the UN performs a dual role in international conflict management. On the one hand, it provides a multilateral channel for the international community to tackle the most intense international conflicts. On the other, it serves as a legitimizing agency for unilateral conflict management initiatives pursued by various state and non-state actors (Rubin 1992). More importantly, while individual state actors are generally not driven by altruistic motives to manage an ongoing dispute, due to its unique international role, the UN has faced greater pressure to achieve objectives that are not prioritized by other actors. Some of these objectives include the containment of escalating conflicts, reduction of human suffering, promotion of international law and the creation of an environment that would garner more constructive relationships between disputants in the near future (Bercovitch 1996). As such goals are largely associated with the most intractable international conflicts, which, in turn, are usually ignored by state actors, the UN is often assigned the role of mediator because no one else is willing (Crocker *et al.* 2004). Consequently, the effectiveness of the UN is constrained not only by its institutional characteristics (such as the voluntary nature of its membership, level of cohesion among its member states and reliance on members' commitments to support UN's initiatives) and the systemic features of the international arena that are dominated by the principles of state sovereignty and of non-interference, but also by the contextual features of the most hostile and intractable conflicts (Fretter 2002). As a result, due to these constraints, the UN has often had to cope with mounting criticism of its inability to pursue desired objectives (Touval 1994).

In light of this mounting criticism, the UN has frequently delegated peace-making responsibilities to regional organizations, which, at the moment, are the most prevalent type of international organization (Pevehouse 2002). The UN Charter provides a list of peaceful means at the disposal of the parties whose ongoing conflict may threaten international peace and security. One of them suggests that the parties should "resort to regional arrangements or agencies" (UN Charter 1945, Article 33/1), and they can do it "either on the initiative of the states concerned or by reference from the Security Council" (UN Charter 1945, Article 52/2). The rationale behind the devolution of peacemaking duties is based on a number of comparative advantages that characterize regional organizations. First of all, promoting peace, security and stability is the *raison d'être* of many regional organizations. They often have specific procedures or specialized bodies mandated to assist their member states in peacefully settling disputes that arise. In some cases, regional organizations employ a variety of policies aimed at preventing the escalation of conflict. For instance, the Organization for Security and Cooperation in Europe (OSCE) has established missions in conflict-affected members states and has provided them with capacity building assistance (including institutional reform, education of public officials, monitoring elections, etc.) aimed at reducing the potential of conflict escalation. Secondly, these organizations commonly share the socio-political, economic and cultural character of the conflicting parties. As they are more sensitive to the realities on the ground, conflicting parties might be more amenable to allowing a regional organization to mediate their dispute than any other international actor (Bercovitch and Houston 1996; Gartner 2013). Similarly, their involvement may seem less intrusive compared to that of a powerful state whose motives, which many include influence reassertion or expansion, may seem too threatening to the conflicting parties. In light of their regional expertise, cultural sensitivity and institutional mechanisms, regional organizations have become increasingly involved in mediating international conflicts. A study conducted by Gartner shows that over the past three decades, their involvement in conflict management activities has nearly doubled (Gartner 2013, 32).

While regional organizations may be able to signal the strong resolve of their member states in averting negative consequences of an escalating conflict, they also face a number of limitations. Regional organizations may lack credibility if they are perceived to be dominated by a strong regional actor. For instance, ECOWAS mediation efforts in Liberia were strongly hampered by Nigerian interests in the conflict. The Nigerian agenda was strongly resisted by Charles Taylor and his NPFL, who saw the process as a method of strengthening the position of Samuel Doe's government (Maundi *et al.* 2006, 111). In other words, rebel groups might reject mediation from an organization in which the incumbent government has an established role and the ability to influence its interests.

Equally, the incumbent government may resist the involvement of a regional organization in which neighboring states, which may be suspected of supporting the rebel groups, have a stronger role. During the civil war in Burundi, Buyoya's government was very suspicious of Tanzania and its president Nyerere's intentions as the lead mediator representing OAU. While the tensions between the two governments increased after a sanctions regime was imposed on Burundi, the mediation process was blocked only once the rebel CNDD/FDD forces moved their headquarters from Zaire to Tanzania (Maundi *et al.* 2006, 78).

Low-key mediators

The last group of potential third parties can be found in actors that are often labeled as 'low-key mediators,' such as private individuals and NGOs. These actors have no coercive power at the international level and rely in large part on being accepted as mediators due to their reputation as successful third parties whose primary interest is ending the conflict itself. Individuals that are not government officials or political actors might contribute to efforts to de-escalate the conflict, through their distinct capabilities, which may including drawing upon a developed network of contacts, and/or previous experience in mediation. The conflict in Aceh, between the Indonesian government and the Free Aceh Movement, was mediated by Martti Ahtisaari who represented neither a state nor an international organization, but a Finish-based NGO Crisis Management Initiative. He was accepted primarily due to his reputation as an experienced mediator who had mediated conflicts in Namibia and Yugoslavia and because of his well-established network in the EU that would be instrumental in the implementation phase (Conciliation Resources 2008). Despite their limited resources, if accepted, these individuals and the NGOs they represent might help reduce the necessary momentum of unofficial talks between conflicting sides and pave the way for a more formal process. The Carter initiative in Sudan helped jumpstart subsequent mediation efforts by the US government. Carter's involvement was based on the expectation that his prestige and influence would reassure the parties of the seriousness of the endeavor, the benefits of participation and the likelihood of some measure of mediation success (Mitchell 1993, 155). Similarly, the Carter Center's initiatives in Burundi (1995) and Congo (1999) laid the fundamental groundwork for subsequent mediation efforts by neighboring states, regional and international organizations (Maundi *et al.* 2006).

NGOs represent a type of actor whose interests are "not as apparent or suspect as the primary players of power politics" (Zartman and Touval 1996, 450). They are usually associated with activities that are instrumental to any peacemaking process, that might range from various forms of humanitarian assistance (such as aiding the areas affected by the influx of refugees or those that were stricken by a natural disaster), monitoring and surveying the the extent to which human rights are upheld and contributing to long-term economic development projects (Dunn and Kriesberg 2002, 195). More importantly, they are often perceived as actors whose primary focus is "the pursuit of peace, including the promotion of the philosophy and techniques of negotiation, conflict resolution, and nonviolence" (Anderson 1996a, 344). The recent proliferation of international non-governmental organizations in various areas around the world has meant that they often find themselves embroiled in an emerging conflict while they are pursuing their specific mandates (Anderson 1996b).

The ubiquity of development, humanitarian and religious NGOs in countries and regions affected by conflict has produced a very valuable entry point to conflicts. Apart from trying to alleviate the problems associated with violent conflicts, NGOs might also possess the necessary capacity, knowledge and expertise to initiate a dialogue between conflicting sides. Due to their long-term objectives in conflict prone areas, they may be very well placed to identify moments at which the conflict is ripe for mediation. Firstly, they can provide valuable contributions by conducting fact-finding missions, through which key stakeholders are identified and their interests and needs are defined. This information can be used to bring the situation into the international spotlight and mobilize different actors to take preventive steps in managing the emerging dispute before it erupts into violence. Simultaneously, NGOs can use their presence on the ground and exploit their developed relationships to induce creative thinking on the part of the conflicting sides, so that they might perceive peaceful negotiations as an attractive alternative to more belligerent activities. As they cannot muster the coercive inducements, neither carrots nor sticks, that are generally available to state actors, NGOs usually rely on emphasizing the significance of previously developed close ties with local actors and the provision of confidential and neutral spaces for discussion (Princen 1992). As such, the conflicting sides that might be reluctant to accept the presence of more powerful state actors in the early stages of conflict (before it has escalated into violence) might find it more useful and less demanding to deal with non-governmental agencies (Dunn and Kriesberg 2002). Therefore, on the one hand, NGOs can be seen as actors able to generate the necessary momentum for the parties to accept mediation activities by more resourceful international actors if required in the future. On the other hand, their activities could complement track one diplomatic efforts and provide venues for lower-level stakeholders that have the ability to influence their decision makers involved in negotiating a comprehensive settlements. The United States Institute of Peace initiative in Tajikistan to forward Inter-Tajiki dialogue between lower-ranking officials from both the government and the opposition strongly influenced the official peacemaking process. One participant stated, "[a]fter six meetings of the Dialogue, it was no longer possible to argue credibly that negotiation between government and opposition was impossible" (Slim and Saunders 2001, 46). As mediation processes should not be regarded as completed once an agreement has been reached, the ultimate evidence of NGOs' utility can be seen in their provision of highly valuable implementation assistance in the form of monitoring early elections, provision of capacity building assistance and developing programs aimed at long-term social reconciliation.

Kriesberg notes that "the recognition of the special capabilities and limitations of various kinds of providers combined with a careful assessment of the most appropriate response or combination of responses, can facilitate effective cooperation in forming a comprehensive approach to bringing about constructive conflict outcomes" (Kriesberg 2002, quoted in Dunn and Kriesberg 2002, 211). Although the various roles, interests and actors might be less blurry in theory than in practice, it is important to note that each peacemaking activity is largely conditioned by an adequate mix of well-coordinated activities conducted by international actors that share a common goal in managing a given conflict. And in order to achieve the requisite level of cooperation and coordination among various actors, this analysis needs to depart by rightfully addressing each actor's capabilities, interests and limitations in any conflict management activity.

The "how" in mediation: mediators' strategies and leverage

The sole *interest* of the third party is not sufficient for the mediation procedure to be efficient. A mediator's ability to influence the mediation process and deliver acceptable solutions is determined by the strategies and leverage that are available. In order to see a particular outcome materialize, mediators resort to different strategies. In the mediation literature, strategy is defined as "a broad plan of action designed to indicate which measures may be taken to achieve desired objectives in conflicts" while behavior refers to actual "tactics, techniques, or instruments" at a mediator's disposal (Bercovitch 2005, 113). The most accepted typology classifies the mediator's behavior and corresponding strategies on an intervention scale and assesses the level of the mediator's assertiveness in the peace process.

Facilitation/communication

At the low end of this scale are strategies labeled as communication (Touval and Zartman 1985; Zartman and Touval 1996) or facilitation (Bercovitch *et al.* 1991; Bercovitch and Houston 1996; Hopmann 1996; Wilkenfeld *et al.* 2005). Using this strategy, the mediator assumes a very passive role in the peacemaking process. As the name indicates, when acting as a communicator or facilitator, the mediator focuses primarily on assisting the parties in communicating more smoothly and facilitates their mutual collaboration while exercising modest control over the actual process of mediation. Given the high level of distrust that conflicts usually generate, disputing parties' decisions are affected by incomplete information about their opponents' preferences and capabilities, which prevents them from identifying mutually acceptable alternatives to their belligerent relations (Fearon 1995; Powell 2002; Hopmann 2001; Beardsley *et al.* 2006). The mediator as facilitator or communicator provides the disputing sides with information that is essential to narrowing down the differences between the parties and estimating the range of mutually acceptable outcomes. In other words, by employing facilitative and communicative strategies, mediators help the disputing parties recognize that they actually have compatible interests. Tactics that are implemented are inconspicuous. Mediators assist the parties in establishing contact, either directly or indirectly through shuttle diplomacy. They elucidate the overall situation for both sides,

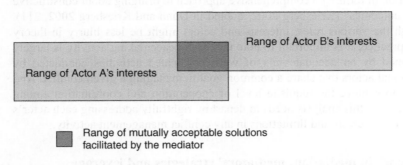

Range of Actor B's interests

Range of Actor A's interests

Range of mutually acceptable solutions
facilitated by the mediator

Figure 1.1 Facilitation/communication.

identify pertinent issues and promote confidence-building measures, all of which help the parties recognize joint gains and the availability of mutually acceptable solutions through negotiations.

Formulation

Even when the parties recognize that they share a range of possible solutions, they still need to agree on a specific outcome within it. Given the high level of distrust that conflicts generate, conflicting parties might perceive potential solutions – even though they are actually within this range of mutually acceptable ones – as mutually exclusive, creating the necessary conditions for an impasse (Beardsley 2006, 63). Faced with zero-sum perceptions and hard-liner bargaining attitudes on the part of conflicting parties, mediators need to assume a more active role in the process. A strategy by which mediators help the parties redefine the issues and propose specific solutions is generally deemed formulation (Touval and Zartman 1985; Hopmann 1996). For Zartman and Touval "formulas are the key to a negotiated solution to a conflict; they provide a common understanding of the problem and its solution or a

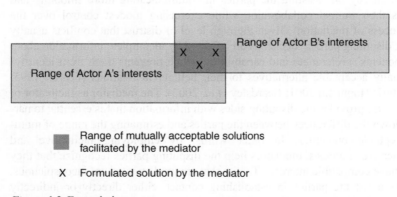

Range of Actor B's interests

X   X
X

Range of Actor A's interests

Range of mutually acceptable solutions
facilitated by the mediator

X   Formulated solution by the mediator

Figure 1.2 Formulation.

shared notion of justice to govern an outcome" (Zartman and Touval 1996, 454). Since persuasion requires a certain level of involvement, the mediator not only acts as a communicator, but also needs to get involved much more directly in the process, by: offering innovative solutions that could downplay those commitments that constrain the parties, emphasizing that unilateral (i.e., belligerent) action is in no one's interest and that the current stalemate requires immediate solutions.

Facilitation and formulation are forms of integrative bargaining strategies that help the actors correctly identify solutions within the overlapping range of possible nonviolent outcomes (Beardsley *et al.* 2006, 63; see Carnevale 1986). In using these two strategies, parties gradually abandon zero-sum perceptions and engage in problem-solving approaches through which they recognize joint gains. In certain conflict, facilitating communication and formulating possible solutions is not enough for the parties to alter their positions and reach a compromise. As numerous studies have shown, less intrusive strategies are most successful in low-intensity conflicts in which parties are willing to settle, but are unable to communicate this willingness to each other (Bercovitch and Gartner 2006; Beardsley *et al.* 2006). However, in cases in which disputants lack the motivation to settle and show an unwillingness to compromise, a more powerful intervention from a third party is needed (Rubin 1980; Hiltrop 1989; Carnevale and Pruitt 1992; Carnevale 2002; Sisk 2009; Bercovitch 2009).

Manipulative mediation 'with muscle'

The most active strategy a mediator might use is referred to as 'mediation with muscle' or 'power mediation' (Fisher and Keashly 1991; Svensson 2007; Beardsley 2009). When mediating with muscle, the mediator becomes 'a full participant' who is able to affect the substance of the bargaining process by presenting incentives or delivering ultimatums to the disputing sides (Bercovitch *et al.* 1991; Bercovitch and Houston 2009; Touval and Zartman 1985). According to Touval, in order to elicit concessions from conflicting parties, mediators are not only expected to offer suggestions and formulas pertinent to the substance of the dispute, but also to exercise influence by creating pressure and providing incentives to compromise (Touval 1982). The mediators may manipulate parties' perceptions by resorting to threats to use coercive action (such as sanctions or military deployment) against them in order to increase the costs of non-compliance and continuation of conflict. At the same time, the mediators may also manipulate the perceptions of the parties by providing incentives in order to increase the attractiveness of a negotiated solution. These incentives may be of a material nature and include provisions of financial and humanitarian aid, development assistance, security guarantees and implementation monitoring; or less tangible incentives such as improvement of international reputation, legitimizing their cause, and/or enhancement of relations with particular external actors (Zartman 2009; Sisk 2009). Threats and promises, or carrots and sticks, are intended to alter the parties' cost-benefit calculations and induce them to recognize viable alternatives within the rapidly developing range of mutually acceptable solutions (Beardsley *et al.* 2006,64).

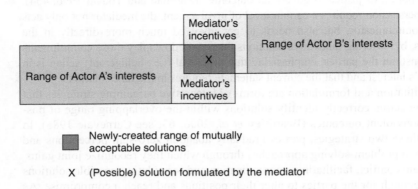

Newly-created range of mutually
acceptable solutions

X   (Possible) solution formulated by the mediator

Figure 1.3 Manipulation (mediation with 'muscle').

There is an obvious difference between facilitation and formulation on the one side and manipulation on the other. The first two strategies employ a variety of methods (such as facilitating communication, distribution of useful information and formulation of a viable solution) such that the disputants can identify an *existing* mutually acceptable solution within their range of available alternatives. The manipulative strategies, however, are used with the aim of enlarging the spectrum of possible solutions that both sides see as preferable to a continuing conflict. Despite their obvious differences, the three mediation strategies are not mutually exclusive. As Beardsley *et al.* note, "mediators always use facilitation in some fashion and rarely use manipulation without also engaging in formulation," however "many mediators will be limited to formulation and/or facilitation due to a lack of resources, their own strategic decisions, or the context of the crisis" (Beardsley *et al.* 2006, 65). The US involvement in mediating conflicts in Northern Ireland and Bosnia show how a choice of strategy is not directly dependent on available resources only, but also on the context in which mediation takes place and the strategic interests that motivate the mediator to get involved. Despite the fact that Mitchell and Holbrooke represented the same entity, their approaches were considerably different: in a protracted, yet not highly violent conflict, involving US allies, Mitchell assumed a process-oriented approach, focused on facilitating communication and exploring joint gains; Holbrooke, on the other hand, resorted to threats and promises in order to promote his credibility and power in a highly violent and destructive conflict that was taking place in an area in which the US wanted to reaffirm its strategic relevance and limit its opponent's influence (Curran *et al.* 2004).

Types of leverage

As international mediators are not just passive actors in charge of facilitating the communication between parties in conflict, but rather an active third party in the process of managing the conflict, their specific characteristics and capabilities will have a direct impact on the mediation outcome. The relative extent of a mediator's influence is generally associated with the resources available to them, which, in turn, are translated into leverage or power. Leverage in mediation is "the ability to move a party in an intended direction," and derives from the very fact that disputing sides need the mediator's assistance in finding solutions to their problems (Touval and Zartman 2006, 436). For Zartman and Touval "leverage is the ticket to mediation – third parties are only accepted as mediators if they are likely to produce an agreement or help the parties out of a predicament, and for this they usually need leverage" (Zartman and Touval 1985, 40). Since leverage enhances the mediator's ability to influence an outcome, mediation could thus be seen as a "process involving the exercise of power" (Bercovitch *et al.* 1991, 15; Smith 1994, 446).

Despite widespread acknowledgement of their being effective forms of leverage, carrots and sticks are not the only types of power related to the resources and relationships that a mediator might bring to the conflict. Carnevale (2002) identified two main forms of power, based on an actor's 'will and skill.' On the one hand, there is the resource-based aspect of social power (strategic strength) and, on the other hand, there is the behavioral aspect of mediation (tactical strength). According to this categorization, "strategic strength in mediation refers to what the mediator has, to what the mediator brings to the negotiation table; the tactical strength refers to what the mediator does at the negotiation table" (Carnevale 2002, 27–28). Tactical strength is exemplified in a mediator's premeditated choice of specific techniques and the ability to follow a particular procedure. The mediator may develop a procedural framework that reduces uncertainties and enhances the trust between the parties. Throughout the process, they can use various techniques to build up momentum and keep the parties committed to compromise. For instance, Eliasson used to "wear-down" the parties by keeping them at the table for many hours (Svensson and Wallensteen 2010, 67). They may control the communication in order to manage emotions between the parties and help them reduce their differences. Finally, tactical strength is also mirrored in a mediator's ability to reduce the negative impressions the parties have of each other and provide face saving measures if needed. Evidently, tactical strength is best reflected in facilitation and formulation strategies.

Strategic strength may incorporate different types of social power. Using French and Raven's (1959) classification of social power, Carnevale identified six types of power that mediators bring to the process: reward power, coercive power, legitimate power, expert power, referent power, information power, and relational power. As mentioned earlier, threats and incentives, which in Carnevale's typology are referred to as reward and coercive power (2002, 29–30), are most commonly associated with powerful mediators and the manipulative strategies they use. According to Inbar, "great power is simply in possession of more 'carrots and sticks' needed to convince the parties to a dispute to resolve their differences than lesser prominent international mediators" (1991, 82). It should be noted that coercion has often been linked with immediate short-term success and less stable outcomes in the long run. Along with the possibly insincere motives that drive parties to accept mediation and the obfuscated future of the bargaining environment, the artificiality of external coercive/reward leverage has been considered a significant liability to the longevity of the solutions achieved through mediation. While carrots and sticks may serve the purpose of increasing the costs of continuing conflict and promoting the attractiveness of a negotiated agreement, their long-term utility is conditioned by the mediator's 'credible commitment' to maintain their presence during the implementation period. In other words, the newly created zone of possible agreements exists as long as the mediators maintain the incentives available to the parties. Thus, as argued by Beardsley, "leverage itself is thus not bad for a self-enforcing peace as long as the impact of that leverage does not wane and leave the actors with time inconsistency problems" (2011, 151).

Given the evident limitations of coercive/reward leverage, mediators may resort to other forms of social power in an effort to co-opt the parties into cooperation. Not all international actors are able to muster hard power that can be used in mediation due to their varied resources and operational capabilities. Reiterating the voluntary nature of mediation, where actors may reject any solution and abandon the process at any moment, mediators may resort to 'softer types' of power in order to alter conflictual relations between the parties and guide them toward a negotiated solution. According to Nye, soft power is "getting other to want the outcomes you want," and is based primarily on three resources: culture (in places where it is attractive to others), political values (when it lives up to them at home and abroad), and foreign policies (when they are seen as legitimate and having moral authority) (Nye 2008, 96; see also Nye 2004, 2011).

Within the realm of soft power, four non-material forms of French and Raven's social power can be observed. These can be categorized as individual, semi-institutional and institutional forms of soft power. The power of expertise, which is based on a mediator's special knowledge or a reputation for having that knowledge, together with the previously mentioned information power, "which makes compliance with mediator's requests seem rational" (Carnevale 2002, 29), are strongly related to the individual characteristics of the person that has been representing a particular international actor/body in the mediation process. On the other hand, referent power through which mediators lead by example,

Table 1.1 Types of power in international mediation

	Hard power		Soft power				
Nye (2008)	Coercive Material		Co-optive Non-material				
French and Raven (1959)	Coercive (sticks)	Reward (carrots)	Legitimate	Information	Expert	Referent	Relation

represents a semi-institutionalized form of soft power as it is based on a third party's status and prestige, but also on its charisma all of which can be used as tools of attraction (French and Raven 1959, 266). Lastly, legitimate power is an influence "driven by belief that the mediator has the right to prescribe behavior, and derives from a norm that has been accepted by the disputants" (Carnevale 2002, 28). This influence is best observed when comparing different types of mediators: a mediation process performed by an international organization is generally deemed more legitimate and carries with it a higher authority than a process carried out by an individual state (Rubin 1992; Touval 1992; Fretter 2002). This is directly related to nature of a mediator's interest in managing the dispute. As previously mentioned, international organizations represent composite entities, so their interests reflect a specific combination of the various interests of their members. This filtering process allows them to promote the image of an actor with a higher degree of legitimacy in prescribing behavior. While incentives associated with coercive/reward sources of power can be deemed artificial because the parties do not internalize them, soft power allows the mediator to 'win the hearts and minds' of the disputants so that they feel that they were not forced to accept a negotiated solution; rather they are the owners of the solution that was reached.

Contextual factors

Geopolitical conditions

To evaluate mediation activities, it is crucial to consider the overall context and conditions that surround the conflict. The first set of relevant contextual factors relates to the geopolitical conditions that govern international affairs. These features are most resistant to any form of change and, as such, they create the operational framework within which conflict management activities are conducted. The distribution and balance of power between international actors together with modes of strategic alignment have a strong impact on the effectiveness of the mediation process. For instance, the support offered by allies or outside patrons may distort the perception of a hurting stalemate. By making the conflict more tolerable, outside support limits the attractiveness of a mediated solution, induces the parties to assume increasingly unyielding positions, thus contributing to the 'freezing' of the conflict (Bercovitch 2005, 108). The conflict in Cyprus is an example of a situation in which the uncompromising support of external patrons induced the parties to view their stalemate as bearable.

Intractable nature of mediated conflicts

The second set of contextual factors is related to the nature of the conflict at hand. Mediation takes place in the most resistant cases, where parties are unable or unwilling to reach a solution on their own. These disputes tend to be long, complex and intense (Bercovitch and Jackson 2001; Beardsley 2010). Their protracted and destructive nature, evidenced by recurrent acts of violence and the use of military means, contributes to the psychological manifestation of animosity, profound sentiments of fear and distrust, exaggerated stereotypes and misgiving among the parties involved. Parties' identities become polarized, often linked to an existentialist struggle where the existence of 'the other' is a direct threat to one's survival. The issues at stake in the conflict become embedded in each party's identity. They create symbols and belief systems that reflect a distinct perception of the conflict and past events. Historical narratives are reaffirmed as the "new scars become old wounds" and proof of primordial hostility (Zartman 2005, 49). Positions and promoted solutions are conditioned by the parties' zero-sum perceptions and competitive attitudes. Even if at one point there was a single salient solution, it lost its relevance due to the failure to implement it. With the passing of the time, conflict becomes engrained in peoples' daily routines and such behavior even becomes institutionalized (Kriesberg 2005). In such intractable conditions, the persistence of the status quo provides a unique opportunity for some parties to maintain their socio-political and economic power. The increased saliency of issues, coupled with a conflict's potentially profitable nature, encourage leaders to accept higher costs. Sunk costs become sources of entrapment, which cannot easily be disregarded (Meerts 2004). As a consequence, parties tend to be less inclined to compromise, making the mediator's job even more challenging.

Evidently, ripening the conflict is not an easy task. As Bercovitch pointed out, "to have any chances of success, and mediation effort requires resources, experience, strong political support, and a considerable measure of luck" (2005, 109). Thus, instead of randomly selecting cases to be mediated, conflicting parties and external actors link their decision to conduct mediation to the likelihood of success (Greig 2005, 249). Past mediation experience may pose a serious challenge to future mediation efforts. One the one hand, failed peacemaking fuels intractability: negotiations lose their appeal as a way out, parties engage in a dynamic of blaming each other for failure and mistrust becomes a norm (Kriesberg 2005). On the other hand, mediation efforts are not isolated events: prior mediation experience or mediation history encourages future efforts, disputants establish a rapport with the mediator and develop a willingness to work with an outsider (Melin 2013, 88). In other words, while failed efforts might discourage parties from relying on mediation as an attractive alternative to confrontational strategies, past experience with mediation in other disputes increases the appeal of mediation as tool of conflict management.

Chances of mediation success increase if the parties to the conflict are open democracies. Domestically these actors have institutionalized third-party involvement in conflict management and are more accustomed to negotiation and compromise. These factors make them more likely to accept the political costs of mediation (Dixon 1993). As the global community democratizes, even non-democracies have become more inclined to accept the democratic practices that mediation promotes. (McLaughlin Mitchell 2002; Crescenzi *et al.* 2011). Since shared democratic norms and practices between disputants and mediators increase the effectiveness of mediation, the level of internationalization of the conflict also conditions the acceptability of mediation efforts. Mediation is thus more likely in interstate than intrastate conflicts because governments involved in civil wars might resist legitimizing the rebel cause by accepting mediation (Melin and Svensson 2009). Armed rebel groups are often labeled as terrorists by incumbent government officials and negotiating with terrorists is a high political liability. As the case of Sri Lanka will show, the government in Colombo was unwilling to engage with the LTTE for decades because they were considered a terrorist organization and not a legitimate political force (Groeneveld-Savisaar and Vuković 2011). And the situation becomes even more complex and difficult to manage as actors on the ground start fragmenting, each faction competing for a more legitimate role (Bakke *et al.* 2012). In principle, the incumbent government's resistance to accept mediation decreases as the relative power of a rebel group increases. And its relative power is not only determined by the number of troops it controls; more nuanced indicators of its power include political development, territorial control, access to natural resources and links with foreign allies (Clayton 2013).

Resistance to accept mediation makes a conflict more protracted and fuels its intractability. And the longer an intractable conflict continues, the more resistant it becomes to mediation. According to Bercovitch and his colleagues, this vicious cycle is better managed in the early stages of the conflict before identities become polarized and new grievances emerge (Bercovitch *et al.* 1991, Bercovitch 2005). However, even when conflicts become very violent and mediators show willingness to mediate, disputants may still reject mediation because it might signal their readiness to bear increasing costs and their resolve to endure in their intentions (Melin *et al.* 2013). In other words, accepting mediation might be equated with showing weakness and might be difficult to sell to constituencies. Thus, if not tackled in their early stages, intractable conflicts become very difficult to manage over time, becoming less and less tractable with every subsequent mediation attempt. Empirical studies have shown that while initial efforts have a high probability of success (32%), after three or four attempts, mediation effectiveness starts to wane (23%) (Bercovitch *et al.* 1991, 13). In situations like this, it is more reasonable to aim for conflict management rather than resolution. As the latter implies not only the elimination of confrontational behavior, but also the addressing of the root causes and trigger mechanisms that generated the conflict in the first place, intractable conflicts in which issues and identities become strongly intertwined make the task of resolution very demanding. Thus, the primary goal in addressing such a conflict is to manage it by containing further escalation (Bercovitch 2005, 104). And this should not be understood as a half-baked approach. As Kriesberg notes, "a well-managed conflict may be a prelude to a fundamental transformation of the conflict" (Kriesberg 2005, 75). Over time, many conflicts tend to dwindle in intensity for a variety of reasons. Parties might realize that their preferred goals have become unattainable or that the methods of achieving them have proved to be overly burdensome and costly. So, following the logic of ripeness theory, as the parties start perceiving a painful impasse where unilateral actions are not yielding expected benefits, they may redefine their expectations and accept alternatives to fighting. Throughout this entire transformative process, mediation may prove to be of crucial importance and conducive to the achievement of different degrees of success.

Understanding degrees of success in international mediation

Most scholars agree that defining success is generally very difficult because the evidence of success or failure is almost always vague (Kriesberg 1991, Kleiboer 1996, Bercovitch 2002). Despite an impressive body of literature on the topic of international mediation, the academic community has thus far been unable to reach a consensus on a comprehensive definition that would unequivocally delineate how to recognize success in international mediation. Even when scholars use somewhat similar definitions, their analyses seem to discuss essentially quite different aspects of success. Academic conceptualizations of success have often suffered from definitions that appear to be quite arbitrary, developed on case-by-case basis and are not based upon a solid theoretical foundation. Bercovitch eloquently described this problem as such:

> Success in conflict management is an elusive quest. Often what appears as successful to one person may be seen as unsuccessful by others. Mediation may seem successful at one time only to be seen as totally unsuccessful months or years later.
>
> (Bercovitch 2007, 301)

This conceptual confusion regarding success in international mediation should not come as a surprise. International mediation processes are not uniform and, as such, it is quite difficult to establish a one-size-fits-all set of criteria with which to assess achievement of the various objectives of mediation. Parties' objectives and goals tend to change throughout the process, so measuring mediation success in terms of parties' goals makes it impossible to formulate a consistent conceptualization of mediation success. On the other hand (and more importantly), so far empirical studies have overwhelmingly treated mediation outcomes – both success and failure – as dependent variables. The focus has rarely been on how to measure success, but rather on which factors influence the outcome of mediation. The bulk of existing studies – particularly those that have explored correlations between a variety of factors and mediation outcomes – have treated success as a dichotomous phenomenon, usually linked to the existence of a signed agreement. In other words, mediation was successful only if parties reached a formal agreement. The fact that the parties accepted mediation in the first place and issues related to the *implementation* of agreements are not incorporated into an understanding of mediation success.

Reaching an agreement is nothing short of a true accomplishment for any mediator. The formalized nature of agreements or settlements allows scholars and practitioners alike to easily identify them and use them as an indicator of a successful bargaining outcome having been reached (Beardsley 2011, 75). However, using agreements as the sole indicator of success might not be suffi-cient to explain the complex nature of the mediation process. Since mediation is a voluntary process and is conducted in the most resistant cases, its very occur-rence can also be treated as a sign of success (Melin *et al.* 2013, 364). In other words, bringing the parties to the table is already an achievement, as it signals their readiness to explore alternatives to fighting. Although parties may use mediation for devious reasons, in order to truly alter confrontational relations, mediators need to highlight the utility of a negotiated agreement and find a way to incentivize the parties to commit to the process. Therefore, *mediation success* is best understood as a significant (or even essential) contribution to de-escalation of conflict, movement towards an acceptable agreement or reconcili-ation, under the prevailing conditions (Kriesberg 1991, 20). Under this definition, mediation success can be observed as a dynamic phenomenon that corresponds to different stages of the mediation process (Greig and Diehl 2012, 104–145; see also Vuković 2014).

The first stage focuses on getting the disputing parties to accept mediation. In preparing for mediation, third parties explore which parties are willing to discuss de-escalation and which parties must be excluded from the process in order to make the process more efficient. Pre-negotiation, as some scholars refer to it (Zartman 1989b; Stein 1989; Saunders 1996) is usually characterized by a 'turning point' in the interaction between conflicting parties. At this point, parties are induced to reconsider viable peaceful alternatives to settle their dispute – thus making the mediation process more relevant and likely to take place (Stein 1989). In this phase, the mediators are faced with the challenging task of acquiring as much relevant information as possible and using this information to tailor an appropriate strategy in the following steps. This informa-tion can be acquired through a variety of methods, ranging from fact-finding missions, diplomatic channels, intelligence reports and secondary sources. In gathering relevant information, mediators need to acquire more than the publically-stated positions that are usually formulated as a comprehensive set of maximalist solutions. More relevant to the mediation process is the information that unveils the parties' fundamental interests and needs that they aim to achieve through conflict. Since this information is an indicator of why parties accept mediation, mediators may use it to increase the attractiveness of a negotiated solution and highlight the ineffectiveness of confrontational methods. Therefore, the first degree of success in international mediation is reflected in the media-tor's ability to transform conflictual relations and de-escalate the conflict by getting the parties to the table.

The second stage of mediation is related to the achievement of a formal agree-ment, regardless of its scope: whether it is a simple cease-fire or a compre-hensive agreement, it just needs to be a product of a mediation process. Once the mediators have acquired the necessary information and the parties have accepted the peacemaking process as a 'way out' of their predicament, they may proceed with the process in a more direct way. The parties start discussing the pertinent issues, which will potentially lead them toward de-escalation. This discussion is strongly conditioned by the information mediators acquired in the preparation stages. First of all, a lack of exploration in the preparation stage already becomes evident in the early phases of discussion and bargaining through inadequate proposals, procedural features and strategies that mediators employ. Second, the mediator's understanding of the issues at stake is reflected in a premeditated choice of how to conduct the talks. Depending on the nature of conflict and the characteristics of the parties, 'strategic sequencing' may start by addressing the most simple and least salient issues, gradually building up the momentum and trust required to tackle the most complex issues; or the parties may first be confronted with the most difficult aspect and subsequently discuss the less complex issues (Lax and Sebenius 1991). Furthermore, the process may also follow the logic of 'nothing is agreed until everything is agreed,' where the parties engage in a bargaining process aimed at creating attractive tradeoffs and package deals by combining various issues that are in the negotiation agenda. Third, the mediators need to have a very clear idea of who their negotiating partners are: they need to identify the most constructive ones and exclude those destructive elements that are less willing to engage in the de-escalation process. Finally, an active mediator needs to be able to control the situation and offer incentives to conflicting sides that might induce them to distance themselves from their initial positions and perceived alternatives and induce them to accept a negotiated agreement.

Mediated conflicts are more likely to result in formal agreements than those that are not mediated (Beardsley 2011, 75; see also Bercovitch and Gartner 2009). Depending on their primary scope and capacity to address the conflict's underlying issues, agreements may take different forms. The least comprehensive form is a cease-fire agreement. As their primary aim is to stop the violence, they represent the first step in creating the momentum required to produce a more comprehensive settlement. However, while they are the simplest form of agreement to achieve, they are also the easiest to break. Due to the fragility of cease-fire agreements, some scholars remain skeptical as to whether or not their achievement can be considered a measure of success, especially when they are not followed by more far-reaching settlements (Greig and Diehl 2012, 105). Partial or robust agreements contain provisions that reflect a greater degree of convergence between the parties. With them, the parties indicate at least a formal willingness to alter their belligerent behavior and agree on specific measures that could solidify peaceful relations.

Reaching an agreement brings us to the final stage of mediation: implementation. In this phase, mediation success is directly linked to the durability of the mediated settlements. Empirical studies show that mediators who commit themselves to maintaining their presence in the implementation phase strongly contribute to an agreement's longevity (Beardsley 2011, 151). In his phase, mediators seek to promote the utility of a negotiated agreement and gain support for the settlement from the constituencies. In order to increase the likelihood of compliance, mediators confer legitimacy and credibility to what was agreed upon (Kriesberg 1991, 25). At the same time, in order to reduce uncertainty between the parties, mediators may prescribe detailed sets of guarantees related to the implementation of the agreement such as setting up demilitarized zones, drafting disarmament provisions and/or employing cease-fire and election-monitoring missions (Fortna 2003). Nevertheless, the durability of settlements should not only be naively associated with a mediator's 'will and skill.' Conflict intensity and the nature of the issues at stake are often the primary reasons why some conflicts relapse into violence (Greig and Diehl 2012, 161). Although mediators might be called in to help improve communication between the parties and assist them in reframing the issues, thereby ripening the conflict for resolution through the creation of various inducements, their impact is highly dependent upon the parties' willingness to compromise. Evidently, the three degrees of success are strongly linked, as the same factors that encourage parties to accept mediation have a strong influence on their readiness to reach a mutually acceptable solution and make it endure over time. Although they do not provide a single measure of success, they encompass the complexities of international mediation as a voluntary and legally non-binding process.

Notes

1 This chapter is based on Vuković (2011), Vuković (2014a) and Vuković (2014b).
2 Galtung argues that we may observe structural violence when "the violence is built into the structure and shows up as unequal power and consequently as unequal life chances" (Galtung 1969, 171). Furthermore, by cultural violence he means "those aspects of culture, the symbolic sphere of our existence – exemplified by religion and ideology, language and art, empirical science and formal science (logic, mathematics) – that can be used to justify or legitimize direct or structural violence" (Galtung 1990, 291).
3 See Ott 1972; Young 1972a; Bercovitch 1984; Touval and Zartman 1985; Holsti 1991; Bercovitch *et al.* 1991.
4 The present definition is derived from earlier formulations put forward by Zartman and Touval (2007, 438) and Bercovitch and Jackson (2009, 35).
5 Some of the most recent mediation activities included: facilitating the Oslo accords between Israel and the PLO (Bercovitch 1997), contributing to the achievement of the Comprehensive Peace Agreement in Sudan (Kelleher 2006) and mediating the conflicts in former Yugoslavia (Simić 1995) and Sri Lanka (Höglund and Svensson 2009).
6 See Danilov 1999; Hyde Smith 2005; Hill 2012.

2   Multiparty mediation[1]

State of the art

Definition

After a nearly two decade long decline, the number of conflicts around the world has begun to increase once again. These conflicts encompass a complex interchange of local and international dynamics coupled with an increased number of actors involved and the goals they bring with them. Most of the conflicts fought in recent years have been intra-state (i.e., civil wars) and one of the most noticeable trends in these conflicts has been the increased fragmentation of the conflicting parties (Themnér and Wallensteen 2013). This poses a serious challenge to any peacemaking process. The creation of various factions increases the number actors whose approval is needed for an agreement to be accepted and, as a consequence, reduces the range of possible solutions. Furthermore, the multiplicity of actors opens the door to a more fluid set of alliances posing a challenge to the negotiation process (Cunningham 2006). To make matters even more complex, these conflicts have been characterized by another conspicuous tendency, unprecedented since the end of World War II: they have been increasingly internationalized in the sense that they saw one or more external states contributing troops to one or all conflicting sides (Themnér and Wallensteen 2014). While in principle external actors may affect an ongoing conflict by trying to manage it or by joining one of the sides in the fight, often these actors also pursue a separate agenda that may not fully align with that of the actors they may officially or unofficially support. In these cases, their presence may compound the adverse effects of an increased number of participants on the peacemaking process. First of all, it may distort the parties' assessment of the extent to which a mutually hurting stalemate exists, as the parties may believe that with external help they may still be able to escalate the conflict and achieve victory through unilateral action. At the same time, external actors may have less of an incentive to negotiate because the costs of fighting they bear are lower. Finally, their involvement brings a separate set of demands to the process, which need to be addressed in order for the conflict to be solved. By reducing the range of possible solutions and diminishing the sense of ripeness, external involvement may contribute strongly to prolonging the conflict (Cunningham 2010).

Evidently, in an international system that lacks an overarching authority, international conflicts often attract the involvement of actors with interests as divergent as the ones discernable between the conflicting parties themselves. As an increase in the use of mediation seems to be less a matter of choice and more a fact of life, the field of international mediation is becoming both diversified and crowded (Crocker *et al.* 1999). The traditional notion of mediation as a process primarily conducted by state representatives has been expanded by the continuous proliferation of new international actors that are willing and able to manage conflicts. Mediation activities are increasingly conducted by international and regional bodies, non-governmental organizations, local actors and eminent individuals. Contingent upon their relative capabilities and willingness to engage, these actors may enter the process at various stages and assume different roles that will have an impact on the overall outcome.

Mediation activities conducted by multiple third parties are commonly referred to as *multiparty mediation* (Crocker *et al.* 1999, 230). They include sequential, simultaneous and composite involvement of more than one external actor in mediating a dispute. The mediation efforts in the former Yugoslavia are an excellent example of sequential multiparty mediation. During the conflict, one actor after another became involved, building upon previous (failed) attempts to mediate a solution. As a result, in the case of Bosnia alone, by the time peace was brokered in Dayton, 144 different third parties had acted as mediators (Greig and Diehl 2012, 77). Multiparty mediation may also occur simultaneously involving many different mediators with various institutional foundations on the ground at the same time. This was the case in the multilevel peace processes in Tajikistan and Burundi in which 'track II' peace initiatives of the local civil society and international NGOs worked in parallel with 'track I' diplomatic efforts by neighboring states and international organizations such as the UN (Hara 1999; Saunders 1999; Iji 2001). Finally, multiparty mediation refers to interventions by ad hoc composite bodies and coalitions. In contemporary international society, which is becoming increasingly multipolar, ad hoc coalitions continuously change shape. The archetypical ad hoc coalitions of states are now complemented by the participation of other international actors. Looking at the reasons why states form coalitions, Frazier and Dixon argue that they "provide states the opportunity to act outside of formal multilateral settings but with some of the benefits of multilateralism such as legitimacy and pooling of resources" (Frazier and Dixon 2006, 391). At the same time, their multilateral composition might also be more appealing to the conflicting sides. Parties may perceive these groupings as not being subject to, guided by or in service of the interest of only one state. As each mediator enters the process with a particular set of resources and interests, the parties may perceive a coalition's activities as more balanced and sensitive to their interests (Gent and Shannon 2010).

Advantages of multiparty mediation

Multiparty mediation has become a very practical solution to modern day conflicts, which require elevated levels of commitment in order to manage them. Since it is rare that a single entity (a state, an international/regional organization, an NGO or an eminent individual) is either willing or able to invest as much as is really required, forming or expanding an existing coalition with other interested actors represents an attractive alternative. First of all, not every mediator enters the process with the same level or type of leverage required to incentivize the parties to adopt a solution. Joining a multiparty effort allows actors to pool in their resources and skills and, as a consequence, increase the overall leverage that can be applied in the mediation process (Crocker *et al.* 2001, 59). Second, a collective effort reduces the costs of mediation for each individual external actor. Acting in the context of coalitions generates smaller shares of fiscal burden and political risk associated with mediation (Böhmelt 2012, 702; see also Beber 2010). Third, collective actions are also perceived as being characterized by increased levels of legitimacy. In the most intractable conflicts, parties might strongly resist single-actor mediation because they may perceive it as being biased toward the other side. By expanding the number of actors, coalitions can include third parties that are sympathetic to the interests of all conflicting sides. As a consequence, the balance achieved increases the legitimacy of the process in the eyes of the conflicting sides. The projected legitimacy permits external actors to exercise their leverage with less resistance, adding to the overall effectiveness of the mediation process (see Tago 2005). Fourth, the participation of influential regional and global actors in the mediating coalition can contribute to 'restructuring' both domestic and regional relationships that may hamper the achievement of a negotiated solution. Although mediators are often interested in preventing or reducing the negative externalities of an escalating conflict, their participation in the mediation process may serve as an important impetus for improving systemic relations between them. By working together on managing a conflict, external actors establish new relations that transcend the dynamics of a particular conflict. As the case of Cambodia will show, external actors interested in managing the conflict developed momentum that helped them to move from confrontational to more constructive relations (see Solomon 1999; Crocker *et al.* 2001, 60).

It should be noted that third parties participating in a multiparty mediating process might assume different roles and responsibilities. The nature of their involvement depends on their interests in the conflict and capabilities they can employ in the peacemaking process. On a scale of assertiveness ranging from low to high, third parties may be active supporters of a mediating process conducted by other external actors, they could be co-chairs assisting the lead mediator or they could be lead mediators themselves. Regardless of the level of assertiveness, each external actor's contribution may prove to be pivotal to the process. Their cooperative involvement not only increases the legitimacy of the process, but also allows for their leverage to be used to create the crucial incentives that have the potential to encourage the conflicting parties to reach a mutually acceptable solution.

Finally, a very significant advantage of multiparty mediation activities is the possibility that different mediators enter the process at a particular stage, according to their resources and capabilities. According to Crocker, Hampson and Aall "when one avenue is blocked, the activities of another mediator or party providing 'good offices' can create a new opening in the negotiation process" (Crocker *et al.* 2001, 63). When the parties reach a deadlock in formal negotiations, under the scrutiny of the public eye, continuing the talks generates high political costs. In such circumstances, less formal talks can be mediated in a non-intrusive fashion, most commonly by low-key actors such as NGOs and eminent individuals. These talks may provide sufficient cover from domestic pressure and can create new opportunities for communication. The ability to extend the talks, by opening new channels through which relevant information can be exchanged and constructive proposals can be promoted, may help the process to break out of the impasse.

The conflict cycle and comparative advantage of different kinds of mediators

Crocker, Hampson and Aall offer a very detailed explanation of the comparative advantage different mediators may exploit depending on the stage of the conflict (Crocker *et al.* 1999, 2001, 2003). In the early phases of conflict, before parties resort to physical violence, combined interventions of non-official actors can help to defuse conflicts before they escalate (Crocker *et al.* 2001, 61). These situations are mainly characterized by diffuse political instability, systemic frustration, tension and suspicion between the parties, who have begun to develop animosity toward each other (see Lund 1996). Given the high level of uncertainty, parties might be willing to talk to each other, but only through an intermediary and only under certain conditions. First, they might be apprehensive about possible mediation activities conducted by other states and international organizations because their involvement can be perceived as interference in internal affairs. At the same time, a process mediated by such high-ranking international actors might internationalize and legitimize the cause of those actors that seek to contest the authority of the incumbent government. For these reasons, we can expect governments to be more responsive to initiatives that offer informal settings for communication, as such environments shield the parties from the pressure of their respective constituencies.

However, these low-key actors often lack the necessary leverage to be effective. Opening new channels of communication might be used by the parties for devious reasons to buy time, consolidate their resources and gain international support for their cause. Lacking the necessary leverage, mediators might not be able to incentivize the parties to reach a mutually acceptable solution. As the conflict continues to escalate, parties become more reluctant to accept the involvement of outside actors. Their relationships and perceptions of each other become even more polarized and antagonistic. They resort to inflammatory rhetoric, start threatening to use physical force and reduce communication to a minimum. As such, reestablishing communication becomes a priority. Once again, low-key mediators (i.e., NGOs) might be useful in establishing communication between the parties without making them lose face since publicly they might be committed to advancing policies that are more conflictual in nature (Crocker *et al.* 2003, 241).

Once communication has been established, it is useful to introduce mediators that have coercive and reward power that can be used in a formal setting (Crocker *et al.* 2001, 62). The use of coercive threats and side payments by third parties might induce conflicting sides to change their preconceived options and convince them to turn away from violence. Without these incentives, parties will have little reason to participate in talks and will be more inclined to continue hostilities as a means of achieving an acceptable solution. Consequently, as the conflict continues to escalate and the use of violence becomes more systematic, the process might require an even stronger presence of mediators with 'muscle' to assert the necessary amount of pressure on parties and lead them away from deadlock. According to Crocker, Hampson and Aall, at this point it is expected that mediators develop inventive and plausible solutions for "confidence-building measures, cease fire monitoring, verification proposals," to make sure that obligations are being met and other types of 'political guarantees' that facilitate addressing the most complex security issues pertinent to the parties (Crocker *et al.* 2003, 242). Under these circumstances success can only be achieved if mediators apply effective procedural control over the process. More importantly, if issues have not been addressed adequately during the negotiation process, this will most certainly cause problems in the implementation period. The participation of multiple mediators is not only beneficial due to the fact that they can lend leverage to the process during the negotiations; rather, depending on their relative capabilities, their involvement may be more crucial in the post-agreement phase when this leverage has to be used in practice. An inability to deliver incentives reduces the credibility of the mediation process, so it becomes crucial to avoid defection of the parties who can produce and put into effect various security guarantees, economic assistance and capacity building provisions that were used to incentivize the parties in reaching a negotiated solution.

Liabilities of multiparty mediation

Free riding is a very common liability associated with multiparty mediation processes. Many parties join the efforts because they do not have to bear the high costs of mediating alone and can still reap the benefits of a successful mediation. Since mediation activities are conducted in the most intractable cases, there is a strong possibility that some parties might avoid taking the blame when the process starts to fail. In such circumstances, the responsibility of tackling the most difficult issues is passed from one actor to another, often ending up in the hands of "the institution of last resort – the United Nations – which frequently has neither the resources nor the support of member states to shoulder the burden" (Crocker *et al.* 2001, 59).

While multiparty mediation permits cost sharing and pooling of leverage, these dynamics are strongly undermined if the parties enter the process without a shared understanding of the conflict and lack a shared sense of a possible solution (Crocker *et al.* 2001, 57). When mediators do not act on the basis of a shared script, they might send mixed signals to the parties. The parties may become confused about the strategies and resources that the mediators intend to use in order to incentivize them toward a solution. More importantly, the parties will lack a clear understanding of which solution is being promoted throughout the process. As the parties start developing the view that mediators might be working counterproductively, they might hijack the process for reasons other than reaching a negotiated solution. Alternatively, they may exploit this confusion to stall and buy time. Parties might also use this opportunity to go forum shopping for a mediator offering a negotiation process that is favorable to their cause (Crocker *et al.* 2001, 57; see Pinfari 2013).

Forum shopping poses a serious challenge to multiparty mediation processes. For instance, the UN Secretary General Ban Ki-Moon noted that "multiple actors competing for a mediation role create an opportunity for forum shopping as intermediaries are played off against each other. Such a fragmented international response reinforces fragmentation in the conflict and complicates resolution" (Ki-moon 2009). Similarly, in his report on "Strengthening the role of mediation in the peaceful settlement of disputes, conflict prevention and resolution," the UN Secretary General emphasized that "competition and disagreement over strategy and funding have permitted parties to forum shop, therefore hampering peace efforts" (A/66/811 2012, pt. 15). As a solution, Annex I of the report entitled "United Nations Guidance for Effective Mediation" emphasizes the importance of coherence, coordination and complementarity of the mediation effort as the necessary ingredients for eliminating the negative effects of forum shopping and improving overall mediation effectiveness (A/66/811 2012, pt. 43–47).

Size and composition of the mediating coalition

Achieving coherence, coordination and complementarity becomes extremely difficult as the mediating coalition becomes enlarged. While some studies suggest that multilateralism increases the likelihood of reaching a negotiated solution (Frazier and Dixon 2006), there might be an inverse relationship between the number of mediators and the probability of creating and maintaining a synchronized intervention strategy. Mediators participating in mediating coalitions not only differ in terms of the leverage at their disposal, they also bring with them diverging interests and understandings of the conflict. The more the number of mediators increases, the more likely it is that the coalition will be characterized by heterogeneous interests and the more complex the relationship between the parties will be (Crocker *et al.* 2003, 252). Böhmelt (2011) argues that with an increase in the number of mediators comes an increase in organizational costs necessary for the achievement and maintenance of cooperative efforts. Multiplication of mediators requires organizational regulation through monitoring mechanisms and sanctions regimes for non-compliance (Axelrod and Keohane 1985, Fearon 1998, Touval 2010). So as the number of actors increases, so too will the difficulties in regulating their cooperation increase. Reflecting on the dynamic of borrowing leverage and increasing organizational costs, Böhmelt finds that both small and very large groups are less effective in mediating disputes. On the one hand, a single mediator or a small group rarely has the necessary amount of leverage to produce the crucial incentives for the parties in conflict. On the other hand, while the bigger coalitions are more likely to possess the necessary leverage, their size makes them more difficult to organize and produces a "greater heterogeneity of interests" (Böhmelt 2011, 877). Therefore, the expansion of the mediating coalition is certainly instrumental to the effectiveness of mediation efforts until the moment the coalition becomes congested and difficult to organize and coordinate.

Although coalitions composed of democratic states might promote the spirit of coherence, complementarity and coordination, these coalitions do not have a significant impact on mediation effectiveness. Böhmelt finds that chances of effective conflict resolution are not driven by regime type (Böhmelt 2011, 877). Shared norms in promoting peaceful methods of managing conflicts may actually contribute to the collective action problems and free riding seen in many democracies. Participation in a coalition of democracies makes collaborative behavior routine, promotes the exchange of crucial information and, most importantly, ensures predictability in decision-making processes. Under such conditions, according to Böhmelt "the more democracies there are as third-party interveners in a dispute, the more likely these states will rely on their fraternal obligation and expect that other democracies will provide more leverage or resources for settling a conflict" (Böhmelt 2011, 877). As experience shows, on numerous occasions, multiparty mediation has been successful even when it was conducted by a coalition composed of democratic and non-democratic states. In some instances, the participation of non-democratic states was essential to delivering the incentives required for the parties to move toward a negotiated solution. Therefore, while convergence of interests and perceptions between mediators helps the process to overcome issues such as forum shopping and commitment problems, effective multiparty mediation is also contingent upon the mediator's leverage, resources and the strategies applied in the process.

There seems to be noticeable variety in the make-up of coalitions. According to data presented by Greig and Diehl (2012), international organizations are more inclined to join coalitions with likeminded international actors. Less than 5% of all mediation activities conducted by international organizations included third parties with opposing interests. Working under the provisions present in Chapter VII of its Charter, the United Nations has been very active in strengthening its interaction with various regional organizations. It has established an office to the African Union and developed two mediation capacity-building programs (2009–2010 and 2011–2012) aimed at strengthening AU mediation capacities. Similar work plans were set up with OAS and OIC in 2011. The UN has also worked very closely with ASEAN, the EU and the OSCE in exchanging know-how, identifying areas of capacity building and establishing useful forms of cooperation (A/66/811 2012, pt. 45–49). At the same time, the UN has been very vocal in highlighting the importance of maintaining a partnership in mediation efforts. For this reason, the UN has conducted annual meetings with regional organizations at the expert level, developed a mediation support network of NGO representatives and formed the Group of Friends of Mediation, composed of 28 member states (A/66/811 2012, pt. 56–60). The UN took all these measures as a way of fostering coherent mediation activities and promoting the need for keeping competing interests within mediation coalitions to a minimum.

On the other hand, around 17% of multiparty state mediations are conducted by coalitions in which participating actors are engaged in balancing their biases (Greig and Diehl 2012, 75). The fact that multiparty state mediation is characterized by greater diversity compared to the efforts of international organizations does not mean that these efforts are predestined to fail. Certainly, it is difficult to imagine that a mediating effort could be successful if conducted by mediators with competing interests that do not wish to cooperate with each other. In cases in which mediators have competing interests and diverse alliances (relationships) with the parties to the conflict, meditation coalitions can be seen as 'teams of rivals.' In these circumstances, effective multiparty mediation is conducted by "negotiating teams that are not necessarily comprised of likeminded, ideological soul mates but are 'teams of rivals' who develop mutual respect and a common understanding that they share wider strategic interests and goals which go beyond the conflict in question" (Hampson and Zartman 2011, 134). Efficiency is dependent upon the mediators agreeing to work as a team. This attitude represents a clear signal of (initial) willingness to cooperate, despite the fact that they still harbor competing biases. The fact that they maintain diverging interests sends a signal to the parties to the conflict that their stakes might be secured (i.e., that they have an ally in the team of rivals), which increases the appeal of the mediating coalition. However, once accepted by the parties, mediators need to develop a sense that cooperation is both possible and useful for the advancement of their interests as well. While they may have diverging interests regarding a particular conflict, they could still develop a sense of convergence based on a broader set of strategic interests that govern their relations. This convergence opens the door to cooperation in the mediation process and subsequent coordination of mediator strategies and leverage.

Cooperation

Conceptualizing cooperation

With all this in mind, the crucial challenges that multiparty mediation processes have to overcome are the (1) achievement of adequate *cooperation* among the mediators themselves and (2) subsequent *coordination* of their activities in the mediation process. Many studies have already demonstrated how cooperative and coordinated interactions between mediators improve mediation effectiveness (Zartman 1989a; Kriesberg 1996; Crocker *et al*. 1999, 2001, 2003; Whitefield 2007; Diehl and Lepgold 2003; Iji 2005; Fisher 2006; Strimling 2006; Böhmelt 2011; Beardsley 2011; Touval 2010; Hampson and Zartman 2011; Heldt 2013). Zartman encapsulates the general argument as follows:

> Conflict management is best carried out in *concert*. If a number of concilia-
> tors are available to the parties themselves and if a number of friends of the
> conflicting parties can *coordinate* their good offices and pressure, the
> chances of success are improved.
>
> (emphases added, Zartman 1989a, 276)

Cooperation can be understood as "a situation where parties agree to work together to produce new gains for each of the participants that would be unavail-able to them by unilateral action, at some cost" (Zartman and Touval 2010, 1). It implies a dynamic through which parties with competing interests decide to pool their resources and capabilities in order to achieve common gains. Cooperation is not coincidental. It represents a conscious and planned course of action through which participants reach an agreement to overcome their incompatibili-ties by working together. When faced with incompatible goals, parties can take one of three courses of action: pursue unilateral action, enter a cooperative arrangement or not (re)acting at all. In international affairs, actors that are focused on preserving the autonomy of their actions may prefer to act alone and follow the maxim 'unilaterally if possible, multilaterally if necessary' (see Touval 2010). The decision to act unilaterally is directly related to the costs of cooperation: parties will decide to pursue unilateral action when the costs of cooperation outweigh the expected benefits. In other words, cooperation is pos-sible when they perceive that it would cost them less to attain their goals by cooperating than to act alone (Zartman and Touval 2010, 5).

The costs of cooperation are multifold. First of all, costs may reflect organiza-tional externalities. While institutionalized multilateralism has the potential to reduce transaction costs by establishing predictable rules and procedures that foster coordinated activities (Keohane 1984, Ruggie 1993), ad hoc cooperative endeavors are much more costly. Outside of established regimes, which regulate cooperation, actors must agree, design and maintain the rules and procedures each time they decide to work together. These decisions are not, however, isolated from the wider network of interactions between the actors. In fact, one explana-tion of why cooperation takes place is the existence of interdependence (Keohane and Nye 1977). Interdependence creates an environment full of precedents and established norms that are of heuristic value when it comes to formulating future (ad hoc) cooperative arrangements. Thus, the organizational costs of cooperation decrease as actors cooperate more over time. The second type of costs derives from the negotiation dynamics that are intrinsic to any cooperative activity. From the perspective of negotiation, cooperation is a process in which participating actors combine competing interests to obtain common ones (Hopmann 2010).

The creation of common interests is a result of a negotiation process through which the parties re-evaluate their original goals. By exchanging the necessary information about their interests and needs, parties redefine their incompatibilities and seek to create joint gains. Establishing joint gains requires parties to abandon their maximalist goals and formulate a solution on the basis of compromise that benefits all of them (Hopmann 2001). Essentially, in order to co-opt the opponent into realizing joint gains, a party needs to give something in return. They do this subject to the expectation that the other side will reciprocate. Thus by agreeing to cooperate, parties willingly settle for less than initially planned. They accept these costs once the benefits of cooperation outweigh them. On the one hand, they may be aware that their unilateral actions are not yielding the expected results. On the other hand, through the process of reframing, parties manage to create value that was not apparent in their initial assessment. More importantly, they realize that this value can be attained only through cooperative endeavors; in other words, the newly formulated value is contingent upon the cooperative participation of the other side. It should be noted that cooperation does not mean the abandonment of previous goals. On the contrary, it is a method of achieving (reframed) goals – which still reflect essential interests – through means other than confrontation (Zartman 2010). Also, it is important to emphasize that both costs and benefits are not only measured in terms of material means. For instance, when parties agree to cooperate, they acknowledge the other party's interests as legitimate. Similarly, by cooperating, parties empathize with each other and recognize that each other's well-being is mutually reinforcing and that they are codependent. Therefore, costs and benefits may also relate to various intangible assets such as security, autonomy, reputation, etc.

The creation of joint gains through cooperation is only possible if the parties are willing to reciprocate. Reciprocity represents an assurance that cooperative behavior will be rewarded with a similar behavior in the future. In an environment characterized by incomplete information, parties will reciprocate only on temporary and ad hoc basis, fearing defection from the other side. In conditions of such uncertainty, cheating represents a safety measure that parties apply in order to protect their interests (see Baldwin 1993). One way to overcome problems of incomplete information and promote the benefits of cooperation is through repetition. Axelrod finds that tit-for-tat strategy – reacting to the opponent's strategy by employing the same one – allows parties to learn about the benefits of cooperation in a very short period of time, as their cooperative behavior is reciprocated to produce joint gains (Axelrod 1984). However, tit-for-tat as a repetitive strategy also has the potential to generate and perpetuate conflict: once the actors start reciprocating confrontational behavior, they become entrapped in a spiral of conflict from which it becomes very difficult to escape. Evidently communication represents a crucial component of cooperation: "the more reliable information of future reciprocity, the greater the chances of cooperation lasting" (Zartman and Touval 2010, 7; Strimling 2006). As mentioned previously, in order to avoid operational costs associated with defining and maintaining principles of cooperation, parties might decide to institutionalize their cooperative interactions.

By creating predictable and pre-arranged frameworks for communication, parties may contribute to a routinized dynamic of reciprocity that does not require immediate returns. According to Hopmann,

> Parties reciprocate cooperation, not so much because they expect an immediate reward but because they have a relationship built upon trust in which they can expect the other to reciprocate whenever necessary at any indefinite time in the future. In this sense, expectations of reciprocity and peaceful change have become a constitutive part of the relationship; they are expected as an inherent part of the relationship and not necessarily because of some expectation of immediate reward.
>
> (Hopmann 2010, 103–104)

In other words, reciprocity is more than a simple process of giving something in order to get something *immediately* in return. Reciprocity takes place on the basis of a coordinated exchange between the parties. Cooperation and coordination are not two distinct phenomena; rather, coordination represents a subset dynamic of the larger cooperative process (Strimling 2006). While both cooperation and coordination imply that the actors involved need to have shared goals, there is still a very clear difference between the two phenomena. A precondition of successful cooperation is that all parties recognize the shared benefits of working in concert. Once acknowledged as beneficial, cooperation opens the doors to the dynamics of coordination, which involves the more mechanical aspects of dividing the labor effectively and clarifying who needs to do what, when and how. In other words coordination is the next step in the process of achieving full cooperation, as parties make sure that they do not cross purposes or stumble over each other in their efforts to accomplish their common goal.

Cooperation in multiparty mediation

In the realm of multiparty mediation, cooperation can be observed in its full complexity. In order to reach a successful outcome, cooperation needs to take place on three distinct yet highly interrelated levels. First, since the dynamics of the conflict impede the parties from negotiating directly (i.e., bilaterally), they have to choose to cooperate with third parties in order to find a mutually acceptable solution. At the same time, since the conflict is mediated by a multitude of outside actors, these actors also need to come up with a 'common script' that will serve as a clear guideline for resolving the dispute. Thus all the third parties need to cooperate amongst themselves and reduce the possibility of sending mixed signals, which might jeopardize the management process. Finally, it should not be forgotten that each outside actor also has a specific interest in resolving the conflict and that this interest is directly related to the mediator's relations with one (or both) disputing sides. For this reason, it is essential that cooperation take place on this third level, as this is the level at which outside actors acquire their added leverage.

When multiple mediators act in concert, they all face dual costs: those of cooperating plus the inevitable costs of mediation. Given the combined costs of multiparty mediation, for cooperation to take place, parties need to know that the benefits will outweigh the costs. It is not uncommon that at a certain point in the process of cooperating, a party decides to defect from the group. Defection may come in different forms – from procrastination to full abandonment of the process – but its distinct features in multiparty mediation processes are: a reluctance to work together; non-recognition of joint gains; and an unwillingness to use the full potential of its leverage and resources to move the conflicting parties toward an agreement. So even while trying to establish a cooperative arrangement parties may create new conflicts: they may realize how incompatible their perceptions of the conflict are; they may disagree about the distribution of costs and benefits; or they could object to the respective contributions cooperation requires (Zartman and Touval 2010, 3). Therefore, it becomes crucial to understand not only why parties cooperate, but also how they arrive at it and how is it maintained.

Game theoretical model

In order to fully understand the complexities of achieving cooperation in a multiparty mediation effort, this section will first provide an abstraction of the process in the form of a game theoretical model. Game theoretic approaches are useful insofar as they allow us to analyze the decisions parties make regarding potential strategies available to them in the mediation process as they pursue the maximization of their expected utilities. Several studies of mediation have already benefited from the use of rational choice models (Kydd 2003, 2006; Maoz and Terris 2006). The intention here is to bring into play those findings to help us understand the general patterns that govern the relations between the parties and the specific decisions they make throughout the mediation process.

Because one of the underlying assumptions is that the nature of cooperation can change over time, this model will utilize the dynamic Theory of Moves (ToM). Brams developed this theory in order to bring, "a dynamic dimension to the classical theory of games, which its founders characterized as 'thoroughly static'" (von Neumann and Morgenstern 1944; 3rd edn, 1953, pg. 44 as quoted in Brams 1994, 1). The first rule of ToM is that a game must start at an outcome, called "initial state" (Brams 1994, 22). The assumption is that from this state, players can aspire to move to a better state by switching their strategies. As Brams explains it, "as they look ahead at their possible moves, the possible countermoves of other players, their own counter-countermoves, and so on, the players try to anticipate where play will terminate" (7). Thus, the game ends when, after a series of "alternating responses," the player who has the next move decides not to switch its strategy (22). Another important rule of ToM is that a player will not move from an initial state if this move "leads to a less preferred final state; or returns play to the initial state" (27). Brams calls this rule "a *rationality rule,* because it provides the basis for players to determine whether they can do better by moving from a state or remaining in it" (28). The last rule is that of "*precedence*," and it implies that once a player makes a move "its move overrides the player who stays, so the outcome will be induced by a player who moves" (28). As each player looks ahead and makes rational calculations of where to move from each initial state, the process ends in outcomes that Brams calls *nonmyopic equilibria* or NME (33).

Brams' theory proves its applicability to the case of mediation by arguing that:

> [s]ome decisions are made collectively by players in which case it would be reasonable to say that they choose strategies from scratch, either simultaneously or by coordinating their choices. But if say two countries are coordinating their choices, as when they agree to sign a treaty, the important question is what individualistic calculations led them to this point. The formality of jointly signing a treaty is the culmination of their negotiations, which covers up the move-countermove process that preceded it. This is precisely what ToM is designed to uncover.
>
> (Brams 1994, 23)

Let us assume that there are two disputing sides – side A and side B – that are unable to negotiate a settlement themselves. The intractable nature of their conflict and the issues at stake draw attention from more than one outside actor that have an interest in managing the peace process. Again, for the purposes of simplification, let us assume that we have (at least) three such players, each one with specific interests in the conflict, leverage they can exert in the peace process and relationships they have with other mediators and conflicting sides. Therefore, let's presume that mediators 1 and 3 are *biased mediators* due to the particular nature of their relationship with parties to the dispute. Mediator 1 is biased toward party A, and has particular leverage over it, so as it is able to move party A in its intended direction. The same relationship exists between mediator 3 and party B. Conversely, mediator 2 is what scholarship refers to as a *pure mediator* that does not have a special relationship with either of the conflicting sides, but nevertheless has a strong interest in resolving the conflict (see Fisher and Keashly 1991). The model will assume that mediator 2 is the only actor that is unwilling to drop out of the process, while actors 1 and 3 might opt for this strategy and thus undermine cooperation within the mediating coalition.

Under all these assumptions, the model prescribes four different scenarios. In the first scenario, all three mediators choose to cooperate throughout the process. In the second and the third scenarios, actors 1 and 3 respectively choose to defect from the group while still maintaining a biased relationship with either A or B. In the fourth scenario, both 1 and 3 choose to defect, leaving the entire mediating process to 2, though they once again maintain biased relations with conflicting sides.

The model predicts that cooperation in the process of multiparty mediation can be explained using an inverted prisoner's dilemma. This dilemma describes a situation in which the conflicting sides (A and B) become involved in the mediation process, regardless of the action of the mediators. In other words, the mediation process will continue even if one mediator decides not to cooperate with the rest of the group. Using the Theory of Moves, we can interpret the model as follows (Table 2.1).

Point (a) is a common starting point for all international conflicts. It is the moment at which a conflict assumes the necessary characteristics to encourage outside actors to become involved. Many studies have examined the phenomena, of who mediates and when and why it occurs (Bercovitch and Schneider 2000; Greig and Regan 2008). As the model shows, here mediation is conducted by one outside actor (number 2) that parties perceive as trustworthy and unbiased. At this point, each biased mediator chooses not to participate in mediation, while still maintaining a biased relationship with one of the conflicting sides. In this case, outside actors avoid both the costs of mediation and of cooperation. At the same time, they still maintain a special relationship with one of the parties to the dispute and thus still indirectly exercise some influence over the mediation process, which is being conducted by actor 2 alone. Theoretically speaking, this outcome is NME, because it creates greater benefits than any other, so in the event that the game starts at this point, rational actors would not move from it. Nonetheless, as only one mediator is involved in the process, we cannot speak of multiparty mediation taking place in this state.

In the contemporary dynamics of international relations, we can expect to observe a proliferation of actors willing to step in and manage a conflict in accordance with their particular interests. Knowing that more benefits can be accrued by joining the mediation coalition, one actor might decide to opt for a cooperative strategy from the beginning. Thus, the game actually starts at point (b), when one biased mediator decides to start cooperating with mediator number 2. In this state, the mediator that does not cooperate with the other two faces smaller benefits compared to the one that chose to cooperate (1,4) or (4,1). Nevertheless, in reality we often see that some actors purposefully choose not to cooperate with other mediators. Why would this be the case? Because their rationality is myopic, actors may fail to recognize that the game cannot revert to point (a), where a non-cooperative strategy would have created far greater benefits. Here the choice of non-cooperation (point (a)) is compounded by the fact that some actors aim to use their biased position to influence the behavior of a

Table 2.1 Game theoretical model

| | | Mediator 1 | |
		Cooperates	No cooperation
Mediator 3	Cooperates	(c) 2,2	(b) 4,1
	No cooperation	(b) 1,4	(a) 3,3

particular side in the conflict and consequently to spoil the mediation efforts of other actors. In fact, as the rule of ToM dictates, the next move is that of a player that does not yet cooperate and its next move cannot be to move the other player back to non-cooperative behavior. Thus they need to realize that the best they can hope to achieve given the game's progress is a move to point (c).

However appealing the non-cooperation decision might appear at a first glance, spoiling the process might actually backfire. When an outside actor decides not to cooperate while others are engaged in mediation, it undercuts its own potential to exercise influence over other actors involved in the mediation and loses the potential to create benefits for itself and its partner side in the conflict. While the biased mediator stays outside the coalition, the side it is supporting might still remain trapped in the process and it is to be expected that in such a situation, it is less likely that potential solutions will be to its advantage. When one side in the conflict is losing through mediation, so will its outside partners, even though they are officially not cooperating in the process. For example, their international reputation might be undermined, as might their leverage to influence future developments in the process. In such circumstances, both the non-cooperative outside actor and its partner party to the conflict will face far smaller benefits than those who opt to cooperate and potentially (through constructive dialogue and exercising necessary leverage) move the proposed solution to their advantage.

Faced with a lower payoff, a rational second biased mediator decides to cooperate, which moves the game to its final state found at point (c), which is the outcome of the game and an NME. Even though in this case their utility is smaller than at point (a) (due to the costs of both mediating and cooperating), they will undeniably experience greater benefits than they would if they were not part of the mediating coalition. In such a setting, each mediator is able to exert a certain pressure on the process and bargain in favor of the side in the conflict with which they have special relations. Biased mediators attain important utility as their partner involved in the conflict gains through mediation. Thus, despite the costs of mediating and acting in concert, the second outside actor still manages to accrue greater benefits through coordinated activities than it would have if it opted for a strategy of defection, assuming that mutual defection is not an option. This is in line with the initial statement that cooperation implies the creation of new gains for each party that were unavailable to them by means of unilateral action, albeit at some cost.

If interpreted in terms of classical game theory, cooperation represents a dominant strategy in this model and the Nash equilibrium is point (c) (2,2). ToM also provides a similar results, given that once the multiparty mediation starts, cooperative behavior produces higher payoffs than defection does and the final state is also at point (c). Overall, cooperation can be identified as a rational strategy that leads to non-myopic equilibria. Once a party chooses to cooperate, short-term goals that induced a party to defect are no longer a priority. Rather, for a rational outside party that received low payoffs from a strategy of defection, cooperation becomes a useful mechanism through which it is possible to limit the other side's utility. In other words, cooperation proves to be decidedly beneficial not only to the process, but to the parties themselves.

Insights from the model and relevance to the process

This model highlights that, for external actors, the employment of cooperative strategies is actually more beneficial than spoiling the process would be. In fact, even the cumulative costs of cooperating and mediating complemented by the potential benefits of acting as a spoiler still do not match the benefits generated by cooperative strategies. Since cooperation is decidedly beneficial not only to the process but to the mediators themselves, it is important to understand what should be done once an external actor opts to defect from a group. As noted by Sisk,

> game theory contributes to mediation strategies through the finding that one can *encourage moderation and deter 'defection'* in bargaining relationships by not allowing a player to gain from a defection strategy, even if it imposes additional costs to cooperation to prevent a defector's gain.
>
> (Sisk 2009, 48; emphasis added)

Discouraging defection is not a simple task, as it implies direct interference in another party's policy objectives. In this case, it is not enough just to issue a reprimand for non-cooperative behavior or warn that such a strategy is not constructive for the overall process of mediation and leave it at that. It is essential that the defecting party come to recognize the benefits of deciding to change its strategy and pursue cooperative strategies.

In his analysis of international mediation in Zimbabwe, Stedman (1991) endorses a polycentric view and notes that both conflicting parties and mediators are rarely unitary actors. According to his study, because conflicting parties are often composed of various factions and splinter groups, an expectation that all of them perceive a 'hurting stalemate' is quite untenable. Rather it is the external actors that show interest in managing the conflict that are the real agents forwarding that perception. In other words, the perception of ripeness often occurs first among the external actors and it is subsequently transposed from them to the conflicting sides. However, given the proliferation of mediators, in order to promote the perception of ripeness, it is crucial that they speak with a single voice (Stedman 1991, 242; see also Kleiboer 1994; Zartman 2001). Fostering a perception of ripeness between mediators can be seen as an essential ingredient in achieving the sense of urgency required to reach the necessary convergence of interests that would allow them to work together to manage the dispute. Existing theories on this topic focus primarily on the significance of inducing a perception of ripe moments on the part of the conflicting sides. Less is known about the mechanisms that generate a perception of ripeness among the external actors. Despite the fact that there are obvious differences in roles, capabilities and preferences between actors internal and external to the conflict, existing notions of ripeness theory could be extended to mediators as well because their competing interests that impede the achievement of cooperative endeavors create a new conflict that needs to be overcome. Managing the conflict between mediators depends on their ability to realize the inadequacy of unilateral action and recognize the utility of cooperation.

Specific foreign policy objectives never exist in a vacuum. They are embedded in a broader set of strategic interests that each actor pursues on the international stage. In that sense, the motivation to manage a conflict is never an isolated decision; instead it should be seen as an element of a more complex network of strategic choices developed by each actor in the international arena. Significant developments on the systemic level caused by pivotal political, social, economic and/or natural events might strongly affect an actor's strategic priorities and encourage them to re-evaluate the guiding principles of their foreign policies. Although such geo-political shifts are largely exogenous to the conflict that is being managed, they still have the potential to alter external actors' interests in mediating the dispute. In some instances, these shifts may lead third parties to the point where their interests in managing the conflict converge. For instance, conflicts taking place in close proximity to each other, at the same time will impact the disputants' decision to accept mediation. According to Kriesberg, as a parallel conflict starts to intensify for one or more conflicting sides, the saliency of their previous conflict may decrease, making de-escalation possible (Kriesberg 1991, 20). During the hostage crisis of 1979, Iran's uncompromising position during the first few months of Algerian mediation was altered as Iran entered a parallel conflict with Iraq. Sick noted that, "as the cost of the Iran-Iraq began to mount, this conflict probably increased pressure on the Iranian clerics to find a settlement" (Sick 1985, 50). A similar argument may be made for external actors. The presence of a parallel conflict that has the potential to affect the external actors' strategic interests may influence their calculations about the ongoing dispute and induce them to find a solution through a cooperative multiparty mediation effort. A solution to the ongoing dispute prevents them from overstretching their capacities by being involved and/or managing several disputes at the same time.

Similarly, disastrous events of natural or man-made origin can upset the established strategies of the conflicting sides: the more devastating these events are, the more costly an ongoing conflict may become, making a negotiated solution an attractive alternative. The peace talks between the government of Indonesia and the Aceh Free Movement reached a breakthrough following the destructive tsunami that hit the area in December 2004. The 'tsunami effect' "was a shake-up in circumstances that meant talks could begin again, on a new foundation" (Large and Aguswandi 2008, 10). Comparable events could also impact the external actors' calculations about an ongoing conflict. If a non-cooperative external actor experiences a tragic event of large proportions, it might find it increasingly difficult and costly to maintain its confrontational attitudes vis-à-vis other external actors in managing a specific dispute. At the same time, it might not be able to invest as much time and resources in a specific conflict anymore. Sharing the costs of conflict management with other external actors becomes an appealing alternative, which, in turn, increases the likelihood of cooperative engagement between the mediators.

Reframed policy objectives may also emerge with the arrival of a new political elite. A change in leadership structure has the potential to foster the subjective perception of a painful deadlock, which may not have been recognized previously despite the same objective circumstances (Stedman 1991). This was the case during the Beagle Channel dispute mediated by the Vatican. The conflict was successfully mediated only once the non-compromising military regime in Buenos Aires was replaced by the democratically-elected president Alfonsín, who ran on a platform of unequivocal support for a negotiated solution (Fournier 1999, 65). Although changes in leadership can be useful indicators of an emerging sense of ripeness between the parties, interpreting these changes is never a straightforward task. As Zartman and de Soto note, "the reasons the new leadership gained power and any accompanying messages must be studied for signs of recognition that the conflict is in a stalemate and it hurts" (2010, 16). Without such unequivocal messages, the establishment of a new elite does not automatically mean that a sense of urgency to resolve a lingering conflict has been created. The new elite might not be able to produce an opening for negotiations or might be deprived of the necessary 'credentials' to act on such a delicate policy preference. At the same time, new elites might be even more reluctant to compromise, making a negotiated solution even more unlikely. Therefore, evaluating the new elite's policy preferences is of great importance to knowing whether or not the parties are likely to find a way to resolve their differences. This principle can be transposed onto a mediating coalition that experiences difficulties reaching common ground on how to proceed with mediation. A change in leadership in one or more of interested external actors might bring to power an elite more willing to compromise with the rest of the international community. If they find the confrontational strategies of their predecessors to be too destructive and ill equipped to yield the expected benefits, they might be inclined to perceive cooperation with other third parties as a more attractive alternative and might thus formulate a new set of foreign policy objectives accordingly. On the other hand, a new elite that promotes a platform of further insistence on uncompromising policies will only reinforce the existing lack of cooperation and common ground between them and other international actors. Thus, to reiterate the earlier argument by Zartman and de Soto, in order to know whether or not the new elite will bring about change that will produce a more cooperative environment, it is important to know if it is sending signals of recognition that the current situation is quite painful and unbearable. The new elite might be apprehensive about the domestic socio-political and economic conditions or damaged international reputation created by the previous regime's confrontational attitude. In these circumstances, improving relations with other international actors may generate gains that could be used to improve the domestic situation and repair a tarnished international image.

Evidently, changes in foreign policy objectives induced by exogenous geopolitical shifts have a trickle-down effect: the mediators' decision to re-evaluate their interests in the conflict is induced by factors that are external to it. However, the more the third parties expand their degree of involvement in the conflict, the more their interests become susceptible to the dynamics of the conflict. Those external actors that provide logistical and/or military support to one of the conflicting parties may experience mounting costs and losses more directly. Even though formally they might act as mediators or external actors supporting the mediation process, these actors could still employ violence as an off-the-table tactic in the same way conflicting parties do. Although a non-cooperative third party might find direct support of one of the sides in a conflict to be in line with its foreign policy objectives, as the conflict dynamics on the ground start to take their toll, the desirability of continuing the conflict may start to wane. In these circumstances, as confrontational strategies have resulted in higher costs than expected benefits, the non-cooperative third party might find that it is in its interest to re-evaluate its approach and seek the attainment of greater benefits via cooperation. It is important to emphasize that once external actors start experiencing a hurting stalemate, they can transmit this message to their partners, regardless of how they feel about it. As mentioned earlier, the involvement of an external supporter distorts the sense of ripeness among the parties (Cunningham 2010), so a message conveyed by outside allies that the conflict is ripe for a mediated solution directly contributes to the possibility that a conflicting party will reframe its approach to the conflict as well. For instance, it was the external supporters of the Patriotic Front and the Government of Rhodesia who first felt the hurting stalemate and put pressure on the parties to agree to a mediated solution (Stedman 1991). They did this because, "the conflict was costing them good relations among other allies, notably other African states and the United States, and their reputation was suffering for not bringing the conflict to an end" (Zartman and de Soto 2010, 16).

The Zimbabwean case clearly indicates that costs of an ongoing conflict are not only material in nature. In fact, as mentioned earlier in this chapter, reputational costs represent a significant aspect of the cost-benefit analysis that actors make prior to cooperating with others. The decision of the parties to the conflict to cooperate is also conditioned by the effects confrontational strategies will have on cooperation with their allies outside of the conflict. For example, the move from confrontation to cooperation that led to a settlement in South Africa in the early 1990s was made because confrontational strategies were isolating the parties from the rest of the international community. On the one hand, de Klerk's government had begun to realize that non-cooperative, old regime policies were no longer able to generate the expected security and level of affluence for the minority and were contributing to further degradation of the regime's international reputation and legitimacy (Zartman 1995, 148). On the other, the fall of the Soviet Union represented an important loss of international support for the African National Congress. According to Zartman,

> To both, engagement in a cooperative strategy brought international support and approval. Although neither party's goals changed in their pursuit of

their conflict, their means shifted to cooperation, induced by the need for cooperation within the international community, without which the confrontation tactics could and would have continued.

(Zartman 2010, 168)

Zartman refers to this as a 'playback effect,' which is "the impact of unilateral action on relations with third parties and potential allies in cooperation at other times and on other issues" (Zartman 2010, 164). While both exogenous geopolitical shifts and changes of conflict dynamics imply that non-cooperative external actors will change their strategies on their own initiative, the playback effect points to the possibility that the initiative for cooperation might come from the rest of the coalition. Zartman suggests that the "international community of relevant bystanders will cooperate among themselves to try to induce a conflicting member to shift to cooperation when it gets too confrontational in pursuing its conflict with another party" (Zartman 2010, 162). It is important to note that defection is a direct expression of an actor's policy preferences, so one way of encouraging a mediator to abandon non-cooperative attitudes is to expose it to pressure exercised by the rest of the mediating coalition. However, since such coercion is costly and often used primarily toward conflicting parties, the coalition may also opt to engage the defecting mediator in a negotiating process. Here, a change in current behavior is achieved through incentives that make participation an attractive option. In other words, building a 'team of rivals' is dependent upon making the necessary trade-offs (Hampson and Zartman 2011, 134). The difficulty of negotiating an effective cooperative arrangement increases with the number of participants. Therefore, it is often useful to narrow down the focus to specific issues and conduct the process only among the selected group of actors that have a direct stake in the particular issues at hand (Hampson 1995). The group may only be expanded by including actors that are able to contribute to the establishment of collective effort. There is no rule specifying where the process should take place. It may be conducted in an entirely ad hoc manner outside of the context of the existing multilateral arrangements. At the same time, the issue could be placed on the agenda of an existing institution that allows for the negotiations to be still held within a small and selective group of actors (Touval 2010, 89). Regardless of where they take place, negotiations on cooperation are not only important because of the compromise required on specific issues, but also in terms of their ability to create pact-building relationships and a sense of shared decision making (Hampson 2010, Zartman and Touval 2010).

Clearly, the responsibility for encouraging an external actor to adopt a shared idea of a solution and to opt for a cooperative strategy is often placed on the rest of the mediating coalition. More precisely, it is the actors who have a strong self-interest in the conflict's outcome that generally take the initiative to negotiate with defectors. They do this in order to avoid the negative consequences of competing interests within the mediating coalition. Reflecting on the game theoretical model presented earlier, cooperation becomes possible when the mediators perceive it to be in their self-interest. The fact that some actors decide not to cooperate can be

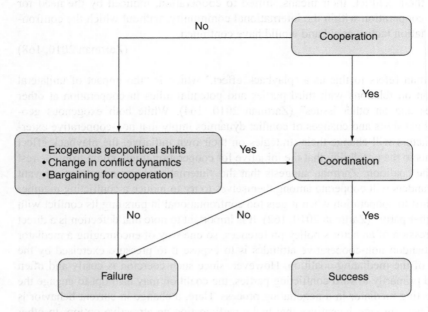

Figure 2.1 Flowchart to success or failure.

explained in terms of myopic rationality. Mediators that see defection as their strategic choice are those that focus on short-term rather than long-term goals. However, the choice to defect will inevitably have an impact not only on the mediating coalition, but also on the overall process, as it might encourage (at least) one disputing side to stop cooperating in the peace process. This dynamic is directly related to the fact that mediators often have a particular relationship with (at least) one of the disputing sides, which prompts them to get involved in the mediation process and correlates the pursuit of self-interest with the promotion of a partner state's agenda. Therefore, when the mediating coalition is faced with a potential dropout from the group, mediators might need to negotiate with the dropout to find a compromise solution that can bridge their conflicting interests in order to (re) establish a cooperative relationship. The outcome of this rapprochement will have a direct effect on the overall mediation effort. More specifically, if the mediators manage to reach an agreement with the dropout, the mediation process is more likely to be successful.

Coordination

Conceptualizing coordination

Even when multiple mediators manage to achieve a convergence of interests in managing a conflict, their efforts to operationalize and synchronize their activities often prove to be at odds. As indicated previously, one of the most challenging aspects of multiparty mediation is the problem of *coordination*. In the case of multiparty mediation, coordination prescribes a method of synchronized usage of the different leverage and resources each mediator has at its disposal in the process in order to create the necessary incentives that would have been unavailable from a single mediator alone. A harmonious employment of various sources of leverage can be instrumental to the effectiveness of the mediation process: where direct leverage is limited, it may be borrowed from others (Crocker *et al.* 1999, 40). A well-coordinated mediating coalition will be able to exploit the comparative advantage of all the mediators through a synchronized employment of different mediation strategies. Coordination among mediators sends a strong signal to the disputing sides about their commitment to manage and resolve the conflict. Strong dedication to alleviating the problem will increase the credibility of the group, reduce the likelihood of sending mixed signals to the conflicting sides and minimizes the chances that the conflicting sides will go 'forum shopping.' As a result, there will be fewer opportunities for procrastination in achieving a negotiated settlement.

Coordination implies different forms of exchange between the actors: information sharing, collaborative analysis and strategizing, resource sharing, formal partnerships and other means of synchronizing and/or integrating activities (Nan and Strimling 2006, 2). Its effectiveness depends on the recognition of the different roles each external actor can play. A developed sense of each actor's contribution to the process has to be clear from the outset. Understanding that each third party can assume a different role, relative to its interests and capabilities, creates a platform upon which their involvement can be coordinated. According to Kriesberg, mutual acknowledgement of each actor's contributions coupled with an explicit differentiation of roles can reduce the hazards associated with having many intermediaries interfering with each other's work (Kriesberg 1996, 351). At the same time, coordination requires a regulated exchange of information about the respective peacemaking efforts and analysis of the conflict from the participating external actors' perspectives (see Fisher 2006). This exchange is important not only in terms of preventing mediators from getting in each other's way; it is also instrumental to creating coalitional memory and the promotion of a sense of learning from previous efforts. Many peacemaking efforts have suffered from the ill effects of uncoordinated activities because they lacked the ability to learn about best practices from previous efforts. An important limitation in this regard is the fact that mediators often do not engage for an extended period of time. If their experiences do not get transmitted to successive or competing third parties, this lack of exchange will contribute to more chaotic and inconsistent peacemaking efforts (Heldt 2013, 13). Finally, effective coordination requires collaborative strategizing and planning of specific individual and collective initiatives based on shared analysis (Fisher 2006, 68).

Leadership

A clear sense of leadership within the coalition helps avoid the detriments of an uncoordinated process. The responsibilities of a lead mediator are: "to set priorities, to ensure those priorities are pursued by all the third-party actors involved, and to provide consistency across phases of a political process" (Jones 2002, 111). Experience has shown that the choice of assigning (or assuming) the leadership role appears to be quite contextual and ad hoc in nature. Kriesberg points out that

> the choice of the person or organizations which take on the leadership or the coordinating role may be made by the adversaries themselves, by the intermediaries, based on assessing who would have the interest and resources, or through a power struggle.
>
> (Kriesberg 1996, 348)

Whitefield goes even further and claims that the appointment of leading actor is not done through a rational process: it is rather a combination of opportunity, conflicting parties' demands, capabilities and resources of interested mediators to sustain that role and their credibility vis-à-vis other members of the international community (Whitefield 2010, 6). The difficulties of establishing a template for selecting a lead mediator derive from the systemic features of international affairs. No actor, be it a powerful state or an international organization, would ever be inclined to readily give up its authority or its maneuvering space in the mediation process (Jones 2002, 112). Despite these limitations, there are certain conditions under which a particular third party may be deemed most suitable to lead and coordinate mediation activities. The "UN Guidance for Effective Mediation" prescribes that the following aspects should be taken into account:

> The decision regarding leadership should be reached through consultation between the relevant entities, taking into account the conflict context and based on comparative advantage. Proximity to the parties should be neither dismissed nor taken for granted as an automatic advantage. Acceptability of the mediating body and their mediator by the conflicting parties and the potential effectiveness of the mediation should be key considerations.
>
> (A/66/811 2012, pt. 47)

Each external actor carries with it a distinct mix of interests and resources into the peacemaking process. These contributions get translated into comparative advantages once they become integrated into a coherent mediating strategy.

The comparative advantage of powerful states derives from their ability to 'play heavy.' According to Sisk, this implies the provision of strongly structured incentives and sanctions against the parties, promotion of diplomatic consistency through maintenance of communication and by sharing relevant information and, if needed, acting as a guarantor in the implementation phase (Sisk 2009, 53). While the value of having a powerful state in the mediating coalition is quite clear, assigning the leadership role to it might prove to be counterproductive. Jones argues that "coordination by a major power will tend to be coordination in support of one party, as distinct from impartial support to the peace process itself" (Jones 2002, 111). The liability of having a mediation process led by a powerful state that supports one of the conflicting parties is quite straightforward: the external support only adds to the leverage of their partners in conflict and distorts their sense of urgency to reach a negotiated solution. However, as stated previously, the potential utility of a biased mediator derives from its ability to 'deliver' the conflicting party with which it has close ties to an agreement. So far, the record of powerful states leading the multiparty mediation processes has been mixed. On the one hand, the cases of Bosnia and Sierra Leone show how crucial the 'heavy play' of powerful states as lead mediators was. In the former, the US conducted effective 'coercive diplomatic efforts' that put an end to extreme hostilities after years of futile attempts made by the UN, the European Union and various regional powers (Touval 1996). In the latter, parallel to the largely ineffective UN coordination efforts, the UK government unofficially played the role of 'lead state,' mustering crucial financial support for the peace process and providing rapid deployment forces in critical periods (Jones 2002, 108). On the other hand, the examples of the Russian-led mediation between Georgia and the secessionist republic of Abkhazia (Whitefield 2010, 15) or the US involvement with the 'Quartet' (the UN, the EU, the US and Russia) in the Middle East (Zartman 2010, 178) show how mediation efforts led by powerful states can be ineffective in terms of producing a mutually acceptable solution.

Political competition between powerful states at the international level has often damaged multiparty peacemaking efforts (e.g., the impact of the 'tug of war' between Russia and the US and its Western allies on the peacemaking processes in Ukraine and Syria). In these conditions, lead mediators are also expected to 'mediate between mediators.' Since it is their responsibility to formulate priorities and see that these priorities are implemented by the participating actors, in the event that external actors develop conflicting views on the distribution of priorities and relative responsibilities, the lead actor might have to first solve this dispute before returning to mediate the ongoing conflict on the ground. In order to do so, the lead mediator needs to possess the necessary authority (Jones 2002, 111). Although it is rare that any actor has absolute authority over all other participants, in recent years there has been a growing tendency to delegate the responsibility of leading a coordinated multiparty mediation effort to actors that have the power to prescribe behavior based on their own legitimacy. In international mediation, legitimacy has often been associated with actions undertaken by international organizations, especially the UN (Touval 1992). Legitimacy can be understood as "a property of a rule or rule-making institution which itself exerts a pull toward compliance on those addressed normatively because those addressed believe that the rule or institution has come into being and operates in accordance with generally accepted principles of right process" (Franck 1990, 24). The UN's 'aura of legitimacy' reflects a perception that the UN is 'the official representative of the world community' and that its actions reflect that community's consensus (Rubin 1992, 265; Touval 1994, 52). Hurd explains this 'symbolic power,' by looking at the role of the UN Security Council: "The symbolic power of the Security Council is evident in the energy states expend on having the Council pay attention to issues of concern to them" (Hurd 2002, 39).

The conferral of coordinating responsibilities to the UN is done not just because of its legitimate power, but also due to a number of more pragmatic reasons: powerful states often delegate this responsibility when confronted with the toughest cases, as they do not want to bear the costs of and take the blame for perpetuating a conflict. Some of them also maintain a degree of influence over the decision-making process by means of the veto power in the Security Council, which inevitably limits the UN's control over the process. As a result, knowing that they retain some influence, powerful states may borrow legitimacy from the UN. Evidently, the UN's effectiveness is highly dependent upon the support of its member states. Whitefield argues that, "when UN mediation is widely supported, its representatives are well placed to convene and build support from relevant external actors" (Whitefield 2010, 7). For this reason, in his statement at the "Security Council High Level Debate on Mediation and the Settlement of Disputes" the Secretary General Ban Ki-moon called on the Council to: (1) maintain unity over the common principles in resolving a conflict; (2) show readiness to use its leverage (e.g., sanctions); (3) demonstrate support for the lead mediator in order to avoid forum shopping; (4) and once the Council has agreed on how to manage a conflict to give the lead mediator the necessary space to work with the parties (Ki-moon 2008). This statement reflects the ongoing challenges that the UN is faced with when leading international multiparty mediation efforts: a near-constant proliferation of international actors able and willing to get involved that bring with them competing interests, coupled with the dwindling authority of the UN, have limited the UN's capacity to effectively conduct the task of coordinating mediation efforts (Jones 2002, 111).

Coordination mechanisms

So far, in order to avoid the detrimental effects associated with uncoordinated mediation, international actors have developed and used various formats that enhance their respective comparative advantage. UN mediation activities have generally been conducted by the office of the Secretary General and his Special Representatives (SRSG). If adequately supported by the member states, given the UN's perceived legitimacy, activities coordinated by UN envoys are characterized by both credibility and coherence. As mentioned previously in this chapter, the UN generally conducts mediation with likeminded actors. For this reason, their multiparty mediation activities have often had a title that includes the term 'friends.' *Groups of Friends* are "informal groups of states that are created to support the peacemaking efforts of the Secretary General and his envoys" (Whitefield 2007, 9). They are established on the initiative of the UN secretariat and member states, with the intention of creating a framework for collaborative interaction. This interaction prescribes a coordinated effort of pooling the leverage of member states in order to assist the peacemaking efforts led by the UN secretariat. States are selected on the basis of their ability to keep the parties committed to the peacemaking process and are expected to be active in "coordinating Security Council and/or General Assembly action on the conflict in question" (Whitefield 2007, 10). Depending on their size, these groups are subdivided into two groups: (1) the smaller groups of interested states, are termed *Friends of the Secretary-General*; they are more flexible when it comes to their engagement, as they tend to participate in activities conducted both at the UN headquarters in New York and in the field; and (2) bigger groups, generally termed *Friends of a country*, due to their size conduct their activities primarily in New York offices (Whitefield 2007, 10). According to Prantl, the groups of friends give the impression of a revived concept of the advisory committees of the 1950s (Prantl 2006). The first group emerged in 1992, in the post-Cold War context, when the UN Secretariat assumed a leading role in mediating the conflict in El Salvador. The group initially consisted of Colombia, Venezuela, Mexico and Spain and was later joined by the United States. The original purpose of this group was twofold: it was put together to accommodate the interests of the rebel group *Frente Farabundo Marti para la Liberación Nacional* (FMLN) and to bypass the preponderant power of the US in the Security Council and balance it in an informal setting (Prantl 2005, 577). The format allowed the UN Secretariat to marginalize the impact of the Security Council, avoid potential deadlocks that could have been created in that setting and offer a way out of the conflict for the US by participating in the peacemaking process without becoming an active participant (Prantl 2005, 577). The relative success of this endeavor prompted the UN secretariat to reapply the concept in various other crises, such as Haiti, Guatemala, Western Sahara and Georgia (see Prantl 2006; Whitefield 2007).

The comparative advantage of these informal groups is that they allow participants to avoid the pitfalls of operating within an existing institutional arrangement, where the distribution of power and decision-making processes have the potential to limit peacemaking effectiveness. While groups of friends are still selected by and operate closely with the UN secretariat, in some instances, states prefer to establish an ad hoc group completely detached from the existing institutional framework of the UN. *Contact groups*, as they are commonly referred to, bring together states interested in a particular conflict, including (but not limited to) the five permanent members of the Security Council, regional actors (both states and regional organizations) and other states that are able to contribute to conflict management activities. The first such group was established in 1977 to assist in the peacemaking process in Namibia. It was a reaction to the UN's inability to manage the ongoing conflicts in South-West Africa. This inability was the result of a mounting pressure coming from recently decolonized states that were outraged by the Western countries' attitude toward South

African apartheid policies (Davies 2007). The three Western permanent members of the Security Council together with Canada and Germany, at that time non-permanent members, formed the Western Contact Group. Not only did the group choose to work outside the UN institutional framework, it also lacked any explicit mandate from the UN. In spite of this, the group maintained contact with the UN secretariat and pursued goals that were in line with the institution's guiding principles and defined objectives. Prantl notes that the interaction between the contact group and the UN was quite constructive:

> The cooperation between the Western Contact Group and the UN turned out to be crucial because the organization provided the seal of legitimacy to the Western initiative. The Western Contact Group and, later, after the adoption of the linkage approach, the United States alone sought to legitimize the substance of negotiations via the process of Council decision making.
>
> (Prantl 2005, 576)

The Namibian experience was later replicated on several other occasions, including Liberia, Bosnia and Mindanao. Even while working outside of the UN framework, contact groups still aspired to borrow legitimacy from the UN. They did this either by maintaining close contact with its Secretariat and/or by conducting some of the discussions within the Security Council. The UN Secretariat, on the other hand, granted this legitimacy knowing that SRSG's peacemaking efforts – which were often conducted parallel to those of the contact group – are dependent on member states' support. Nobel Peace Prize winner Martti Ahtisaari, UN Commissioner for Namibia at the time of the formation of the Western Contact Group, comments on the delicate relations between the UN and external actors that form contact groups:

> Mediators need to be realistic and include the support from the major actors concerning a conflict: 'There is a sort of realism involved that you need some of the major actors. If you can't have their support, I would not even start a mediation exercise....' Whilst the international community does not need to stand 100 percent behind the mediator's ideas, they need to support the process in general.
>
> (Herrberg and Savaloainen 2009, 7)

These efforts point out a number of important factors that influence the effectiveness of contact groups. If the members of the contact group are able to reach consensus about the methods and goals of their joint endeavor, the process will inevitably benefit from an increased level of influence and borrowed leverage. This consensus does not necessarily need to reflect an absolute symmetry of interests among all participating actors; it is inevitable that some interested states will pursue a more complex set of goals than others, especially if they are directly affected by an escalating conflict. Yet the real convergence that must be achieved within the group requires a shared interest in mediating a peaceful solution that is acceptable to all sides and, more importantly, a clearly defined idea of what this solution should look like. Put differently, while each third party may maintain their potential bias of actor, the group requires the development of a common sense of a bias of outcome. The bias of actor may be exploited, together with other forms of leverage that each third party contributes to the collective endeavor, to deliver the conflicting parties to the envisaged outcome.

Overall it appears that unless there is a compatibility of interests between powerful states and other mediators (both international and/or regional organizations and small and/or medium-sized states) successful coordination of mediation activities cannot take place, thereby undermining the chances of success. In light of this limitation, it appears that the crucial element of properly executed coordination in multiparty mediation is that the lead actor has the necessary degree of legitimate power to guide the mediating coalition's activities and the necessary degree of compatibility of interests with major powers (Jones 2002, 90). As the following case studies show, the lead actor being perceived as legitimate increases the likelihood of mediation success. In cases where the mediation efforts were guided and coordinated by international organizations and small and medium-sized states, mediation success was still subject to the ability of those actors to construct a set of policies and preferences that were compatible with the interests of most powerful states that were involved as third parties in the peacemaking process. In other words, compatibility of interests between various actors increased the internal legitimacy of the mediating coalition. More importantly, the coalition's external legitimacy was not challenged by the disputing sides because the coalition was able to act on the basis of a common platform.

Note

1 This chapter is based on Vuković (2012) and Vuković (2014a).

3   Tajikistan[1]

The lengthy peace process that put an end to a violent civil war in Tajikistan represents a fairly successful case of multiparty mediation in which the activities of external actors were "exceptionally well coordinated" (Barnes and Abdulaev 2001, 11). This was an extremely complex process in which the essential contributions to the resolution of the conflict came from a wide variety of actors. Most of the rounds of talks, supported by the OSCE, were held under the auspices of the UN, while observer states took turns hosting them, thus providing a substantial contribution toward reaching an agreement (Iji 2001). At the same time, the process also benefited from the participation of different non-state actors and was aided by a very dynamic second-track dialogue process[2] that came out of the US–Soviet Dartmouth Conference (Rubin 1998; Saunders 1999).

Nevertheless, among all the different mediators involved, Russia and Iran played a pivotal role in the peace process. According to Iji, "it was their collaboration that moved the intractable conflict in Tajikistan toward a settlement" (2001, 365). Both countries had strong interests in the conflict and highly developed relationships with warring parties, the combination of which allowed them to assume the role of potentially effective third parties. Barnes and Abdullaev point out that "with an interest in the outcome of the war, they became in effect 'secondary parties' to the conflict ... although they contributed initially to the war effort they later became vital resources to the peace process" (Barnes and Abdullaev 2001, 8). According to Hay, the main three reasons for the breakthrough in the negotiations were: conflicting parties were exhausted from continuous fighting; Russia and Iran managed to reach a convergence of interests to promote peace in Tajikistan; and the security concerns created by the Taliban taking over of Kabul (Hay 2001, 39). These factors allowed for a UN-led and coordinated multiparty mediation effort to produce a mutually acceptable solution for the parties in conflict.

Therefore, the peace process in Tajikistan potentially represents a case of multiparty mediation in which eventual success was directly dependent upon the interests of powerful neighboring states, regional geo-political conditions, and international organizations' legitimate power to coordinate the activities of multiple third parties.

The nature of conflict

Sources of intractability

Tajikistan's physical geography (it is a landlocked, mountainous country) prompted the creation of several culturally diverse groupings. Although the majority of these groups are "a part of the Iranian cultural world and are predominately Sunni Muslims," the mountainous terrain "has always made travel between different regions difficult ... creating a significant obstacle to communication as well as social and economic integration" (Akiner and Barnes 2001, 18). The simplest distinction between the various ethno-cultural groupings in the country can be made between the populations that have lived in the flatlands in the northern part of the country, which "in ancient times were part of the rich urban-based culture of Transoxiana," and populations that inhabited mountainous areas in the rest of the county, which resulted in a creation of "strong localized identities" (Akiner and Barnes 2001, 18).

Until the USSR assumed control over the territory in the 1920s, there was almost no contact between the populations of these areas. The first decade of Soviet rule widened the gap between the different communities (Roy 2001). Especially important was the impact of different policies that were drafted in Moscow, which treated the northern part of the country quite differently than the rest. While the plains in the north were gradually industrialized and modernized, the mountainous regions were largely ignored and therefore populations that lived there not only maintained and strengthened their local identities, they also continued to live as their ancestors did for centuries. In principle, the most significant political, social, and cultural traits of contemporary Tajikistan were formed during Soviet rule.

Development of deep feelings of distrust and mutual hatred

Already in the early 1920s, Basmachi fighters from the mountainous areas demonstrated their intent to stop the advancement of the Soviet Union into Central Asia. In order to suppress any form of resistance, "the Red Army massacred more than 10,000 Tajiks and Uzbeks between 1922 and 1926, according to official estimates" (Akiner and Barnes 2001, 19). Large parts of the population found refuge in neighboring Afghanistan, in an attempt to escape "violent purges, forcible resettlement and collectivization, and religious persecution" (Idem). According to Akiner and Barnes, "these events had a lasting effect that contributed to the conflict dynamics which emerged during the civil war in the 1990s" (2001, 19).

In the early 1930s, the Soviet regime started promoting collectivization and industrialization policies, which required a forcible transfer of people from the central and eastern areas of the country to the north. While these policies produced the first migratory dynamic in the country's history, there was no evidence of any integration between populations. Rather, such policies "generated conflict by stimulating inter-group competition and sharpening perceptions of social differ-ence" (Akiner and Barnes 2001, 19). Forced relocation and mixing of the people from different regions transformed the previously loose regional affiliations into a "more fixed group identity based on regional origin" (Roy 2001, 23).

Despite continuous efforts by central authorities in Moscow to organize Tajikistan along secular-socialist lines, most of the population, particularly in the predominantly rural areas, maintained their clan loyalties and religious observ-ances (Hiro 1998). According to Roy, "these networks have commonly been used to maximize access to and control over resources and they were translated into the political and administrative structures of the Soviet Union" (Roy 2001, 23). Even the politics of the local Communist Party revolved around the regional divide. In a centralized, one-party rule system, the only method of career advancement was loyalty to the party elite. The party endorsed "administrative territorial divisions" and was "grouped around district, province and republic level committees" (Roy 2001, 23). The combination of established clan loyalties and party association was the source of political factionalism. While ideological differences were virtually non-existent, political division followed the territorial cleavage, which emphasized regional administrative divisions. For Roy, "this generated inter-regional antagonisms in the struggle for access to power, goods and other benefits" (2001, 23).

Internal characteristics of the conflicting sides and the creation of irreconcilable positions

From the beginning of the Soviet rule, the power in Tajikistan was concentrated within two regions – Sogd or Sughd, also referred to as Leninabad in the north, and Khatlon in the southeast. Leninabad was by far the region that produced the largest number of public officials. While representatives from other regions held various powerful positions in the Soviet system, "all the first secretaries of the Tajik Communist Party from 1946 to 1991 were Leninabadis" (Roy 2001, 23). Due to their administrative positions, apparatchiks from Leninabad were able to develop very strong ties with the ruling elite in Moscow and enjoyed the benefits of a much more advanced regional economy than the rest of the country.

On the other hand, the politically completely marginalized and economically deprived southwestern region of Gorno-Badakhshan, bordering Afghanistan, became a breeding ground for clandestine Islamist movements. What started off as an underground network for Islamic worship that rejected the authority of the official state-controlled Islamic structures became a movement that slowly began assuming a political agenda. Despite some differences,

> by the early 1990s an alliance was formed between the leaders of the distinct Islamic factions who made up the Islamic Renaissance Party (IRP): the new radicals (led by Said Abdullo Nuri), and what was at the time Tajikistan's offi-cial religious establishment (led by Khoji Akbar Turajonzoda).
> (Akiner and Barnes 2001, 20)

Throughout the 1980s, regional, political and economic disparity, turmoil in neighboring Afghanistan, and proliferation of opposition forces posed acute challenges to the authorities in Dushanbe. Along with Islamic movements, the underground political scene also generated various secular, socio-political movements, such as the Democratic Party of Tajikistan (DPT), which initially had a very strong following. The first clear signs of popular dissatisfaction materialized in street riots in February 1990, at which point participants attacked ethnic Russians and other Europeans while shouting: "Long live the Islamic Republic of Tajikistan" (Hiro 1998, 20). However, while most people in Tajikistan considered Islam to be of crucial importance to their socio-cultural heritage, it seemed that "most did not support the creation of an Islamic state" (Akiner and Barnes 2001, 20). It appeared that even local religious leaders were not convinced that movements such as the IPR represented the only and the best alternative to the decaying one-party rule of the Communist Party.

In principle, in the last two decades of the twentieth century, the political elites in Tajikistan failed to find adequate policies with which to tackle the mounting problems of inter-regional disparities. According to Abdullo, the crucial challenges that the country was facing as the Soviet system was eroding were "disparities that had arisen from the increasing economic role of southern population, the demographic structure of the population, ideological diversification, and unequal participation in political decision-making in a country dominated by a northern political elite" (Abdullo 2001, 48).

Employment of repressive measures

By 1989, inter-group skirmishes over the allocation of scarce resources escalated into violent clashes. Inter-ethnic confrontations between Tajiks and other ethnic groups – mainly Uzbeks and Kyrgyz – become more regular. After a series of protests, Tajik replaced Russian as the official language. This action drove large parts of the Russian minority to flee the country. Xenophobic sentiment continued to linger, and on several occasions sparked violent protests – such as those against the re-housing of Armenian refuges in Dushanbe (Abdullaev and Barnes 2001, 83).

Following the dissolution of the USSR, the Tajik Supreme Soviet declared Tajikistan's independence on September 9, 1991. At the same time, facing strong public pressure, the central authorities recognized and licensed several opposition movements such as IRP, the DPT, and the Rastakhiz (Resurgence) People's Organization. A 14-day rally in Dushanbe "[brought] an estimated 10,000 protesters on to the streets" calling for multiparty elections (Abdullaev and Barnes 2001, 83). All the opposition parties took part in the November 1991 presidential elections, which were eventually won by the Communist Party's candidate from the Leninabad region, Rahmon Naiyev. The election results were immediately contested by all opposition leaders who accused the ruling elite of rigging the process and taking advantage of disproportionate access to resources.

Following the election results, the opposition intensified its contestation of the communist regime and especially Naiyev's decision to create a government consisting only of Leninabadis from Sughd and Kulyabis from the Khatlon region. In May 1992, demonstrations prompted Naiyev to exercise his emergency powers and form a 'presidential guard,' which also consisted only of Leninabadis and Kulyabis. Attempts to counter the pressure from the opposition turned into a military confrontation that led to some deaths (Iji 2001, 360; Abdullaev and Barnes 2001, 83). As the situation deteriorated, Naiyev tried to appease the opposition by accommodating them within a coalition government. However this experiment was not long lived and only managed to outrage the neo-communist elite, driving the country into full-blown conflict. As Dushanbe was occupied by opposition forces, Naiyev urged the Community of Independent States (CIS) to send peacekeeping troops.

For Russia, this situation was absolutely unacceptable. So without any hesitation, it helped neo-communist forces from Kulyab reclaim Dushanbe and push the opposition forces toward the Tajiki-Afghan border. In the meantime, the dissatisfied communist elite replaced Rahmon Naiyev with Emomali Rakhmonov from Kulyab who formed a government predominantly composed of a loyal cadre from Leninabad and Kulyab. By the spring of 1993, the repercussions of the intense fighting were more than 30,000 dead and more than 300,000 displaced (Hiro 1998).

Involvement of international actors and their interest in the conflict

Russia

In July 1993, 25 Russian border guards were killed during an offensive by opposition forces that took place along the border with Afghanistan. Moscow's exasperation was best expressed by an irritated president Yeltsin, who publically questioned Russian policy objectives up to that point, asking: "Why did we not have a plan to protect this border, which everyone must understand is effectively Russia's, not Tajikistan's?" (Hiro 1998, 20). It was evident that the Kremlin's strong line now regarded the Tajik–Afghan border as "an advanced Russian base" (despite the fact that it is 1,450 km from Russian territory) "that can protect Russia from the infiltration of guns, narcotics and Islamic fundamentalism" (Hiro 1995, 15). Already, in August 1993, the new doctrine was put into effect through Russian-Tajik military cooperation, which paved the way for 25,000 Russian troops to be located in Tajikistan out of which 17,000 were positioned along the border with Afghanistan. The second step was taken in November 1993, at which point the Tajiki government signed a document that subordinated its finances to Russia (idem). Tajikistan remained the only newly independent country in Central Asia that continued using the Russian ruble as the only official currency. It was clear that the Tajiki government's survival depended directly on Russian support.

Officially, the Russian military maintained a neutral stance in the Tajik civil war. However, there are numerous claims that "the army supported pro-government forces with vehicles, ammunition and weapons" (Abdullaev and Barnes 2001, 93). Again, officially the Russian government indicated a clear interest in maintaining and developing official relations only with the Tajiki government. However, from 1993, as many members of the opposition, especially those from the DPT, found refuge in Moscow, Russian officials started encouraging the parties to talk, and Russia subsequently acted as a key sponsor of the inter-Tajik negotiations (Abdullaev and Barnes 2001, 93).

Iran

In order to counterbalance the asymmetric power, the Islamic-democratic coalition sought external support from Iran. The special relationship between the two countries mainly revolved around cultural and religious issues: Tajikistan was the only new, Farsi-speaking Muslim country in Central Asia. However, despite implicit appeals to Iran, manifestations of Islamic slogans – that echoed the Iranian revolutionary days – were only a symbolic indicator of radicalization of the pro-Iranian Islamic agenda. In reality, the Islamic-democratic opposition "neither believed in the possibility or desirability of an Islamic alternative nor was it even united in a preference for and ideologically tainted political model for Tajikistan" (Mesbahi 1997, 143). The common agenda for the opposition forces was a pursuit of a democratic political system founded on a new constitution. From the beginning, it was absolutely clear to the authorities in Teheran that Tajikistan was not 'ready' for an Islamic revolution, due to its Soviet heritage which largely dissociated the population from Islam, and regional/clan fragmentation. At the same time, Iran was faced with wide-ranging and formidable regional and international consensus, promoted by Russia and the US, on the issue of the Islamic threat and Iranian influence in Tajikistan (Mesbahi 1997, 148). Iran's reluctance to fully promote an Islamic agenda in Tajikistan created problems for the opposition forces. Authorities in Teheran refused to provide armaments when they were most needed and, on occasion, failed to provide direct rhetorical support for the opposition through diplomatic means (Mesbahi 1997, 150). Nevertheless, Iran remained the biggest and most influential outside actor that voiced undisputed support for the opposition.

Both Russia and Iran had obvious leverage over the conflicting sides. Adequate use of such power represented a crucial resource that would allow the mediating coalition to produce the necessary incentives to leverage the government and the United Tajiki Opposition (UTO) toward a mutually acceptable solution. However, in order to produce such incentives, biased mediators need to assume a cooperative attitude. Accordingly, while cooperating with other mediators, biased mediators are useful as they can use their special relationship with one conflicting side to influence its behavior, positions, and perceptions thereby moving it toward an agreement.

Finally, reflecting on Russia and Iran's formation and projection of interests vis-à-vis Tajikistan, the country was of great strategic importance for both regional powers. As indicated in the theoretical chapter, once third parties show an intent to cooperate with each other, in order to produce the necessary incentives and successfully manage the conflict, third parties need to coordinate their activities and adequately use the leverage that is at their disposal in order to guide the parties toward a mutually acceptable solution. The intent to adequately apply necessary and available leverage is directly related to the strategic importance of the country as perceived by the third parties involved. The stronger the mediators' strategic interest in the conflict, the greater the chance of successful mediation through a coordinated effort by mediators in a coalition. The prospects of employing adequate (and necessary) leverage in order to steer the two conflicting sides toward an agreement will be explored further in the remainder of this chapter.

Involvement of the UN

According to Goryayev, "the UN was recognized as the leading international body driving the peace process and *coordinating* international responses to the crisis" (Goryayev 2001, 32; emphasis added). The UN already became involved in September of 1992, when it dispatched the first fact-finding mission to explore the conflict dynamics more closely. Once the mission reported in detail about the high level of violence – defining the turmoil as civil war – the UN decided to dispatch a new mission (in November 1992), which also interacted with representatives of neighboring states. These first consultations paved the way for future cooperation between the UN and neighboring countries that were able to exert the necessary political, economic, and military influence over the conflicting parties in order to move them toward a peaceful solution. By January 1993, the Secretary General established a small United Nations Mission of Observers in Tajikistan (UNMOT), mandated to monitor the situation on the ground and ascertain the positions of all concerned parties. The information provided by UNMOT prompted the Secretary General to appoint a full-time Special Envoy "mandated to concentrate on achieving a ceasefire and establishing the process of negotiations for a political solution" (Goryayev 2001, 34).

Goryayev points out that "over a period of seven years, the Special Envoys/ Representatives and their staff were responsible for designing the negotiation process, maintaining contacts with all parties to the conflict and integrating the efforts of other countries and organizations" (2001, 34). While lacking muscle, the UN was able to provide leadership in coordinating the activities of various third parties (Iji 2001, 347). The mediation process showed that the Special Envoys were highly devoted to maintaining and strengthening their relations with the officials from the neighboring countries. Regular communication and consultations with the observer countries created an opportunity for the UN negotiating team to "inform the governments on the negotiations, to *coordinate* plans and actions, and to prepare for future rounds of talks" (Hay 2001, 40;

emphasis added). Such actions generated the requisite degree of trust in the activities conducted by the UN and assured the neighboring countries (particularly Russia and Iran) that the UN-led negotiations would not endanger the interests they had in the region. According to Hay, "the consultations with observer governments kept them informed, engaged and confident that the Tajik delegations and the mediators were taking their views and interests into account" (Hay 2001, 42).

Throughout the process, the UN mediating team was not only in charge of facilitating the communication between the belligerents, they were also in charge of formulating proposals and drafting the initial text of the agreement. In order to assure the interested states, and Russia and Iran in particular, the UN mediators "often coordinated the compromise solutions they proposed" which "helped the observers to feel a sense of ownership over the negotiating process" (Hay 2001, 43). These trust-building efforts generated reciprocal attitudes among the observing countries. For the UN mediators, it was crucial to have the support of the powerful states, especially Russia, which had strong military, political and economic interests in the region. For this reason, the UN team regularly informed and consulted the Security Council, which generated strong support for the SRSG's mediating efforts from within the Security Council.

While well equipped to perform the mediator roles of communicator and formulator, the UN lacked 'muscle' in the mediation process. The only leverage it had was that of legitimacy. As pointed out by Iji, "the UN's legitimate and moral authority served as a complement to the incentives supplied by Russia and Iran" (2001, 376). This was especially important when the two conflicting parties showed no interest in compromising. Under such critical conditions, UN mediators would stop the negotiation process and consult the neighboring countries' officials – especially those from Russia and Iran – share their formulas, draft new proposals, and "request them to use their leverage with the parties to encourage them to compromise" (Hay 2001, 43). Therefore, the necessary conditions for successful coordination – the required level of legitimacy and compatibility of interests between the international organization and major powers – were present and greatly contributed to the success of the mediation process. However, in order to arrive at the required degree of cooperation, both major powers first needed to achieve a mutual convergence of interests. This was neither a simple nor a quick endeavor.

Multiparty mediation

Initial lack of cooperation between third parties

In the context of this disproportional constellation of forces, where the government had the upper hand due to its support from Moscow and the opposition had failed to find similar support elsewhere, Russia saw an opportune moment to initiate inter-Tajik negotiations under UN auspices. Reflecting on the previously illustrated game theoretical model, at this point the multiparty mediation process starts and the 'game' is at point (b), where the mediator indicates the intention of cooperating with other third parties – in this case Russia showing its intent to use the good offices of the UN – and manages to reap comparatively higher benefits than those third parties that are not part of the multiparty mediation endeavor – in this case, Iran. The benefits stem directly from the ability to guide and direct the process in a way that is compatible with the 'cooperative' mediator's interests, particularly as these interests are not counterbalanced by the involvement of the other 'non-cooperative' mediator.

Since the attacks on the border station in July 1993, in spite of the strong line assumed by the Russian army and President Yeltzin, the Russian ministry of foreign affairs was exploring the possibility of finding a settlement through negotiation. Acting as communicator and facilitator, Russia established direct contact with the opposition leaders that found refuge in Teheran. Resorting to shuttle diplomacy, Russian envoys managed to encourage both sides in the conflict to start negotiations (Gretsky 1995; Iji 2001).

The first round of talks was held in Moscow between April 5–9, 1994. The two sides managed to agree on an agenda for the rounds of negotiation to follow, classifying three categories of issues that needed to be tackled: political settlement, refugees and internally displaced persons, and the structure of the government of Tajikistan (Iji 2001, 360). From the start, a substantial discrepancy over the 'sequencing'[3] of these issues emerged. The government wanted first to see the mutiny end and find a solution to the refugee problem, while the opposition called for an "all-party council to govern the country and the legalization of opposition parties" (Iji 2001, 360).

The second round of talks was held in Teheran, between June 18–28, 1994. The key issue on the agenda was the achievement of a ceasefire. Despite the initial readiness to come to an understanding regarding the ceasefire, the parties failed to agree on a timeframe for its implementation. Once the talks had failed, the government abruptly decided to hold a referendum on the new constitution and presidential elections, scheduling both for September. Irritated by this move, the opposition intensified its military operations along the border with Afghanistan and the situation deteriorated even further.

Russia was not happy with the ongoing conflict, especially as it was endangering Russian troops located in the country. It decided to resort to manipulative strategies in order to force the government to sign a ceasefire agreement and to postpone the elections and referendum (Hay 2001). At the same time, Iranian diplomats used the same tactics with the opposition leaders. Shortly thereafter, a ceasefire was reached at a consultative meeting in Teheran in September 1994. According to Hay, the deputy foreign ministers of Russia and Iran "were instrumental in convincing the respective Tajik delegations to sign the Drat Agreement on a Temporary Ceasefire prepared by the UN negotiating team" (Hay 2001, 40). The compatibility of interests between two major powers, coupled with the coordinating efforts of the UN whose position did not run counter to those of the major powers, were the necessary conditions for achieving the agreement. The armistice was eventually extended until February 1995 during the third round of talks in Islamabad, held between October 20–31, 1994 (Iji 2001). This provides a clear example of how a cooperative and coordinated effort by biased third parties can produce sufficient incentives to leverage the disputants toward an agreement.

However, despite these important contributions to achieving a cessation of hostilities, Russia was still not fully committed to brokering a negotiated solution to the conflict. According to Iji "Moscow helped jump-start the negotiations, move them forward, and focus the attention of the parties on talking rather than fighting, but was not prepared to pressure Rakhmonov strongly enough to accept power sharing with the opposition" (2001, 366). This attitude sent mixed signals to its partners in Dushanbe that were focused on regaining power through new elections (presidential in November 1994 and parliamentary in February 1995) and a referendum on the constitution (February 1995) that excluded the participation of the opposition parties. The government's decision reduced the already fragile confidence the opposition had in the peace process, so the spotlight once again shifted toward the frontlines. Evidently, the lack of the strong presence of Iran in this phase of the process had a direct negative effect on the opposition forces. They were clearly experiencing comparatively lower payoffs from the peace process (as predicted by the game-theoretical model), which in turn induced them to resort to violence in order to improve their negotiating position.

As the belligerent activities escalated, the two conflicting sides agreed to meet in Moscow in April 1995 to discuss the possibility of extending the armistice. The opposition accepted the talks under the condition that they would lead to more substantial negotiation over a potential political settlement. On the eve of this meeting, Russian Foreign Minister Kozyrev issued a statement addressed to Russians living outside Russia which included the following: "we have at our disposal an arsenal of methods to defend our compatriots" (Hiro 1995, 15). The opposition understood this as a direct warning and walked out of the UN-chaired meeting. Motivated by this unyielding Russian position, Tajik President Rakhmonov reacted in a self-assured tone and offered to meet the opposition leader, Said Nuri, from IRP, "any time, anywhere" (Hiro 1995, 14).

After this statement was issued, a series of summits and rounds of talks were held. On most of these occasions, these talks only served as an outlet for both sides to channel their disagreement without achieving any substantial progress. Evidently, the government still had an upper hand in the peace process, especially given the overwhelming role of their Russian partners. They were, however, hurting on the battlefield, as the opposition resorted to violence to distort the status quo balance of power at the negotiating table where they were still experiencing lower payoffs. Again the lack of a substantial Iranian presence in the peace process was hurting the UTO.

Of the series of summits and rounds of talks, the agreements on refugees and prisoners of war achieved during the fourth round of talks in Almaty (May 22–June 1, 1995) are worthy of mention. Another important event was the signing of the Protocol on the Fundamental Principles for Establishing Peace and National Accord in Tajikistan, which was the result of the Rakhmonov–Nuri summit facilitated by Iran in Teheran on July 19, following indirect talks through the UN envoy. This protocol served to "[delineate] the road to and the overall shape of a final settlement" (Iji 2001, 362). Despite Iran's contribution to drafting the protocol, its mediation potential was still not fully realized. Teheran still maintained financial and political support in addition to their somewhat clandestine military assistance to the Islamic-democratic coalition. Iran's biggest hope was to create "an effective contestant against the Rakhmonov regime, although Teheran continued to be very careful to maintain good relations with the government side" (Iji 2001, 366). While both sides in the conflict started sending signals of readiness to start negotiating on political issues, fighting on the ground never actually stopped. Evidently, the conflicting sides used violence as an off-the-table tactic, in order to improve their bargaining position.[4] As the situation deteriorated, the subsequent (fifth) round of talks held in Ashgabat, Turkmenistan – November 30, 1995 and between July 8–21, 1996 – focused mainly (again) on finding an agreement on a ceasefire.

It was evident that neither side was fully committed to negotiating a peace agreement. Even though the peace process had been underway for more than two years, high levels of mutual distrust still existed. The opposition questioned the legitimacy of the neo-communists' participation in negotiations as an official government, given the alleged electoral fraud that had taken place over time. Its military success throughout the conflict was impressive, proving to Iran that its support was worthwhile. On the other hand, the government did not recognize opposition forces as an equal partner with whom they would not only negotiate, but also eventually share power. The government did not have to look far to find support for its claims. Russia was "most unlikely to let Tajik Islamist share power in a country which it regards as crucial to its own security" (Hiro 1996, 14). Clearly, while outside support was still available for their respective unilateral solutions, the Tajik parties participated in negotiations only 'half-heartedly' (Iji 2001, 366).

As argued earlier, when the mediating coalition is faced with conflicting interests, if one mediator decides to defect from the group dynamic, this will have an important impact on the dynamics of the peace process between negotiators. At the same time, Russia and Iran still did not have a shared idea of a potential solution to the conflict, which would have helped them to push the parties toward a peaceful solution to their dispute. If mediators do not reach a convergence of interests, the conflicting sides will be induced to defect from negotiations, making it more likely that the peace process will fail. In the case of Tajikistan, this was unequivocally indicated by the unyielding positions of both the government and the UTO. Neither side was inclined to show any intent to compromise and abandon maximalist claims in the peacemaking process.

Convergence of interests between third parties

Just when the peace process was approaching a severe deadlock in September 1996, violent events in nearby Afghanistan produced sufficient cause for Russia and Iran to settle the conflict in Tajikistan (Abdullaev and Babakhanov 1998; Abdullo 2001). The storming of Kabul was the 'last straw' that induced Russia to rethink its policy objectives that supported a military solution to the conflict. By then, the neo-communist regime in Dushanbe was in a state of serious decay, while the opposition forces were gaining momentum on the battlefield. Acknowledging the weakening of its military forces and its inability to fight Muslim insurgents – a lesson learned in a 20-month long conflict in Chechnya in 1995–1996 – Russia determined "the cost of further military involvement in Tajikistan to be too high" (Iji 2001, 366). Since the Tajik–Afghan border was still considered to be 'a Russian border,' Moscow urgently needed a stable Tajikistan to serve as a buffer zone against the threat of Islamic fundamentalism coming from Afghanistan (Iji 2001, 367).

Iran was also prompted to modify its policy objectives in Tajikistan. Despite the temporary military success of the opposition forces, it was already clear to Teheran that the chances of an armed seizure of power were extremely small. And even in that case, in the eyes of policy makers in Teheran, Tajikistan was never ready to be modeled into an Islamic state. For this reason, Iran was always very careful to maintain a relationship with the government in Dushanbe, at least in terms of the cultural and religious dimensions. According to several observers, "Iran attached more importance to the maintenance of good relations with Russia than to the creation of an Islamic state in Tajikistan" (Iji 2001, 367). In fact, just in order to preserve good relations with authorities in Moscow, Teheran never provided all the assistance requested by the opposition forces (Mesbahi 1997). So when the Taliban militia gained power in Afghanistan, Iran immediately realized that the conflict in Tajikistan needed to be resolved as soon as possible. For Iran, a stable Tajikistan represented a solid shield against the regime in Afghanistan the existence of which was "adverse to their interests because of geopolitical, ethnic and religious reasons" (Iji 2001, 367).

Given these novel developments, the two lead states had a converging interest in resolving the conflict in Tajikistan. In this case, both Russia and Iran shared an idea of the final outcome of the conflict: the final agreement should be based on a power-sharing arrangement between the government and the opposition (Hiro 1998). As Iji noted, "such coincidence of interests and positions rendered possible the joint mediation by Russia and Iran in the Tajik conflict. ... Once Russia and Iran became serious about settling the conflict through a cooperative mediation effort, the negotiation began to gain momentum" (Iji 2001, 368).

In fact, both states took the conflict resolution process much more seriously. Using the particular leverage at their disposal as biased mediators and lead states, they resorted to manipulative strategies in order to move both conflicting sides toward an agreement. In cases in which outside actors have a strong strategic interest in a country or region, which prompts them to manage a conflict, the stronger the mediators' strategic interest in the conflict, the greater the chances of successful mediation through a coordinated effort by mediators in a coalition. As indicated previously, Tajikistan possessed all the characteristics of a strategically important zone for both Russia and Iran. Therefore, well-coordinated action taken by both Russia and Iran soon brought results. Both conflicting sides, exhausted by continuous fighting, saw a military solution to the conflict as an unattainable goal. Eventually, as their sponsor states definitely stopped providing assistance for military action, both the government and the opposition started taking the option of actually negotiating a solution much more seriously. Thus, Rakhmonov and Nuri, each one experiencing increasing pressure from the outside patron states, agreed to meet and discuss the most delicate issues of the peace agreement. By December 1996, they managed to find a mutually acceptable formula for peace. In the following rounds of talks, hosted by Iran (Teheran, January 6–19, 1997) and Russia (Moscow, February 26–March 8, 1997), thanks to the well-synchronized activities of powerful states, the parties managed to overcome all their differences in opinion, agreed to make important concessions regarding the future power-sharing arrangement, and paved the way to the actual peace agreement which was signed on June 27, 1997 in Moscow. According to Hay,

> the personal contribution of Russian Foreign Minister Primakov and his deputy Mr. Pashtukov, were invaluable for reaching agreement on the Protocol on Military Issues in March 1997, one of the most important documents of the process. The direct involvement of Iranian Foreign Minister Velayati facilitated the signing of Protocol on Refugees in January 1997.
>
> (Hay 2001, 40)

What was even more remarkable was the fact that Russia and Iran were not only focused on putting pressure on the negotiators, they also used all necessary means to create a proper atmosphere for the negotiations. Of particular importance for them was the isolation of the spoilers[5] who had problems accepting the proposed power-sharing solution. An unprecedented demonstration of Russian dedication to achieving and upholding the peace settlement happened in August 1997, when Russian air forces bombed a garrison of governmental forces led by generals unhappy with the peace agreement and the power-sharing arrangement it prescribed. Evidently, Moscow was "deadly serious" about helping Rakhmonov implement the peace treaty (Hiro 1997, 14).

Looking back at the game theoretical model, the apparent convergence of interests moved the process to point (c). In other words, the process reached the NME. The convergence of interests was a direct result of a series of factors. Evidently, a strong geo-political shift will induce the defecting mediator to change its strategy and engage in a cooperative meditation effort to manage the conflict. The storming of Kabul by Taliban forces represented a serious geopolitical challenge for both Russia and Iran. While the Tajik civil war could be treated as an isolated conflict that could be contained within a region without any fear of it spilling over to other countries, neither third party showed any intent to push for a more peaceful solution to the dispute. However, the projected and feared spillover effect stemming from Afghanistan induced Russia and Iran to rethink their policies toward the region and thus find a stronger interest in stabilizing the situation in Tajikistan as soon as possible. Therefore, the convergence of interests between two mediators was the direct effect of a serious geo-political change in the region and the causal link between Taliban occupation of Kabul and Russia and Iran's convergence of interests can be deduced.

At the same time, an increase in the cost of supporting a war induced the defecting mediator to change its strategy and engage in a cooperative meditation effort to manage the conflict. Both Russia and Iran found the costs of perpetuating the war unbearable and not in their self-interest. As indicated previously, Russia in particular was harmed by the ongoing warfare and this realization directly induced Moscow officials to rethink their policies regarding the peace process in Tajikistan. Therefore, the causal linkage between increasing costs of supporting warfare and convergence of interests between third parties can be observed. Once Russia and Iran realized that a military solution to the conflict was unattainable, they were able to reformulate their policies toward their partners, using specific power at their disposal, and leverage them through a cooperative endeavor to find a mutually acceptable solution. While Iran was less affected by the costs of war, it was more prone to rethink its policies toward the conflict due to the ineffectiveness of its strategy to produce any outcome that was in line with its self-interest. The same can be said about Russia's change of attitude: when a mediator's defecting strategy produces high costs in the mediation process for the state it supports, this will induce the defecting mediator to change its strategy and engage in a cooperative meditation effort to manage the conflict.

Notes

1 An earlier version of this chapter was published as a case study in Vuković (2012).
2 Saunders (1999) identifies three distinct yet highly interrelated levels of peacemaking and peacebuilding processes that took place in Tajikistan. While each level was instrumental for the achievement of a peaceful solution, this chapter primarily focuses on the "level I" or "track-one" peacemaking process which was characterized by the participation of the highest ranking officials from the Government of Tajikistan and United Tajik Opposition.
3 For the discussion on sequencing see Lax and Sebenius (1991).
4 For the discussion on the use of violence during negotiations see Sisk (2009).
5 See Stedman (1997) for a discussion on spoilers in international conflict resolution.

4 Namibia

A much different case of multiparty mediation occurred throughout the 1980s in Southern Africa. The peace settlement signed on December 22, 1988 at the UN headquarters in New York by officials representing Angola, Cuba, and South Africa, which granted Namibia its long-awaited independence, represented the successful conclusion of an eight-year-long, US-led diplomatic endeavor that engaged a multitude of international actors. The intricate dynamics of the Cold War era coupled with regional problems dating back to the League of Nations, were reasons enough for the US to understand that acting alone was not sufficient and that its mediatory clout, even as a superpower, was finite (Crocker 1999, 229). In order to guide all parties involved in the regional imbroglio toward a settlement, they needed the much broader diplomatic involvement of various global and regional players.

Looking back, it appears quite clear that the peacemaking process could not succeed without valuable diplomatic input provided by members of the Western Contact Group (the United Kingdom, France, West Germany, and Canada), frontline states (Tanzania, Zambia, Zimbabwe, Mozambique, and Botswana) and the UN and its sub-organizations (Iji 2011). According to Crocker, "the multiparty character of the mediation was designed to neutralize the obstruction of competing parties and states, and add reach, credibility, and access to international and regional efforts" (Crocker 1999, 207).[1] Moreover, on the systemic level, the rapprochement between the USSR and the US broke the deadlock in the negotiation process and contributed to the US mediation initiative (Berridge 1989, Wood 1991, Pycroft 1994). When the Soviet Union radically altered its policy objectives and "abandoned reflexive obstructionism" in order to "do creative things together" (Crocker 1999, 239), the peace process managed to overcome Cold War constraints and move the parties toward a settlement for a longstanding problem in Southern Africa. The rapprochement between the US and the USSR was very important for the peacemaking process. It allowed for US-led mediation (primarily conducted by Chester Crocker, who at that time was the US Assistant Secretary of State for African Affairs) to achieve the necessary level of legitimacy and consequently produce success via a well-coordinated peace process. Thus, despite the fact the US acted as a biased mediator with a specific set of interests it aimed to promote in the peace process, its role was acceptable to both the disputants and the other powerful state (USSR) (Berridge 1989, 469). However, in the mentioned period, as the Soviets priori- tized their interests in Afghanistan, they left policy leadership on Angola to the Cubans and their Angolan allies (Crocker 1993). Thus, next to an improved climate in US–Soviet relations, a critical change of position made by the Cuban government, which had its own independent agenda and a strong military pres- ence in Angola, was of pivotal importance for the peacemaking process.

Therefore, the case of Namibia provides a unique opportunity to observe a situation in which the outcome was dependent upon the interests of external actors and global geo-political conditions. At the same time, the case will also show how intrinsic dynamics of warfare induced multiple mediators and actors on the ground to achieve the necessary level of convergence of interests and, through a peace process coordinated by a powerful state, produce a mutually acceptable solution to the conflict.

The nature of the conflict

Sources of intractability

The territory of present-day Namibia was occupied by Germany after the Berlin Congress in 1878 and remained in its possession until the end of the Great War when the League of Nations decided to transfer it to South Africa as a 'Class C' mandate which stayed to administer the territory as an integral part of the gov- erning state (Zartman 1989a, 174). After a series of events in the post-World War II period, and the growing global pressure toward decolonization, in 1968 the UN changed the name of the territory of Southwest Africa to Namibia. Soon after, in 1971, following several appeals and rulings in favor of South Africa, the International Court of Justice ruled South Africa's presence there illegal (Crocker 1999, 207). However, the real challenge to the South African presence in Namibia arose after a sudden Portuguese withdrawal from the region in 1975, leaving Angola completely vulnerable to a subsequent Soviet-backed, Cuban intervention. The link with the events unfolding in neighboring Angola proved to be of crucial importance to the mediation process that would follow, as both aspects – the power vacuum in Angola and Namibia's claim of independence – would eventually be linked and managed jointly by international actors.

Development of deep feelings of distrust, mutual hatred and irreconcilable positions

During the wave of decolonization after the Second World War, in the territories of present day Angola and Namibia, several groups formed with national liberation as their main goal. Each one embodied a particular societal mark and was inclined to promote a specific socio-political agenda. During German colonial rule, the Herero community of central Namibia and the Nama from the south were subjected to brutal exploitation and genocide (Olusoga and Erichsen 2010). As early as the

1920s, when the territory was transferred to a South African administration (at that time a British dominion), the ideal of an independent Namibia started to emerge. In fact, a few thousand Hereros managed to escape the German "extermination order" of 1904, finding refuge in present-day Botswana (Vigne 1987, 87). According to Vigne, "it was through the efforts of exiles that Namibians themselves were able to bring the issue of Namibia to the attention of the UN, despite the virtual imprisonment of the majority of their own country, and the exile of many more" (1987, 87). The growing sense of Namibian nationhood was further strengthened in the midst of the global wave of decolonization, resulting in a strong resistance to South African rule. Colonial hardship was further aggravated with the introduction of apartheid policies in 1948. During the 1950s, several political movements emerged including the South West Africa's People Organization (SWAPO) – an inexperienced, populist, and non-aligned movement – and the South West African National Union (SWANU) – a sophisticated, perhaps elitist, and Peking-oriented movement (Vigne 1987, 88). The turning point came about in 1964, when the newly formed Organization of African Unity (OAU) put forward a direct challenge to both movements centered upon their readiness to take up arms against the South African occupation. SWAPO's 'yes' led to its recognition, while SWANU's refusal to accept the risks of armed struggle meant the withdrawal of OAU support (Vigne 1987, 88). As a result, SWAPO emerged as the "sole and authentic representative of the Namibian people" in the eyes of the UN (A/RES/3111, 1973; A/RES/31/146, 1976).

Like many African countries, from its inception, Angola represented a conglomerate of different peoples and groups, each with its distinct history and traditions (Meijer and Birmingham 2004, 10). Their shared experience started in large part with the Portuguese colonial expansion in the region. Under the colonial regime, the Angolan society was subjected to highly discriminatory legislation, which "separated the indigenous population from a tiny elite of 'civilized' individuals (or *assimilados*) who enjoyed some of the rights of Portuguese citizens" (Meijer and Birmingham 2004, 11). These racial and discriminatory politics unquestionably left an important mark on the future societal dynamics in Angola. Social cleavages that were generated by the colonial rule conditioned the future relationships between different social groups, which were characterized by high levels of mistrust and suspicion.

While in Namibia SWAPO was able to assume the role of the "sole and authentic representative" of the people, which was able to challenge South African rule, in Angola things were quite different. The territory was affected by an ongoing rivalry between various elites. Over time, three very strong groupings emerged, all promoting the idea of national liberation. The National Front for the Liberation of Angola (FNLA), led by Holden Roberto, was initially the strongest one, reflecting the aspirations of the elites from the north, primarily from the hinterland of Kinshasa, while still maintaining some cultural links with the old Kongo kingdom (Meijer and Birmingham 2004, 12).

The Popular Movement for the Liberation of Angola (MPLA), emerged from the territory populated by the Mbundu people from the surroundings of Luanda, but it also included several urban communities of both indigenous and mixed-race descent. Finally, the Union of Total Independence of Angola (UNITA) led by Jonas Savimbi, promoted the economic interests of the Ovimbudu people and their merchant leaders from the southern *planalto* (Meijer and Birmingham 2004, 12). However, according to Meijer and Birmingham, "to a large extent the ethnic identification of these movements has come about as a result of conscious political maneuvering by each leadership rather than as a genuine expression of popular sentiment and aspiration" (2004, 12). The promotion of particular interests was only aggravated by the power vacuum left after the end of Portuguese colonial rule, as each movement aspired to establish power over the entire country.

Internal characteristics of the conflicting sides and employment of repressive measures

The anti-colonial struggle in Angola started in the early 1960s and was characterized by methods of guerilla warfare. Since none of the armed movements was able to seriously challenge the colonial rule, they tried to outmaneuver each other on the political and diplomatic level. For this reason, the nationalist movements were very eager to attain the necessary support from abroad. The FNLA managed to secure the backing of some of the African countries, the US, and China, and in 1962 it established the Revolutionary Government of Angola in Exile (GRAE), which was initially recognized by OAU as a legitimate representative of Angola and a successor of the colonial rule (Meijer and Birmingham 2004, 13). However, despite being much weaker militarily, by 1975, the MPLA managed to outmaneuver the FNLA diplomatically and shift the OAU support in its favor.

Both movements suffered strongly from internal fractionalization. Especially vulnerable in this regard was FNLA, whose government in exile suffered a serious hit in 1964 when Jonas Savimbi – Minister of Foreign Affairs at that time – accused the FNLA of being militarily ineffective, dependent upon the US, and affected by nepotism and the authoritarian leadership of Holden Roberto (Meijer and Birmingham 2004, 13). He went on to visit a number of states – interestingly enough, mainly communist ones – in search of support. In 1966, he established UNITA. Meijer and Birmingham point out that "by exploiting the feelings of exclusion in Angola's largest ethnic group, the Ovimbundu, Savimbi built up his own constituency in the centre and south of the country" (Meijer and Birmingham 2004, 13).

The first Angolan war – which was part of a greater Portuguese colonial war – was brought to an end in 1974, not because of the effectiveness of anti-colonial movements, but due to the growing pressure and dissatisfaction of the public in Portugal. In fact, the process of decolonization was a direct result of the April 1974 military coup that overthrew the Salazar-Caetano regime in Portugal. As Portuguese control over Angola was decreasing, sporadic violence broke out across the country. During the turmoil, the armies of the MPLA, FNLA, and UNTA jointly patrolled the country with the aim of preserving peace (Meijer and Birmingham 2004). In January 1975, thanks to strong international pressure, the Portuguese authorities and the three movements signed the Alvor Accords, which prescribed the establishment of a transitional government, a new constitution, elections, and independence for Angola. The accords soon collapsed, however, creating a pretext for a power struggle between three factions.

At the same time, although in exile, SWAPO was challenging South African rule in Namibia. Over time, the movement opened offices in several cities across Africa, eventually opening one at the UN. Although very active on the diplomatic front, SWAPO received the necessary 'push' to resort to violence only with the ruling of the International Court of Justice (ICJ) on the issue of Namibia's independence. The Court started deliberating on the issue due to South Africa's refusal to transfer the territory to a UN Trusteeship Council. Ethiopia and Liberia had asked for a "contentious judgment" of South West Africa and in 1966 they received a favorable advisory opinion from the Court. However, this only caused further complications, as months later, the Court reversed its earlier opinion stating that the two countries had 'no *locus standi*' and that the case was inadmissible (Vigne 1987, 89). Although numerous international partners tried to persuade SWAPO to resort to legal means and use the UN system to gain the necessary support for independence, at that moment it was clear that SWAPO could only secure independence through fighting (Vigne 1987, 90).

On July 18, 1966, the same day the ICJ reversed its earlier opinion, SWAPO declared its intention to start a military campaign against South Africa. The movement was already preparing for this move and the first units entered northern Namibia in August 1966 (Vigne 1987, 90). The movement was undertrained and poorly equipped to confront the South African forces. Nevertheless, they were resolute in their aims. In the midst of the early military campaign, SWAPO still tried to rally international support. The reversed decision of the ICJ, which South Africa proclaimed as its victory, motivated the members of the UN General Assembly to pass Resolution 2145 and terminate the current mandate which was conferred by the League of Nations. As South Africa had failed to fulfill its obligations as laid out in the mandate, it no longer had the right to administer the territory and henceforth South West Africa would come under the direct responsibility of the UN (A/RES/2145, 1996). Bypassing the Security Council, the General Assembly also established a '*de jure*' government of the territory with a commissioner as its executive and renamed the territory Namibia (Vigne 1987, 92). This decision was strongly objected to by South African trading partners from the West.

It was an unwritten rule during the Cold War that each liberation movement in Africa would be associated with a specific ideological camp. Despite often being labeled as a member of the 'Casablanca Group' – which included the African National Congress (ANC), Liberation Congress of Mozambique (FRELIMO), the MPLA and Zimbabwe's African People's Union (ZAPU) – SWAPO tried to establish a distinctive and non-aligned position. According to Vigne, there were two reasons for this: first of all, due to a long history of oppression and genocide, the Namibians "felt themselves as yet ill-equipped to serve as equal partners with the imperial powers of East and West"; and secondly, while rejected by the US and UK, SWAPO was very hesitant to accept the authority of the USSR (Vigne 1987, 92). SWAPO's initial choice to assume a non-aligned stance was aimed at preserving internal unity – something that other liberation movements could only aspire to. Nevertheless, in the midst of Cold War super-power rivalry, SWAPO's struggle against South Africa provided sufficient motivation for the Soviets to support its cause. Over time, SWAPO's ties with the Soviets improved and strengthened, which made them highly unpopular with the US and its Western allies.

While unable to garner international support from the powerful Western states, the situation turned in SWAPO's favor with another ICJ ruling. In 1975, the ICJ passed a new advisory opinion, this time stating that the continued presence of South Africa in Namibia was illegal. It called on the UN member states to recognize the illegality of South African presence and refrain from any acts that could imply the legality of its administration in Namibia. At the same time, South Africa was obliged to withdraw its administration from Namibia (ICJ 1975). Despite objections from some Western states, the illegality of South African rule in Namibia was clearly established.

The events in neighboring Angola, where the Portuguese were agreeing on a transfer of power and accepting the independence of its former colony, inspired SWAPO to continue its struggle against the South African regime. However, the situation in Angola soon became more complicated. Following the collapse of the Alvor Accords, the power struggle between the three main factions became extremely violent. Thanks to external support from the Soviet bloc, on November 11, 1975, the MPLA declared Angola's independence and installed Agostinho Neto as its first president (Meijer and Birmingham 2004, 10; Pycroft 1994, 242). The FNLA and UNITA were excluded from the newly established government, which in fact was a socialist, one-party regime. Gradually, the new system, which was organized along Marxist-Leninist lines, received international recognition, though not from the US (Meijer and Birmingham 2004, 13).

By the end of the 1970s, FNLA followers were integrated into the system thanks to a rapprochement between the MPLA and Zaire's President Mobutu Sese Seko, who was very close to the FNLA's leader Holden Roberto. The FNLA army, which at one point represented a foreign-armed force with thousands of recruits, "disintegrated without being formally disarmed or demobilized" (Meijer and Birmingham 2004, 15). This left UNITA as the main contender for power in Angola. With the collapse of the Alvor Accords, UNITA began receiving support from South Africa, at first in a clandestine form. By 1983, the partnership with UNITA became an official policy of the government in Pretoria (Meyer 2004, 82). At the same time, the fact that UNITA was fighting a Marxist-Leninist regime was enough reason for the US to directly support the movement.

The turmoil that followed saw a simultaneous unfolding of three different armed conflicts. The first one was the bush war along the Namibian border with

Angola between the South African Defense Force (SADF) and the SWAPO. The second and third conflicts saw the SADF involved in the Angolan civil war, where it assisted the UNITA in fighting the MPLA, which enjoyed Cuba's unequivocal support. The US mediation efforts mainly tackled the problem of resolving conflicts involving the South African and Cuban military presence both in Namibia and Angola and concentrated on a settlement that would see withdrawal of foreign forces from both countries. By then, as far the Angolan civil war was concerned, "no external party had the standing or legitimacy to force its mediation on the Angolan parties, still less to create yet another linkage of the external to the internal Angolan issues" (Crocker 1999, 224).

As the conflict in Vietnam was approaching an end, Angola and Namibia became a fertile ground for another super-power proxy war. In fact, as Pycroft notes, "the influence of super-power rivalry became one the defining characteristics of southern African regional politics" (1994, 242). According to Meijer and Birmingham, "each side was not so much defending a specific interest in Angola as playing out geo-political rivalry" (2004, 15).

Involvement of international actors and their interests in the conflict

Soviet Union

The unfolding situation in the region provided enough reason for the Soviet Union to advance its ambition of implementing the 'Brezhnev Doctrine' in southern Africa. Under that doctrine, the détente and peaceful coexistence with the 'imperialist camp' were a result of a favorable shift in the balance of power and a form of struggle between the two systems. For Moscow, the agreements between the two global powers were a reflection of Soviet success in the "diplomatic struggle of the two worlds" (Mitchell 1978, 381). Brezhnev even stated that "détente by no means annuls the battle of ideas" (Brezhnev cited in Mitchell 1987, 381). According to Mitchell, under the Brezhnev doctrine, "the Soviet support for national liberation movements, particularly in southern Africa, is presumably based upon the assumption that the general crisis of capitalism makes the West more vulnerable to pressure" (Mitchell 1978, 381). In other words, the success of the liberation movements was perceived as a means to an end, which was the increasing weight of the Socialist system in world politics (Mitchell 1978, 381).

Following the rationale of the Brezhnev doctrine, the Soviets used the turmoil and instability that emerged during the collapse of Portuguese colonial rule in Angola to advance their role at the global level. Pycroft noted that

> the victory of the Soviet-backed MPLA over the South African and United States assisted UNITA and FNLA forces in the first round of the Angolan civil war in 1975 and 1976 provided the Soviet Union with a foothold in southern Africa, which it improved through support for the MPLA

in Angola, SWAPO in Namibia, the African National Congress (ANC) in South Africa, and Frelimo after independence in Mozambique.

(Pycroft 1994, 242)

The Soviet (and Cuban) support for the MPLA started as early as the 1960s, but was initially insufficient to allow the MPLA to challenge Portuguese colonial rule. Over time, Soviet support became fundamental to the MPLA's cause. The heavy armaments that were provided to the movement in the most delicate moments of the civil war in 1975 were of crucial importance to the MPLA's success in obtaining control of the capital and declaring Angola an independent country. In 1976, the USSR established even closer relations with the MPLA by signing the Treaty of Friendship and Cooperation (Meijer 2004, 86). At its first congress in December 1977, the movement transformed itself into a Marxist-Leninist party signaling its unquestioned affiliation with the Soviet bloc.

Cuba

Cuba was another close ally of the MPLA. Cuban interest in the region started with Che Guevarra's visit to Central Africa in 1964. During the 1975 civil war, Cuba assisted the MPLA, by first sending military advisors and eventually by dispatching troops in response to South African intervention in support of UNITA. By February 1976, Cuba had dispatched around 14,000 troops to support the MPLA, with a clear intention of consolidating Soviet influence in the region (Meijer 2004, 87). Although the leadership in Havana welcomed Soviet cooperation in this conflict, Cuban involvement was rooted in an independent agenda and had its own rationale. Anatoly Dobrynin, who was the Soviet ambassador to the United States at that time, stated in his memoirs, that the Cubans sent their troops to Angola "on their own initiative and without consulting us" (Dobrynin 1995, 362). In fact, according to Gleijeses, "by deciding to send troops, Castro challenged the Soviet leader Leonid Brezhnev, who opposed the dispatch of Cuban soldiers to Angola.... Indeed, it took two months for Moscow to provide crucial logistical support to airlift Cuban troops to Angola." (2006, 8). Although the US and other external actors initially viewed Cubans in Angola as Soviet proxies, this was never fully the case. Kissinger noted:

> At the time we thought he [Castro] was operating as a Soviet surrogate.... We could not imagine that he would act so provocatively so far from home unless he was pressured by Moscow to repay the Soviet Union for its military and economic support. Evidence now available suggests that the opposite was the case.

(Kissinger 1999, 816)

Cuban involvement was mainly motivated by its opposition to the South African backed white minority rule. The Cubans wanted to prevent any possibility of apartheid policies spreading over to Angola and the consolidation of white domination over black majority in Southern Africa (Gleijeses 2006, 8). After Angola became independent, Cuba continued to provide much-needed military support, but it also assisted the government in rebuilding the country by providing it with engineers, teachers, doctors, and civil servants (Meijer 2004, 87). Cuban ability to push South African troops out of Angola was not only a significant military accomplishment. According to Gleijeses, it was the real beginning of Namibia's war on independence (2006, 9). Although SWAPO started its activities already in 1966, their efforts gained the needed momentum only after the advancement of Cuban and MPLA troops in Angola. As a general from South African forces stated, "for the first time they [the SWAPO rebels] obtained what is more or less a prerequisite for successful insurgent campaigning, namely a border that provided safe refuge" (citation taken from Gleijeses 2006, 9; see Geldenhuys 1995, 59).

United States and 'linkage strategy'

American interests in intervening in the conflict were also primarily political and revolved around the 'Reagan Doctrine.' The doctrine had anti-communism as its *raison d'être* and promoted the idea of supporting anti-communist resistance around the world (Oye *et al.* 1987). Even during the Angolan civil war in 1975 and 1976, the US assisted the anti-communist movements. In principle, in southern Africa, the Reagan administration tried to promote the policies of 'constructive engagement' – which were introduced by Assistant Secretary Chester Crocker in 1981 – with the primary aim of countering the Soviet presence in the region (Crocker 1992; Davies 2007). Under this policy, "any leader that was opposed to Soviet ideology and expansion was courted by America" (Pycroft 1994, 243). The US found a close ally in South Africa's Prime Minister P.W. Botha (who would later become president), who was engaged in a struggle with the Soviet-backed SWAPO in Namibia. The policies of constructive engagement for the South Africa government had a dual impact: on the one hand it was an opportunity for South Africa to regain the Western support it had lost and on the other, it offered a dose of legitimacy for the government's disruptive actions both domestically and in the region.

According to Pycroft, "for Angola, the most significant component of constructive engagement was the US's introduction, in 1982, of 'linkage' into negotiation for Namibia's independence" (1994, 243). In a nutshell, the linkage meant that an independent Namibia could not be achieved without the withdrawal of Cuban troops from Angola, thus tying together the fate of two countries. In principle, the US was interested in achieving a smooth, peaceful, and stable transition from colonial rule to self-government (Zartman 1989a, 182). The main dilemma the US faced was choosing between a continued apartheid South African sovereignty over Namibia, strongly opposed by the international community, or a UN-endorsed independence for the territory, which would most likely also entail a pro-Marxist, SWAPO government in Namibia. By the mid-1970s, as South African policies became incompatible with principles cherished by the US administration, policy makers in Washington realized that any further resistance to Namibian nationalism, which had the backing of the UN, would only backfire in the long run. Thus the key concern of the US was to prevent a war from escalating even further. The US feared that any intensification of fighting would only draw their Soviet rivals into the conflict, making it necessary for the US to align with apartheid South Africa, a scenario they absolutely wanted to avoid.

With the help of partner Western states in the Security Council – France, the United Kingdom, Canada, and West Germany – in September 1978, the US managed to pass UN Security Council Resolution 345 that prescribed a "set of complex arrangements for the territory's transition to independence under South African administrative control with simultaneous UN monitoring and supervision" (Crocker 1999, 214). Once the framework for upcoming peacemaking activities was set up, in 1981 the new Reagan administration took on the task of reestablishing "coordinated working relations among the Western Five" or the Western Contact Group, whose global leverage and reputation would became useful in the context of the upcoming peace-making efforts (Zartman 1989a; Iji 2011).

South Africa was very skeptical about the intentions of the US and its allies in Southern Africa, given the apparent UN advocacy of Namibia's independence and growing support for SWAPO on the East River. However, the greatest contributor to Pretoria's unease was a lack of reaction by the US and its allies to the Soviet-Cuban intervention in Angola. Until then, the West had hesitated to include the Angola question in the peacemaking equation for determining Namibia's final status. It was deemed as rather dangerous to address the issue of the Cuban presence in Angola and consequently lose Angola's assistance in the Namibia negotiations, as it was feared that the rest of the international community might see this as Western countries' prioritization of the communist question over the one of decolonization in Africa. From a practical angle, the West was aware that addressing the Cuban presence in Angola would necessarily provoke Moscow to react, at least on a diplomatic level.

However, despite these concerns, it became apparent to the new US administration under President Reagan that perpetuating this logic would only keep the peace process in deadlock, as South Africa made it quite clear that its cooperation in the process directly depended on the extent of the Cuban presence in the region. Even Angolan leaders recognized the connection between Namibian and Angolan events when they stated that "Cubans could leave Angola *after* Namibia's independence under Resolution 435" (Crocker 1999, 216). So the US chose to take a risk and decided to restructure negotiations in order to include the Angolan factor as well. According to Crocker, the 'linkage strategy' had two advantages: "a far better chance to nail Pretoria down to a firm commitment on Resolution 435 and an appropriate US response to Soviet extension of the Brezhnev doctrine to the Third World, including Africa" (Crocker 1999, 216). The US hoped that a well-coordinated mediation effort, which put diplomatic pressure on the Soviet–Cuban–Angolan group, would weaken the current Soviet martial policies in Africa.

Therefore, while the stage for mediation was set, the US still needed some type of compliance, even tacit, from the Soviets. In other words, the potential success of mediation efforts was directly related to the ability of the Soviets to use their biased position to leverage their partners in conflict to change strategies and opt for a peaceful settlement of the dispute. At the same time, the willingness to leverage both Cubans and Angolans toward an agreement would indicate that the US and the USSR had managed to establish a common idea of resolving the conflict through mediation and thus indicate Soviet willingness to participate in US-led and coordinated mediation activities.

In reality, Moscow had quite limited interests in Namibia, or as Zartman puts it, "no interests to lose or defend and everything to gain" (Zartman 1989a, 183). Its involvement in the conflict was incomparable to the levels achieved in Angola; its involvement was based on arming SWAPO forces and providing modest amounts of training for them. In principle, the USSR was unconvinced that South African acquiescence to a negotiated independence for Namibia was actually achievable. Nevertheless, the Soviet Union had been more appreciative of conflict resolution on the issue, with its objections giving way to active support, as it was less willing to sustain the costs of continued conflict than one would expect (Zartman 1989a, 184). In fact, Moscow's stance on the issue drastically changed over the span of eight years, departing from straightforward obstructionism of every Western effort to find a solution, to fundamental cooperation with the US that eventually helped steer the parties toward a peace agreement.

This shift in policy was a direct result of a dramatic change that occurred with Gorbachev's accession to power and his new 'perestroika' policies (Shearman 1987). Although the US-led mediation attempts were never formally objected to by the Soviets – as a result of the détente and coexistence prescribed by the Brezhnev doctrine – and albeit important mediation milestones that were reached in the early and mid-1980s, the mediation process was still far from reaching a comprehensive peace agreement because the mediators did not have sufficient leverage over the warring parties. The Soviets had obvious leverage over the MPLA and Cuba, but in light of the Cold War power rivalry with the US, they were unwilling to use it to assist the US in mediating the conflict. In fact, under the Brezhnev doctrine, Soviets saw the US's inability to mediate the conflict as a reflection of the 'imperialist bloc's' decreasing global power and – since the bipolar dynamics of the Cold War were a zero sum game – an indication of the increasing Soviet influence in international relations. The rapprochement between the USSR and US that happened during Gorbachev's mandate was more a result of a larger geo-political shift in Soviet policies toward the US and its allies than anything else.

Multiparty mediation process

Initial lack of cooperation between third parties

Moscow's tendency to unequivocally hamper any Western initiative was already on display during the preparation of Resolution 435. In the face of clear support by SWAPO and frontline states for the proposed text, Soviets backed off and abstained from vetoing the text in the Security Council. However, once the resolution was adopted, Moscow became its strongest promoter, now opposing any modification of the text. Thus, the US intention to link questions of Namibia and Angola was strongly opposed as it represented "nothing less than an attempt to block Resolution 435, to force capitulations of Angola and its departure from the socialist camp, to join forces with Pretoria in creating a pro-Western security zone, and reverse the tide of history in Southern Africa" (Crocker 1999, 234).

The Soviet position was rapidly transposed on to the Angolan–Cuban joint communiqué in February 1982, a statement that officially proclaimed that Angolans and Cubans would decide upon a timeframe for Cuban withdrawal from the country only *after* Namibia was granted independence.[2] Angola wanted to be assured that Cuban withdrawal would not allow for invasion by South African troops, as had already occurred on two occasions, in 1976 and 1979, when withdrawal was interrupted by South African attacks on Angola (Zartman 1989a, 212). The US was aware that the linkage strategy introduced the necessity to accommodate Moscow in the process, as its leverage over the Angolans and Cubans might turn out to be instrumental for a successful outcome.

Increased UNITA military activities amplified Angola's need for stronger backing by its allies. By 1982, the number of Cuban troops increased to about 25,000, and the government in Luanda signed arms supplies agreements with the Soviet Union in mid-May 1983 and early January 1984 (Zartman 1989a, 219). As the MPLA was strongly dependent upon Soviet and Cuban support, the US administration assumed that any Angolan position and proposal had been 'cleared' in Havana and Moscow (Crocker 1999, 235). Since the Soviets refused to negotiate directly with the US, officials in Washington opted for a more cautious approach. Crocker points out that during these years, US and Soviet officials held a series of 'informal exchanges' on Southern Africa, in which the US aimed to "avoid surprises, to probe for constructive openings and offer Moscow a chance to bid and to explain to US purposes and indicate how they might serve the interests of both sides" (Crocker 1999, 234). However, the initial exchanges did not produce any results as Moscow was insistent on bringing up legalistic issues and was unwilling to suggest any alternatives, emphasizing their support for the most recent Angolan positions.

Authorities in both Luanda and Pretoria were having difficulties to find a compromised solution, as any such move was perceived as dangerous to national interest and to the strength of their positions on the battleground. It was a clear 'game of chicken' between the parties, as they were unwilling to make the first move fearing the reaction of the other side. The US became fully aware that the conflict was still not 'ripe' for resolution and that they were unable to achieve a settlement on their own (Zartman 1989a, 214–225). Quite problematic for the US was its lack of leverage, especially a lack of 'sticks' to induce authorities in Pretoria to compromise. Dissatisfied with the South African reluctance to cooperate, the US adopted limited sanctions against Pretoria in 1985 as a reaction to their apartheid policies and started considering the option of providing clandestine support to the

UNITA forces. Until then, the US had only a limited ability to support UNITA because of the Clark Amendment to the US Arms Export Control Act from 1976 that barred the US from aiding any paramilitary activity in Angola (Berridge 1989). The intention was to put pressure on Luanda and Havana, and indirectly on Pretoria, and make them realize that the linkage strategy was a good alternative to complete isolation. The Amendment was repealed in July 1985 and already in 1986, the US provided UNITA with ten million dollars in direct military aid. The assistance progressively increased to 80 million dollars under the Bush administration (Pycroft 1994, 245). According to Pycroft, "the increased US commitment to UNITA came as South Africa began reassessing its commitment to retaining control over Namibia, and therefore questioning its need to maintain UNITA as a bargaining chip in the linkage equation" (Pycroft 1994, 245). Nevertheless, South Africa, motivated by success on the battlefield in 1985, still did not see this as a plausible alternative. Two important events, one at the global level and one on the battleground, changed things dramatically.

Convergence of interests between third parties

With the arrival of Gorbachev to power in 1985, the Soviet Union started an important transition in relation to its regional policies. The new Soviet leadership began publicly calling for 'political solutions' to regional conflicts (Shearman 1987, 1111). The articulation of the new, post-Brezhnev, foreign policy of the Soviet Union was secondary to the need to concentrate on reforming the Soviet economy and society. According to Pycroft, the expensive foreign adventures in places such as Afghanistan and Angola had to be reduced as they were producing unbearable costs to the crippled Soviet economy, while at the same time the Soviet Union was quite willing to achieve "a limited rapprochement with the US to facilitate access to Western finance and technology" (Pycroft 1994, 244). It should be noted that these were only initial steps that did not immediately imply a reduction in opposition to US proposals (Crocker 1999, 235). In fact, the Soviet Union continued to publicly challenge US-led initiatives, asking for the process to be conferred to the UN, the African Union, and the Non-Aligned Movement. More importantly, the Soviet Union discouraged any Angolan cooperation with Washington and "criticized UN Secretariat officials for undertaking quiet probes of Luanda's latest thinking on a linkage-based settlement" (Crocker 1999, 235). Mediators' inability to reach convergence of interests was leading the process into a deadlock. For the US, this meant that the greatest obstacle to a smooth mediation process was not Luanda's positions, but rather Moscow's lack of cooperation. In March 1987, after consulting its allies, Angola decided to resume direct talks with the US. In order to strengthen its negotiating position, Moscow advised Luanda to undertake a massive offensive against UNITA (Crocker 1999, 236), using violence as an off-the-table tactic to improve his negotiating position. Evidently, the non-cooperative strategies of one of the mediators induced the party to the conflict that it supported to defect from the peace process as well.

However, the strategy proposed by the Soviets actually backfired. The Soviet-Angolan assault in late 1987 was a fiasco, with thousands of Angolan troops killed and a large portion of Soviet military hardware either destroyed or captured. As the costs of supporting the conflict were increasing, while still maintaining a hard line on US-led endeavors, Moscow grew frustrated with a continued conflict and became open to fresh ideas introduced by Castro during the 70th anniversary of the Soviet revolution in November 1987. One of the crucial implications of the Gorbachev shift in foreign policy was that the MPLA could no longer depend upon 'unqualified support' from the USSR and Cuba. A deteriorating economic situation in the Soviet Union induced officials in Moscow to reconsider overstretching their military involvement around the globe. Pycroft notes that "although there was a commitment from the Soviet leadership to maintain the military presence in Angola to counter UNITA and South Africa, pressure began to mount on the MPLA to find a negotiated settlement" (Pycroft 1994, 244). While Soviet military support was quite substantial, it came at a high cost. The MPLA had to finance this military support with oil and diamond revenue, to the severe detriment of the country's economy. Almost 65% of Angola's national debt was with the USSR and the presence of Cuban troops was costing the country 250 million dollars a year (Pycroft 1994, 244).

On the other hand, the MPLA had sufficient reason to believe that it could find partners in the West. First of all, the US was the largest importer of Angolan goods – especially oil – with trade worth more than two billion dollars in 1990 (Pycroft 1994, 244). Secondly, the fact that the regime in Luanda was not recognized by the US did not prevent close contact from being established between the US State Department and the MPLA (Berridge 1989, 470). In fact, Crocker was quite interested in having the MPLA at the negotiating table, and for this reason he initially even opposed the repeal of the Clark Amendment, as he feared that this would drive the MPLA away from the talks (Berridge 1989, 470). Nevertheless, the US' unyielding support of UNITA's cause was a direct indication to the MPLA that a military victory was virtually impossible and that a negotiated settlement should be sought (Pycroft 1994, 245).

While acknowledging Cuba's decision that its forces would have to leave Angola, Soviets maintained a firm position that Angola would not be "thrown to wolves" (Crocker 1999, 237). Despite these affirmations, the Soviet Union still did not propose any viable alternative to the linkage strategy. It was the Cubans, who did not participate in the latest military debacle, that made two crucial choices. First, Havana decided to shift the unfavorable balance of power created with the latest SADF-UNITA victory over their allies and sent 15,000 fresh troops to Angola's border with Namibia. By mid-1988 there were close to 50,000 Cuban troops in the region. It was a clear signal to South Africa that celebration time was over and that a military solution to the conflict was far from being easily attainable for Pretoria (Berridge 1989; Pycroft 1994). Second, in the mid-1987 Cuba made a decisive shift and made its bid to join the talks. This enabled the US to conduct talks with a joint Angolan-Cuban delegation starting in January 1988.

Ultimately, the US produced the necessary 'stick' that induced South Africa to engage in negotiations. As the Soviet influence in Southern Africa was decreasing, the need to have South Africa as an anti-communist ally was called into question. This prompted the US to gradually start reconsidering its relationship with South Africa. Especially problematic were the apartheid policies of the Botha administration. In October 1986, the US Congress passed the Comprehensive Anti-Apartheid Act, which imposed a strict set of economic and trade sanctions on South Africa. These policies greatly harmed the South African economy, plunging the country into recession (Pycroft 1994, 245). Mounting problems, both on the battlefield and domestically, induced the officials in Pretoria to find a way to "re-establish favorable relations with the international community and stave off further sanctions" (Pycroft 1994, 245). Thus, South Africa started signaling readiness to join the negotiations with the US and, together with Angola, started drafting a proposal on the timetable for the withdrawal. In other words, Pretoria was looking for an 'honorable exit.' The situation was slowly becoming ripe for resolution: the parties were entering a hurting stalemate as it was clear that a military solution to the conflict was unattainable for any of the parties; thus they started perceiving negotiations as being a 'way out' (Zartman 1989a).

An important consequence of the linkage strategy was the gradual exclusion of SWAPO and UNITA from the peace process. The isolation of the two movements was not done because of their predisposition to spoil the process, but was a calculated decision by Crocker to design a proper 'party arithmetic' that would include all the parties relevant for the achievement of a negotiated settlement and exclude those whose presence could be problematic and disputed. The plan was to create a sequence of steps: first a regional settlement was supposed to be negotiated between states and not movements, after that parties to each conflict were expected to conduct internal peacemaking. According to Berridge,

> the South Africans pressed for SWAPO's exclusion because of their hatred of it, and found the United States receptive because this would make it easier to reconcile UNITA – which had a vital interest in developments in Namibia as well as in Angola – to being excluded as well.
>
> (Berridge 1989, 472)

With both Cuba and Angola willing to talk to South Africa, the US decided to accommodate the Soviets in the peace process while hoping to "neutralize residual obstructionism" and hopefully obtain "valuable insights and even help" (Crocker 1999, 237). In present circumstances, with the new policy outlook of the Gorbachev administration, which voiced the need for policy solutions and was coupled with Moscow's unwillingness to assume any more military costs in the region, the US opted for a careful approach. In April 1988, three in-depth, US–Soviet consultations were held, and as a final result the Soviet Union decided to publicly support a US-led mediation process for the first time. In return, the US bestowed them with 'observer' status which was never fully defined. Meetings with the Soviets continued throughout the tripartite negotiations mediated by the

US. It was tripartite (Angola–Cuba–South Africa) because Cuba explicitly asked to be included in the talks as a part of the Angola team. As underlined by Crocker, US–Soviet meetings soon moved from "debates about the shape of an acceptable settlement" to more practical issues of "how the two sides might advance those points agreed on and how current obstacles could be handled" (Crocker 1999, 237).

Full exploratory meetings between three sides and the US started at the beginning of May 1988 in London. The first meeting saw an immediate Angolan offer of a four-year Cuban withdrawal from Angola and a one-year withdrawal of SADF from Namibia. Before the troop withdrawal, however, the proposal called for a preceding stop to US and South African support for UNITA. The South African delegation responded with a counterproposal asking for a Cuban withdrawal before Namibian independence and at the same time reconciliation between MPLA and UNITA (Zartman 1989a, 230). Fortunately, parties agreed to evaluate each other's proposals, so they decided to meet again in Cairo at the end of June 1988. In the meantime, a series of US–Soviet consultations intensified, bearing more fruit than ever before. During their meetings, both sides explored the options for strengthening cooperation between the three parties in the peace process. According to the Soviet sources, the US guaranteed South African implementation of Resolution 435 if the Cubans withdrew their forces from Angola within three years in return. During a Reagan–Gorbachev summit in Moscow in May, the two sides agreed to deliver a peace settlement within four months – in order to celebrate it at the tenth anniversary of Resolution 435. The two global powers, each backing a particular side in the conflict, had achieved the necessary convergence of interests that allowed for a coordinated mediation process to take place (Zartman 1999, 230).

This coordination was best demonstrated during the talks in Cairo, which almost broke down due to an unexpected Cuban and Angolan 'ideological tirade' regarding apartheid policies of South Africa. The Soviet delegation immediately exercised necessary pressure on its allies and brought them back to the point of negotiation (Zartman 1989a, 231). Thanks to this unprecedented move by the Soviets, the next talks in New York saw all the parties work on the actual text of the settlement. The three sides started increasing levels of cooperation and opted to neglect the timetable of withdrawal in favor of 'indispensable principles' for the final settlement. These included:

> aspects of cooperation (aid) for development, right to peace, right to self-determination, non-aggression, non-interference, non-use of force, and respect for territorial integrity and inviolability of frontiers, as well as recognition of roles – the United States as mediator and permanent members of the Security Council as guarantors.
>
> (Zartman 1989a, 231)

The principles were later ratified by all three sides and by SWAPO. After this, negotiations focused on finalizing details regarding the timetable for the withdrawal.

Also as a sign of willingness to elevate cooperation to the highest level, US officials continuously briefed Soviet colleagues about the "mediator's priorities and game plans" (Crocker 1999, 238). The US hoped that by providing essential information, Soviets would play their part and induce Angola and Cuba to reach an agreement with South Africa on the timetable. At the same time, Moscow also intensified communication with South Africa and contributed to the overall super-power encouragement for authorities in Pretoria. Ultimately, through their consultations, US representatives convinced the Soviets to terminate their requests for a suspension of US support for UNITA and encouraged them to put pressure on Angola to achieve national reconciliation with UNITA. This closed the circle, as all the issues were covered by the peace process. Shortly after, following a very painstaking negotiation on the details of withdrawal, on December 22, 1988, Cuba, Angola, and South Africa signed a peace agreement at the UN headquarters in New York.

Just as in the case of Tajikistan, the US and USSR acted as biased mediators in the sense of the game theoretical model presented earlier. As long as the US and the Soviet Union were unable to achieve a convergence of interests in managing the conflict, any attempt at finding a peaceful solution was unsuccessful, as a mediator's defection was perceived as a sufficient reason for the conflicting parties not to commit to the peace process. At the same time, biased mediators are useful in terms of the effectiveness of the process, as long as they maintain cooperative behavior with other mediators, as they can use their special relationship with one conflicting side to influence its behavior, positions, and perceptions and consequently move it toward an agreement. However, the process also witnessed a considerably different dynamic of multiparty mediation from the one that took place in Tajikistan. The crucial difference between the two cases concerns the leadership role of coordinating mediation activities. While in Tajikistan this role was filled by the Special Envoys of the UN, in the case of Namibia, the leadership role was assumed by the US.

Although the US as a powerful state had a clear set of interests to promote in the conflict and an undeniably biased attitude toward particular conflicting sides (UNITA and South Africa), it managed to be an effective coordinator for two reasons. First of all, over time its mediation activities were recognized as 'indispensible' even by the disputants with whom it had no special relations (the MPLA and Cuba). This generated the necessary level of legitimacy required to prescribe behavior. In fact, this status was publicly and explicitly accepted by all the parties in conflict who considered the US-led mediation to be one of the 14 principles that were crucial to the peaceful settlement of their conflict (Berridge 1989, 469). At the same time, it acquired the necessary degree of consent and convergence of interests with the USSR (which was the key patron state of both the Angolan MPLA and Cuba). This (causal link) allowed for the coordination to be effective even though it was conducted by a biased, powerful state.

The convergence of interests was induced by a larger geo-political shift that occurred once (the new) leadership in the Soviet Union realized that past geo-political preferences were not generating sufficient returns in the conflict: the conflict was too costly and the parties were not getting any results from the mediation process. Such a change in perceptions was further strengthened by the stalemate reached between Cuban and South African forces and their partners in Angola and Namibia. It was a clear indication that a military victory in the conflict was unfeasible and that the present, non-cooperative strategy in the peace process was not producing any substantial results that would overturn the military stalemate.

Notes

1 The main focus of this chapter is on US-led mediation initiatives, and US–Soviet relations within this process. Nevertheless, the critical strategic contributions of the UN and the UK and to a lesser degree of Zambia and Tanzania, to the US-led mediation should be emphasized as well. The US mediation borrowed leverage from these actors wherever and whenever it could be done (Crocker 1993).
2 According to Gleijeses,

> having pushed the SADF out of Angola [in 1976], the Cubans hoped to withdraw their troops gradually, giving the MPLA time to strengthen its own armed forces (known as FAPLA) so that they could take over the defense of Angola. This was the message that Cuban Defense Minister Raúl Castro brought to Luanda on 20 April 1976. He told Neto that the Cuban government proposed that "gradual steps should be taken to withdraw the troops over the next years – 1976, 1977, 1978 – until only military instructors remained." Neto accepted the Cuban timetable with only minor changes, including that "the Cuban military doctors presently in Angola remain and continue to offer their valuable services".
>
> (Gleijeses 2006, 9–10)

5   Cambodia[1]

Civil war in Cambodia involved four different Khmer factions and each one had an outside sponsor state (Solomon 1999). Despite its reputation from the war in Vietnam and the bipolar constraints of the Cold War, the US was seen as the most 'neutral' member of the Security Council, "with the political influence and resources to help structure the settlement" (Solomon 2000, 4). At the moment the US-led peace talks took place in the final months of 1989, the government in Phnom Penh was headed by Hun Sen, whose faction assumed power thanks to a Vietnamese military incursion into Cambodia in December 1978 which over-threw the Khmer Rouge regime (Hampson and Zartman 2012, 4). The pro-Vietnamese government, named the People's Republic of Kampuchea (PRK), was backed only by the USSR and its allies and did not enjoy the support of the West. Also, it certainly did not have good relations with the authorities in Beijing. China was concerned about Vietnamese expansionist policies, interpret-ing them as Soviet efforts to contain Chinese influence in South-East Asia. Once dethroned, the Khmer Rouge fled to the jungles along the border with Thailand and thanks to Chinese support, started an insurgency campaign against Viet-nam's client regime (Solomon 1999, 284).

Given its experience with Vietnam and the positioning of the Soviet Union in the matter, the United States chose China as its partner. It was clear to the US that China was interested in improving its international reputation after the June 1989 events at Tiananmen Square and thus that it would be more willing to cooperate with the US even at the cost of distancing themselves from the Khmer Rouge (Hampson and Zartman 2012, 6). The two sides managed to reach initial convergence of interests in supporting a future coalition government led by Prince Sihanouk, who had governed Cambodia in its first decade as an inde-pendent state, only to be toppled by Khmer Rouge forces in 1963. Ironically, Chinese acceptance of Sihanouk was coupled with a request to allow for the Khmer Rouge to be included in the future power-sharing arrangement. The US did not object to this, as it wanted to keep the Khmer Rouge engaged in the peace process, fearing that they might otherwise act as spoilers. At the same time, the US was confident that if the Khmer Rouge agreed to participate in the future political life of Cambodia, its unpopularity with local people would cer-tainly not allow them to gain power through elections.

Nature of the conflict

Sources of intractability

During French colonial rule, Cambodia was a relatively peaceful area. The majority of its population was ethnic Khmers and Buddhism was the most dominant religion. At the same time, almost a fifth of the country's inhabitants were ethnic and religious minorities. Interestingly, these minorities also had a distinct work-related role in the society. As Kiernan points out, "Vietnamese, Chinese, and Muslim Chams worked mostly in rubber plantations or as clerks, shopkeepers, and fisherfolk, while a score of small ethnolingusitc groups, such as the Jarai, Tampuan, and Kreung, populated the upland northeast" (Kiernan 2002, 483). After World War II, the colonial rule was gradually challenged and resisted by organized independence movements of Vietnamese (Viet Minh) and nationalist Khmer Issarak (independence) forces. Over time, the lengthy anti-colonial struggle produced a Vietnamese-sponsored, Cambodian communist movement, the Khmer People's Revolutionary Party (KPRP), which received "increasing though not unchallenged" support from the Issarak nationalists (Kiernan 1985, 2002). As the KPPR slowly acquired leadership over the Issarak membership, several anti-communist movements started emerging. By 1952, these anti-KPRP movements started campaigns of massacres targeting ethnic Vietnamese and Cham populations (Kiernan 1985).

Cambodia became independent in 1953, as a result of the French defeat in the First Indochina War. King Norodom Sihanouk, who according to Hampson and Zartman (2012) was a mercurial figure, immediately assumed a foreign policy of neutrality. This was a carefully calculated decision in the midst of Cold War dynamics. As Kiernan points out, he tried to accommodate the communist forces and acknowledge their role in Cambodia's struggle for independence, while at the same time he was fearful of their potentially disruptive behavior if the country was to assume a more pro-Western stance (Kiernan 2002, 484). The policy of neutrality was also aimed at maintaining a peaceful relationship with neighboring Vietnam.

In the first decade of Cambodia's independence, Sihanouk's policies of neutrality managed to appease both the moderate nationalists and veteran communists, transforming the country into a one-party kingdom (Kiernan 2002, 484). Dissatisfied forces – both from the left and from the right – either found refuge in Vietnam or headed for the hills deep in the countryside waiting for an opportune moment to return. Veteran leaders of the demobilized KPRP – who generally came from rural, Buddhist and pro-Vietnamese backgrounds – were gradually replaced by a group of younger, urban, Paris-trained, anti-Vietnamese militants headed by Saloth Sar, Ieng Sary, and Son Sen. According to Kiernan's accounts, "from the jungles of remote northeast, the new party leadership planned an armed rebellion against Sihanouk's regime, ignoring his independent nationalism and labeling him a U.S. puppet" (Kiernan 2002, 484). Fearful for its survival, Sihanouk's regime started employing harsh policies against all leftist forces pushing the moderate communist veterans to join the new young leaders of KPRP.

Development of deep feelings of distrust and employment of repressive measures

However, the biggest threat for Cambodia's stability in the mid 1960s came with the intensification of the US campaign in Vietnam. The border between the two countries was flooded with Khmer and Vietnamese-communist refugees escaping Saigon's and the US' advancement. By 1967, the communist forces under Saloth Sar's leadership – now renamed the Communist Party of Kampuchea (CPK) – started a small scale insurgency which provoked a disproportionate response from the government. The Cambodian countryside was dragged into a civil war. Unable to cope with the challenges brought about by the war in Vietnam and CPK's rebellion, Sihanouk's government was toppled in a military coup led by General Lon Nol on March 18, 1970.

Seeking refuge in Beijing, Sihanouk found allies in the CPK and its leader Saloth Sar who started using his 'code name' Pol Pot – or Brother Number One (Kiernan 2002, 485). The country was immediately renamed into the Khmer Republic and Lon Nol became its first President. Under his directive, the army started a campaign of massacres of ethnic Vietnamese, forcing around 300,000 to flee across the border to Vietnam. According to Kiernan, this set the precedent for intensified "ethnic cleansing" by the Khmer Rouge – a colloquial term used for the CPK (Kiernan 2002, 485).

In fact, although assisted by the Vietnamese army as a reaction to the US' support for the Republican forces in their anti-communist campaign when the Vietnamese conflict spilled over to Cambodia,

> the Khmer Rouge central leadership attacked its Vietnamese allies as early as 1970, killed a thousand Khmer communist returnees from Hanoi, and in 1973–74, stepped up violence against ethnic Vietnamese civilians, purged and killed ethnic Thai and other minority members of CPK regional committees, banned an allied group of ethnic Cham Muslim revolutionaries, and instigated severe repression of Muslim communities.
>
> (Kiernan 2002, 485)

In the meantime Lon Nol's government was losing credibility and support, as its policies were tainted with numerous cases of corruption and a repressive military regime. Continued fighting with the communists culminated in 1975, when Khmer Rouge forces seized the capital Phnom Phen – one of the bastions of Lon Nol's power – deported its two million residents to the country side and established a new state of Democratic Kampuchea (DK) (Kiernan 2002, 485).

The new regime immediately started applying severe policies of mass deportations of people from urban areas into agricultural labor camps in the northwestern part of the country, eventually doubling the population of that area. Unbearable living conditions caused the deaths of tens of thousands of people. At the same time, the Khmer Rouge started purging the former Khmer Republic officials, army officers, civil servants, and even the peasants from the northwest who were related to the officials from the former regime. By 1979, more than a million people had died due to starvation, poor living conditions, and extreme repression (Gordon 1986). Under attack were also numerous minorities. Between 1975 and 1979, more than half of the ethnic Chinese population – around 250,000 people – had perished, more than 100,000 Cham Muslims were killed or had starved to death, and more than 10,000 Vietnamese were killed and the remaining 100,000 Vietnamese expelled from the country (Kiernan 1985).

The Khmer Rouge also conducted sporadic incursions into Vietnamese territory. The cross-border attacks motivated Vietnam to intervene, invading Cambodia on 25 December 1978 and taking over Phnom Penh on 9 January 1979 (Gordon 1986). Officials and forces loyal to the Khmer Rouge once again fled to the mountains, leaving the country in the hands of Heng Samrin and his rebels supported by 150 000 Vietnamese troops. The country was again renamed, this time to the People's Republic of Kampuchea (PRK). Finding refuge in the sanctuaries mostly along the country's northern and western borders with Thailand, the Khmer Rouge continued to challenge the new government and the Vietnamese military for more than a decade (Gordon 1986, 66).

Internal characteristics of the conflicting sides and creation of irreconcilable positions

The new governing elite consisted primarily of former Khmer Rouge officials – such as Hun Sen and Chea Sim – that defected to Vietnam in 1978 (Bergquist 1998, 93). Their policies largely avoided "[stressing] Cambodian grandeur at the expense of Vietnamese intentions and took a more realistic view of power relations between the two states" (Chandler 1998, 17). Due to its dependency on Vietnamese support, Cambodia remained quite isolated from the international community throughout the 1980s.

In fact, while ejected from power, Pol Pot and his Khmer Rouge managed to maintain its strong international backing from China and the US. By 1982, together with the royalist National United Front for an Independent, Neutral, Peaceful, and Cooperative Cambodia (FUNCINPEC) led by the exiled Prince Sihanounk, who had the strong backing of both China and the US, and a non-communist movement the Khmer People's National Liberation Front led by Son Sann, the Khmer Rouge successfully formed an exiled Coalition Government of Democratic Kampuchea (CGDK) (Solomon 2000, 15; Chandler 1998, 17). They were joined by a shared hatred of Vietnam and a dependence on foreign support.

Involvement of international actors and their interests in the conflict

The irreconcilable positions of various Cambodian actors cannot be properly understood without a careful assessment of diverging interests and standpoints of major international and regional powers. In fact, the years that followed actually saw a conflict on three levels, which not only included the overthrown

Khmer Rouge and the new Heng Samrin regime, but also Vietnam, China, the USSR, the US, and their numerous allies. Solomon points out that as early as the 1970s, "Indochina became a cockpit of the global rivalry between the Soviet Union and China that developed after the breakdown of their alliance in 1960" (2000, 10). Thus the first two levels of conflict are what Gordon refers to as 'East-East' struggle, as they embodied a clash within the communist ideological camp. On the one side, there was the obvious struggle between two communist groups in Cambodia – the Khmer Rouge and Heng Samrin's PRK. This struggle had a second, more regional level, which saw the conflict between China and Vietnam – again two members of the communist bloc. According to Gordon, in February 1979, as "punishment" for Hanoi's invasion of Cambodia, China launched a brief attack on several northern provinces of Vietnam (1986, 66). The tension between two regional powers increased over time, resulting in Chinese leader Deng Xiaoping's public threat of a second invasion of Vietnam unless Hanoi withdrew its forces from Cambodia (Gordon 1986, 67; Solomon 2002, 11).

Sino-Vietnamese/Soviet rivalry

China and Vietnam have had a long-lasting rivalry in the region. As Gordon points out, this has always been an uneasy relationship, as "the Vietnamese have never doubted that the long-term challenge to their independence emanates from Beijing, and the Chinese have always regarded Vietnam and Indochina as their nation's 'soft underbelly'" (Gordon 1986, 67). The name Vietnam comes from the Chinese term 'An nam' which means 'Pacified South' (Gordon 1986, 68). Vietnam's regional expansionist ambition to unify all of Indochina was strongly opposed by China. Beijing perceived this scenario to be a direct threat to its national stability – in fact almost all the French colonial advancement toward China over the course of centuries had been conducted from the south. Therefore, in 1954 during the Geneva conference, which was convened as the French were defeated by Viet Minh, the Chinese "consistently opposed" a unified Indochina and instead "strongly endorsed the concept of separate Indochinese states" (Gordon 1986, 67). During the conference China's position was well in line with the positions of other major powers: the French tried to preserve as much influence as possible, thus conceding only the northern territories to an independent Vietnam; the US followed its French allies; and so did the Soviet Union, hoping to gain French support for banning German rearmament in Europe. Facing pressure from all sides, Vietnam accepted the creation of Cambodia and Laos. As Gordon points out, "Prince Sihanouk knew at that time, the legitimacy given to Cambodia's independence at Geneva (as well as that accorded Laos) owed much to China's support" (1986, 68).

Hoping to establish a strong and lasting influence in Cambodia, Vietnam trained and supported a vast number of high-ranking members of the Khmer Rouge during their uprising against the republican regime. However, as soon as he got to power, Pol Pot, quite suspicious of Vietnam's plans, commanded a series of purges to be executed with the aim of ousting the 'Hanoi Khmers' and on several occasions tried to alter the border with Vietnam. More importantly, "he had Chinese support from the outset" (Gordon 1986, 69). These provocations eventually resulted in a Vietnamese intervention which put an end to the Khmer Rouge regime.

In its regional power-struggle with China, as a result of the 1960 Sino-Soviet split, Vietnam managed to find a strong ally in the Soviet Union. Moscow had been Hanoi's strongest ally since the war with the US. Thanks to Soviet financial assistance – which amounted to about two billion dollars per year – Vietnam was able to keep its economy afloat and sustain the Cambodian occupation. In return, the Soviets could use the strategically highly important Vietnamese naval and air bases in Cam Ranh Bay and Da Nang (Gordon 1986, 67). The tensions between two communist super-powers lasted until the end of the 1980s. As recorded by Solomon,

> as late as 1989, Deng Xiaoping told President Bush that Moscow's relationship with Vietnam and Cambodia were a threat to China because they represented a continuation of Soviet efforts to "encircle" his country going back to the Khrushchev and Brezhnev eras.
>
> (Solomon 2002, 11, fn 4)

In order to counter the Vietnamese presence in Cambodia, China openly supported the Khmer Rouge. In 1984, Xiaoping stated "I do not understand why some people want to remove Pol Pot ... [I]t is true that he made some mistakes in the past but now he is leading the fight against the Vietnamese aggressors" (cited in Kiernan 2002, 488). Throughout the 1980s, China supplied the Khmer Rouge with 100 million dollars in weapons on a yearly basis (Kiernan 2002, 488).

United States

The US involvement in Indochina during the Sino-Soviet alliance in the 1950s was aimed at containing the spread of the influence of communism. In the 1960s, this policy resulted in a lengthy, costly, and most importantly unsuccessful attempt to hamper revolutionary nationalism under the communist banner in Vietnam and Cambodia. Between 1969 and 1973, the US bombed Cambodia extensively, hoping to cut off the North Vietnamese supply routes and contain the expansion of the Khmer communist forces (Bergquist 1998, 100). The US also provided 'active support' to Lon Nol in overthrowing Sihanouk, whose foreign policy of neutrality the US perceived as "insufficiently supportive of US interests" (Bergquist 1998, 100). However, in 1972 after the Sino-Soviet split, Washington found "a common cause with China in shared opposition to the expansionist Soviet Union and its allies" (Solomon 2002, 12). In 1975, during a visit to Indonesia, President Ford announced that "despite the severe setback of Vietnam ... the United States intends to continue a strong interest in and influence in the Pacific, Southeast Asia and Asia. As a whole we hope to expand this influence" (cited in Kiernan 2002, 487). This statement was not aimed at China because during the same visit Kissinger added,

> we believe that China does not have expansionist aims now.... Their first concern is the Soviet Union and their second Vietnam ... the Chinese want to use Cambodia to balance off Vietnam ... we don't like Cambodia, for the government in many ways is worse than Vietnam, but we would like it to be independent. We don't discourage Thailand and China from drawing closer to Cambodia.
>
> (cited in Kiernan 2002, 487)

The US 'winked semipublicly' (to use Brezinski's term) at the Chinese in support of their aiding the Khmer Rouge. In 1979, Kissinger revealed the following: "I encouraged the Chinese to support Pol Pot. Pol Pot was an abomination. We could never support him, but China could" (cited in Kiernan 2002, 487).

According to Kiernan, it was for "geopolitical reasons, while the Cambodian genocide progressed, [that] Washington, Beijing and Bangkok all supported the continued independent existence of the Khmer Rouge regime" (Kiernan 2002, 487). This common cause with China induced the US to promote the policies that isolated the PRK internationally after the overthrow of Pol Pot in 1979. They held on to Cambodia's seat in the UN, assigning it to the Coalition Government of Democratic Kampuchea – thus absolving the Khmer Rouge of the crimes perpetrated by their genocidal regime (Chandler 1998, 17; Kiernan 2002, 488). Throughout the 1980s, the US strongly opposed any effort to investigate the Khmer Rouge and their genocidal regime. US Secretary of State Schultz even called the Australian initiative for a dialogue over Cambodia "stupid" and declined to support Australian Foreign Minister Hayden's proposal for an international tribunal (Kiernan 2002, 489). He even stressed his opposition of conducting peace talks that would include Vietnam, warning the neighboring states "to be extremely cautious in formulating peace proposals for Kampuchea because Vietnam might one day accept them" (cited in Kiernan 2002, 489). Even the new administration, under President Bush, had no problem with the Khmer Rouge and actually proposed that they be included in the future government of Cambodia (Kiernan 2002, 489). Together with China, the US sponsored the two smaller anti-Vietnamese, Khmer resistance movements led by Prince Sihanouk and Son Sann. At the same time, it did not object Beijing's support of the Khmer Rouge, as both countries were "determined to prevent Hanoi from consolidating its client government in Phnom Penh led by a former Khmer Rouge commander Hun Sen" (Solomon 2012, 12).

The combination of these different positions resulted in a clear stalemate. On the one side China, supported by the US, insisted that Vietnam immediately evacuate Cambodia, on the other, Vietnam, supported by the Soviet Union, asked for clear guarantees that Khmer Rouge would play no role in future governmental arrangements and that China abandon its policy of threats toward

Hanoi. As noted by Gordon, "the involvement of the outside major powers, introduces to the Indochina conflict the classic formula for explosive international politics, in which external states often have a greater impact on developments than those directly involved" (1986, 67). It was clear that the powerful outside power had both the leverage to guide the belligerents towards a mutually acceptable solution and a strong interest in achieving an outcome compatible with its strategic goals.

Multiparty mediation process

Initial lack of cooperation between third parties

Early contact between Prince Sihanouk and Hun Sen had already taken place in December 1987. They met in Paris to discuss the possibility of formulating a power-sharing arrangement between the two non-communist movements and the Hun Sen regime. Although this had the potential to end the war, it was rejected by the US and China "on the ground that it excluded the Khmer Rouge and legitimized the Vietnamese-backed regime already in power" (Chandler 1998, 19). It was obvious that any solution to the conflict would have to include all four Khmer factions. More importantly, any future negotiations had to tackle a number of questions that had to be compatible with the interests of the major powers. These issues were: the withdrawal of the Vietnamese troops from Cambodia; demobilization of paramilitary forces; establishment of measures that would prevent potential retaliatory activities; and a formula for organizing the elections which would produce a legitimate and internationally-recognized government (Chandler 1998, 19).

The importance of powerful outside actors was immediately evident during the first regional forum on Cambodia held in Jakarta in 1988. The meeting was attended by all Southeast Asian states and only managed to produce the necessary guidelines for any future settlement (Ratner 1993, 5). The new talks were scheduled to take place in Paris in a year, but this time with the direct involvement of major powers. As Chandler points out, from the beginning the Paris agreements were worked out by foreign powers that exercised tight control over the factions and the form the final settlement would take (Chandler 1998, 19).

As previously explained, the US and China had a shared goal in opposing Vietnam's occupation of Cambodia, while at the same time they openly supported different anti-Vietnamese factions in the country. The Bush administration knew that open support for the Khmer Rouge was a liability, so in an attempt to block the recognition of the Vietnamese-installed government of Hun Sen, the US adopted a policy of supporting the Coalition Government (Sihanouk–Son Sann–Khmer Rouge) as the legitimate incumbent government in Cambodia (Solomon 2000, 20). As noted by Solomon, who was Assistant Secretary of State for East Asian and Pacific Affairs and was to be appointed as a US envoy in the peace process at the time, "the evolution of great power cooperation on a Cambodia settlement was complicated in early June 1989 by the violent events at Tiananmen Square ... overnight our official contacts with China became a domestic political liability" (Solomon 2000, 20). These events sparked widespread criticism of the Chinese government. In the days that followed, in an attempt to improve their international reputation, the Chinese became extremely sensitive about their continuing support for the Khmer Rouge. As Solomon points out,

> the criticism increased Beijing's interest in a political settlement of the Cambodia conflict in a way that would distance China from Pol Pot and his movement. Nonetheless, China's strategic objective remained consonant with that of the United States: to prevent Vietnam from establishing hegemony over all of Indochina.
>
> (Solomon 2000, 20–21)

The looming convergence of interests between the US and China was pushing the mediation process in a direction that was unacceptable for Vietnam and its partners in Phnom Penh. Reflecting on the game theoretical model, the peace process was at point (b). Cooperative behavior – as illustrated in the model – was producing much higher payoffs to the Chinese, as all of their priorities and interests were promoted through the process.

The Paris Peace Conference was held in August 1989 and was attended by 18 countries and four Cambodian factions (Chandler 1998, 19). According to Solomon, the US "was not inclined to take the lead on Indochina issues," rather it was inclined to support the French and Indonesians (that organized the conference) in their preparations (Solomon 2000, 21). For the Paris conference, the US had a list of five goals that had to be included in the peace settlement:

> an immediate ceasefire and the eventual termination of all foreign military assistance to the Khmer factions; the formation of an interim administration headed by Prince Sihanouk; the establishment of a process that would culminate in the internationally supervised election of a new constitutional government the voluntary return of the large Khmer refugee population in Thailand; and the creation of an international control mechanism to implement a settlement process monitored by the UN.
>
> (Solomon 2000, 24)

The Vietnamese, on the other hand, were aiming at a much different solution. Solomon refers to this position as "a partial solution" to the Cambodian Conflict. The Vietnamese wanted "to limit the international involvement in a settlement to verification of the withdrawal of their troops, perhaps some oversight of an election, but no arrangement that would weaken the authority of their client regime" (Solomon 2000, 24).

The US and China proposed a 'quadripartite' government that meant unequivocally a transfer of a quarter of Hun Sen's power to the Khmer Rouge. Vietnam expressed its strong opposition to the inclusion of Khmer Rouge not only in the future governmental arrangement, but in the peace process itself. They were concerned that in the event that the Khmer Rouge would get a role in the future power-sharing arrangement, a possibility would be created for them to return to power and subsequently retaliate. Vietnamese Foreign Minister Nguyen Co Thach, stuck to the idea that "only Hun Sen government, intact had the power to prevent the dreaded Khmer Rouge from fighting their way back to power" (Solomon 2000, 25). In other words, Vietnam was quite opposed to the 'quadripartite government.' Solomon points out that this position had "little resonance among the conference participants, who generally supported the view that the best way to constrain the Khmer Rouge was to give them some stake in a political process subject to international supervision" (Solomon 2000, 25). As Vietnam was not showing signs of cooperating, Hun Sen's delegation continued requesting that the potential Vietnamese withdrawal be "linked to the guarantees of a non-return to power of the Khmer Rouge" (Chandler 1998, 19). As Chandler points out, "this was simply interpreted as political maneuvering on the part of the SoC [abbreviation for State of Cambodia] to stall the peace process" (1998, 19).

According to Bert, China was not enthusiastic about the Khmer Rouge's return to power, however it used it as a bargaining chip, recognizing that "the Khmer Rouge was the only force in Cambodia capable of standing up to the government militarily, and it used the KR to achieve its objectives, either encouraging them with arms support or pressuring them to participate in negotiations" (Bert 1993, 329). Thus the main Chinese strategic interest was to have Cambodia free of Vietnamese influence, which was largely in line with US interests and those of the ASEAN countries (Bert 1993, 330). As noted by Kiernan, "China's involvement brought Khmer Rouge protégés to center stage" (Kiernan 2002, 489). It was obvious that any agreement would require unanimity. With veto power in their hands, the Khmer Rouge could both obstruct any compromise and, while stalling negotiations, rearm and improve their military power. Kiernan shows Pol Pot's briefings to his generals in which he indicated his intention to delay elections (which were one of the issues that was discussed in Paris) until his forces controlled the countryside:

the outside world keeps demanding a political end to the war in Kampuchea, I could end the war now if I wanted, because the outside world is waiting for me. But I am buying time to give you, comrades, the opportunity to carry out all the tasks. If it doesn't end politically and ends militarily, that is good.

(cited in Kiernan 2002, 489)

Thus during the Paris talks, representatives of the Khmer Rouge insisted that their rule was not characterized by genocide and indicated their support for a coalition government under Sihanouk as the only way for Cambodia to regain its sovereignty lost in a Vietnamese "colonial" rule through Hun Sen (Hampson and Zartman 2012, 6). Although Vietnam was experiencing noticeable pressure, it still did not perceive any utility in accepting the terms proposed by the US and China. At the same time, the uncompromising position of China led the Khmer Rouge to also assume an uncompromising position. The unyielding positions of main sponsor states led the peace conference to failure, as each of their client movements was unwilling to compromise. Clearly, in the event that mediators are unable to reach a convergence of interests, the conflicting sides will be induced to defect from negotiations, making it more likely that the peace process will fail. In fact, in light of the imminent failure of the peace talks "on the ground in Cambodia, the Khmer Rouge, the Khmer People's National Liberation Front (KPNLF), and Hun Sen's State of Cambodia were launching new tests of military strength" (Solomon 2000, 31). Particularly symptomatic of this was Vietnam's lack of convergence of interests with the rest of the mediating coalition – especially the US and China – which was driving the process into a deadlock (Solomon 2000, 84). At the same time, the Vietnamese unyielding position was creating lower payoffs for the Hun Sen government, as they were experiencing stronger pressure from the rest of the conference to accept the 'quadripartite government.' As a result, Hun Sen's government opted to continue pursuing unilateral belligerent activities against other Khmer factions, minimizing the likelihood of a peaceful solution.

However, a significant change took place when Moscow "delivered a secret warning to the Vietnamese that it would no longer subsidize Vietnam's occupation of Cambodia and its tug-of-war with China" (Hampson and Zartman 2012, 5). Soon after that, Vietnam announced that it would withdraw its troops from Cambodia. This significant change in conflict dynamics was strongly related to an earlier, larger geo-political shift in Moscow's foreign policy that saw the rise of Gorbachev to power. Similar to the previously described case of Namibia, the new Gorbachev doctrine saw the developments in Southeast Asia as an opportunity to strengthen its relations with China.

During a speech in Vladivostok in 1986, primarily aimed at the Chinese audience, Gorbachev pointed out that the Soviet Union should abandon the policy objective of being as strong as any possible coalition of states opposing it. It was an indication that the Soviet Union could not economically sustain the strategy of maintaining parity with the US, Europe, China and Japan combined (Nguyen 1993, 285). Thus he suggested a pact between two continental powers, united by their real or imagined grievances against the West, which Nguyen calls "Eastern Rapallo" (Nguyen 1993, 286). Gorbachev emphasized that both countries had similar priorities in terms of improving their domestic economies and thus it was of mutual benefit to mend their differences and engage in constructive economic relations (Shearman 1987, 1101). Knowing that Soviet support of Vietnam had been perceived as a direct threat to Chinese interests, in 1985, Gorbachev informed the General Secretary of the Vietnamese Communist Party, Le Duan, that Moscow wished to see an improvement in Vietnam's relations with China. Two years later, Duan's replacement, Nguyen Van Linh, was informed that Moscow believed a solution to the Cambodian question rested in "national reconciliation and unification of all patriotic forces in Kampuchea" (Shearman

1987, 1101). Although important and novel, these early changes in Soviet positions did not generate sufficient pressure to provoke a change in Vietnam's position. Nevertheless, Vietnam slowly began feeling isolated from the international community.

The withdrawal of Vietnamese troops – promised to the Soviet Union – only aggravated the conflict between the government and insurgent forces. The resistance forces slowly gained ground from Hun Sen's troops, putting significant pressure on the Vietnamese and Hun Sen to explore the possibilities of a peaceful settlement. Vietnam already announced its plans to withdraw troops from Cambodia in April 1989. However, the withdrawal was conducted in stages, as the last troops left the country only after the first Paris talks, in September 1989 (Ratner 1993, 5). Yet, in light of waning Soviet willingness to support Vietnamese policies in the region and the high costs of the occupation, the withdrawal paved the way for more substantial talks (Bert 1993). Such developments suggest that an increase in the cost of supporting the war might induce the defecting third party to change its strategy and engage in a cooperative mediation effort to manage the conflict. This will be further analyzed in the remainder of the case.

Convergence of interests between third parties

The United States became aware that a good way to detach various Khmer factions from their outside sources of support was by transferring the problem to an in-tune Security Council P-5 that could induce the warring parties to compromise. Solomon points out that "the Paris Conference had had an ambiguous outcome regarding a role for the United Nations in a peace process, some proposed it, a few opposed it" (Solomon 2000, 34). According to Hampson and Zartman (2012), the US had two reasons for transferring the problem to the UN. First of all, in case the peace process succeeded, the US wanted to avoid being the sole actor responsible for Cambodia's post-conflict reconstruction and it wanted to see the financial burden shared with other countries. More importantly, "the only way to wean the various Cambodian fractions from their regional and great power backers was through a concerted P-5 team-based effort that would, in effect, force Cambodia's factions to compromise and make concessions at the negotiating table" (Hampson and Zartman 2012, 6). The strongest opponents to this US position were Vietnam and the Hun Sen regime. In their eyes, strong involvement of the UN would undermine Cambodian sovereignty. The only way to prevent the Khmer Rouge from retaliating, they argued, was to preserve the integrity and military capabilities of the current Hun Sen government.

The US initiated the creation of momentum among the five permanent members of the Security Council and a framework for future UN involvement in Cambodia was emerging. Between January and August 1990, the P-5 held six rounds of talks. During the first session that took place in Paris, all participants unanimously accepted the US draft which indicated a need for enhanced UN involvement, especially in the context of the verification of the withdrawal of Vietnam's forces, monitoring of the elections, assistance in the protection of human rights and a smooth repatriation of refugees (Solomon 2000, 40). However, this early convergence of interests also revealed major obstacles to achieving a settlement. Among the most complex ones were: the issues of security, in light of continuous fighting between various Khmer factions; transitional government until the elections could be organized; and Cambodian sovereignty.

On the issue of security, the P-5 concurred

> to stabilize a cease-fire, contending military factions should be put under the UN control in cantonments where they would be disarmed and eventually reorganized into a national army under the authority of the Cambodian government that would emerge from the elections.
>
> (Solomon 2000, 42)

The problem of a provisional administration for the country was solved with the establishment of the Supreme National Council (SNC). On this matter the Chinese insisted that they would not support any settlement that did not provide for an active role for the Khmer Rouge. The US was quite apprehensive of the future role of the Khmer Rouge – especially in light of increasing public outrage at the US's indirect support for the Khmer Rouge – as this would legitimize its past doings. The solution was achieved in assigning "individuals representing the full range of Cambodian public opinion and deprived of any operational authority" to the SNC instead of organizations and movements (Solomon 2000, 42). Thus, while the Khmer Rouge would not be represented as a separate body, it would still have one of its officials as a full member of the Council. According to Solomon, "this gave the Chinese sufficient political leverage to "deliver" their client to the settlement" (Solomon 2000, 42). However, as the negotiations between the P-5 progressed, it became quite obvious that the Soviet Union and China were unable to find a mutually acceptable formula regarding the degree of UN involvement in implementing the peace agreement. On the one hand, the Soviets refused to accept any significant role for the UN, referring to respect for Cambodian sovereignty, which was a euphemism for the concern that strong UN involvement could endanger the government's chances in the upcoming elections. On the other hand, the Chinese were asking for complete disarmament of the government, claiming that such a move would serve the purpose of creating equal chances for everyone in the elections, while in reality Beijing was trying to weaken Hun Sen's chances (Hampson and Zartman 2012, 7; Solomon 1999, 2000).

While the Soviet Union and China were struggling to find an agreement, the United States was experiencing a serious challenge on the domestic front. Solomon recounts that "during the fall of 1989, and into the spring of 1990, domestic political pressure in the United States had been building against any agreement that would seem to legitimize the Khmer Rouge by including their leadership in a settlement plan, much less increase the party's chance of returning to power by some combination of military and political maneuvering" (Solomon 2000, 44). The strongest hit to the US position came in April 1990. Following a screening of a documentary on ABC news, which claimed that US financial support intended for Prince Sihanouk was ending up in the hands of the Khmer Rouge, a bi-partisan group of US Congressmen wrote to then Secretary of State James Baker demanding a radical change in US foreign policy. They asked for an immediate termination of support for Prince Sihanouk and the Khmer Rouge and a subsequent shift in preference toward Hun Sen and his pro-Vietnamese government. The letter stated that "China is the problem, not the solution in Cambodia" and that US policy "should be based, first and foremost, upon preventing the return to power of the Khmer Rouge" (Solomon 2000, 44–45). The congressmen threatened that in the event that "the administration did not shift its approach to a Cambodian settlement away from Sihanouk's coalition, Congress would cut off all financial support for the noncommunist resistance – FUNCINPEC and the KPNLF" (Solomon 2000, 45).

This radical shift – also known as 'the Baker shift' – in the US' position was first announced to Soviets during the fifth P-5 session in Paris in July 1990. Baker stated that the US intended to withdraw its recognition of the representatives of Cambodia's coalition (that included Sihanouk and the Khmer Rouge) in the UN (Hampson and Zartman 2012, 8). He also indicated that the US was considering initiating consultations with the Vietnamese government and their partners in Cambodia (Solomon 2000, 46). The shift represented a political bombshell for the negotiation process. It was clear that the US was about to switch sides and put forward policies much closer to those of Vietnam and the USSR.

China was very concerned that this change would cement Hun Sen's position and jeopardize the momentum that was already created in the peace process. Privately they even admitted that the 'Baker shift' caused a great deal of confusion amongst the Chinese leadership (Solomon 2000, 46). Thus the Chinese decided to push more strongly for the achievement of an agreement within the P-5, as a way of keeping the Khmer Rouge involved in the political settlement (Solomon 2000, 46). Interestingly, reflecting on the game theoretical model, the Chinese choice to stay in the mediation process prevented the process from reaching a potential myopic equilibrium and consequently move the mediation efforts into NME. Vietnam for its part, apprehensive of the Soviet decision to improve its relations with China and stop supporting its cause in Cambodia, saw this as a chance to achieve a greater convergence of interests with the US. In light of the new policy priorities, the US officials openly indicated their readiness to improve bilateral relations with Hanoi under the condition that they accept a UN-managed settlement for Cambodia. Isolated Hanoi was also well aware that it had to "give up on Ho Chi Minh's dream of an Indochina Federation ... and to normalize relations with China on Beijing's terms" (Solomon 2000, 78). As a result, Hanoi became more inclined to compromise and explore constructive ways to engage all of the Khmer factions in future political processes. At the same time, China was careful not to make a move that would shift the blame for spoiling the process to them. For this reason, authorities in Beijing decided to put pressure on the Khmer Rouge telling them to "stay on the course and reach a political settlement" (Hampson and Zartman 2012, 8).

In August 1990, at their sixth and last meeting in New York, all the members of the Security Council accepted a framework agreement that "formally recognized that there could not be a settlement without the participation of all factions and that the Khmer Rouge had to be included to avoid the continuation of the civil war" (Hampson and Zartman 2012, 8); that the UN would take over the role of a transitional government until the elections are organized; that Cambodia's sovereignty would be 'embodied' in a Supreme National Council composed of individuals; and that this body would not have any authority before the UN-monitored elections would take place (Solomon 2000, 47). It was a strong indication that all the major powers – the US, China, and Russia (that represented Vietnam's interests) – managed to achieve a convergence of interests with regard to solving the conflict. In terms of the theoretical model, the process was now at point (c), as each party evidently achieved less than what it initially set out to, but more than what was to be gained from non-cooperative behavior. As Solomon points out, the challenge was now to "convince the conflicting parties to accept the settlement" (Solomon 2000, 47).

Once the P-5 plan became public, the Chinese Vice Foreign Minister visited Hanoi to convince his Vietnamese colleagues to support the framework. According to Solomon, the initiative failed because the Vietnamese Foreign Minister Thach "gratuitously insulted the visiting Chinese envoy in an effort to keep the diplomacy deadlocked" (Solomon 2000, 74). After this incident, in September 1990, Chinese and Vietnamese officials started a series of secret bilateral negotiations in order to resolve their differences. As a result of these consultations, the "extremely nationalistic" Thach retired from his position in June 1991. Soon after that, Sino-Vietnamese relations "were fully normalized" (Solomon 2000, 75). Unfortunately, there are no public records of these meetings. However their frequency in such a short period of time – according to Solomon (2000, 74, fn 53) there were four secret meetings between September 1990 and the spring of 1991 – was a clear indication of the two sides' readiness to exit the lingering quagmire of their bilateral relations. Once reconciled, both sides exercised "irresistible pressure" on their Cambodian partners – Hun Sen for the Vietnamese and Khmer Rouge for the Chinese – to accept the compromises in the interest of the settlement (Solomon 2000, 78). In August 1991, it was clear that all parties had accepted the proposed framework. As all major regional and global actors that were involved in the peace process showed the intention of resolving their differences and exiting Indochina, the signing of a final settlement plan happened in a matter of days. Within two months, specific details of the plan were discussed and the agreement was ratified in Paris on October 23, 1991.

As a direct participant in the peace process, Solomon points out that "it is clear that the parallel and mutually reinforcing reconciliations of 1991 between Beijing and Moscow, and Beijing and Hanoi, made possible the fundamental political deals that enabled the Perm Five's peace plan for Cambodia to fall into place" (Solomon 2000, 78). The evident convergence of interests was a direct result of the mediators' ability to negotiate a solution amongst themselves. At the same time, the constructive role of China, the Soviet Union, and Vietnam in the multiparty mediation process was best observed in their ability to influence their client Khmer factions and move them toward a mutually acceptable solution. However, this role was only fulfilled once the parties managed to reach a convergence of interests: the Sino-Soviet rapprochement that culminated with a P-5 agreement that was a result of a major geo-political shift represented by the rise of Gorbachev to power; and the Soviet decision to stop financing the Vietnamese 'tug of war' with China and change its strategies toward Beijing. Similarly, the Sino-Vietnamese rapprochement was also the result of a geo-political change – waning Soviet influence induced Vietnam to seek new partners in the US and China – and awareness that the costs of supporting the war through occupation were becoming too high, particularly as the Soviets cut their financial support.

The intra-P-5 negotiations that generated the convergence of interests, while conducted under the US leadership, benefited greatly from the legitimacy of the UN. In fact, the US used the legitimacy of the UN to guide the conflicting communist super-powers to an agreement. At the same time, the US was able to take the leadership role only once its goals did not jeopardize those of the other P-5. In fact, the compromise solution that was achieved within the P-5 indicates that each side had to accept less than what they initially aimed to, confirming the dynamics described in the model that a cooperative solution will still produce some costs.

Note

1 An earlier version of this chapter was published as a case study in Vuković (2012).

6   Kosovo[1]

Contemporary conflict management scholarship describes the situation in Kosovo as an undeniable case of intractable conflict (Burg 2005). It is character-ized by contention over the rights of self-determination, sovereignty, and territo-rial integrity. It persisted over time which led to the development of psychological manifestations of deep feelings of distrust and mutual hatred, manifested in the employment of destructive means, violence, and a refusal to yield to endeavors aimed at reaching a political settlement. All of this is indic-ative of its undeniably intractable nature. The case of Kosovo offers a unique opportunity to explore two distinct phases of the peace process within the same conflict, which despite the inevitable change of actors (vis-à-vis their leadership) still did not produce any success.

The nature of conflict

Sources of intractability

As Burg observes, "the dissolution of Yugoslavia can be attributed to the effects of several mutually reinforcing conflicts" (Burg 2005, 184). The key feature of all these conflicts can be found in mounting ethno-nationalism among the various peoples of Yugoslavia, which was caused by unresolved historical dis-putes and by contemporary conflict on political and economic issues. Increasing claims to self-determination in Kosovo were directly linked to both territory and ethnic identity. A territorially compact Albanian ethnic majority was defying domination by the Serb minority and the existing political regime in Belgrade.

The ease with which justifiable economic and political issues were able to inflame temporarily subdued ethno-nationalism and provoke internal conflict was undoubtedly proven in 1968, when frustration over the economic situation in the province aggravated the nationalistic strife between the Albanian popula-tion in Kosovo and Serbian authorities in Belgrade. In fact, by the late 1960s, the situation in Kosovo was quite dire – it was the most underdeveloped part of Yugoslavia in terms of all socioeconomic indicators with the highest rate of illit-eracy, 36% were officially illiterate, while a much larger number was not working literate (Ramet 1992, 189).

In 1974, Yugoslav federal authorities managed to appease the claims for self-determination in Kosovo, by granting the province a high degree of autonomy and a status as a federal unit, although formally it was still a province within the republic of Serbia. Gradually the Albanian population was emancipated and assigned to high administrative positions. According to Ramet, it was at this moment that "the Albanians were becoming restless ... when the slow beginnings of reform had become unmistakable – a confirmation of Machiavelli and Crane Brinton's proposition that repression becomes intolerable once reforms are begun" (1992, 190). In fact, the level of underdevelopment in Kosovo was continuing to fuel popular restlessness. Once again, socio-economic issues were easily translated into political agitation, which culminated in a series of riots, subversive activities and the use of violence across the entire province in 1981. These demonstrations resulted in more than 1000 deaths and many more injuries (Ramet 1992, 196). The protestors now publicly echoed revolutionary tones that flirted with separatism: Kosovo reconstituted as a republic or utter secession (Troebst 1998). The federal authorities reacted without delay, tightening their grip on the province.

The development of deep feelings of distrust and mutual hatred

In the coming years, anti-Albanian sentiment reached every aspect of society. The authorities expanded their list of potential suspects and several thousands of Kosovo Albanians were prosecuted for separatism between 1981 and 1987. Fueled by the stories of exiled Serbs from Kosovo, Belgrade media started publishing articles covering Albanian atrocities, which genuinely and irrevocably contributed to the development of stereotypes of Kosovo Albanians in the eyes of the Serbian audience. The exaggerations in storytelling went so far that Belgrade newspapers started labeling the crisis in Kosovo as "ethnic cleansing" of Serbs (Banac 2001). By 1986, Serbia was inflamed with nationalism, peaking with the infamous Memorandum of the Serbian Academy of Science and Arts that lamented over Serbia's faith in the Yugoslavian community and echoed a direct warning about the imminent loss of Kosovo. The hatred so rampant that Serbs began boycotting Albanian shops and trade with Albanians, which cut down their sales by as much as 85% (Ramet 1992, 199).

The employment of repressive measures

The consistent demographic decline of the Slavic population in the province invigorated nationalistic rhetoric and policies of the new party elite in Belgrade. The underlying aim of Serbian nationalists that assumed the highest ranks in the party (at the republic level) was the implementation of a program that would reduce the number of Albanians in Kosovo (Banac 2001). The accession of Slobodan Milošević to power in 1987 signaled a new and more dramatic escalation of the conflict in Kosovo. He intervened in Kosovo with heavy security forces and revoked the province's autonomy. Under 'emergency measures,' ethnic

Albanians were forced out of public institutions (Ramet 1992; Troebst 1998). Serbian authorities intensified the policy of dismissal of Albanians from jobs in public enterprises. According to statistics from that time, more than "100,000 Albanians were fired from factories, mines, schools, hospitals, judiciary, cultural institutions, media public services, municipal and regional authorities, etc. and replaced by Serbs, Montenegrins, or pro-Serbian Albanians" (Troebst 1998). Serbian authorities issued orders to outlaw all Albanian political, cultural, sport, and media organizations and associations. Albanian students were expelled from universities and a new curriculum in the Serbian language and with Serbian text-books was imposed. Albanians were not allowed to make any transactions on real estate markets without special permission from the authorities (Caplan 1998, 751). Repressive measures and violence, exercised by the security forces, distinguished Kosovo as the region with one of the worst human rights records in Europe at that time (Nizich 1992).

The creation of irreconcilable positions

The expelled Albanian political elite started developing new forms of organization and resistance. The Albanian political leaders in Kosovo developed a strategy of non-violent resistance and established 'parallel' state structures in the province. In 1991, an underground referendum was organized in which almost 100% of participants – all of them Albanians – voted in favor of an independent Kosovo. This motivated the elites to declare the Republic of Kosovo to be an independent and sovereign state. At the same time, emboldened by the referendum, members of this 'parallel government' organized both parliamentary elections in which the Democratic League of Kosovo (LDK) won an absolute majority (89%) and presidential elections that confirmed LDK's leader Ibrahim Rugova as the indisputable leader.

From then on, Kosovo was a clear example of segregation in Europe (Banac 2001). On the one hand, there was the official Serbian regime that excluded ethnic Albanians from nearly every aspect of society and a 'shadow state' established by ethnic Albanians. The Serbian authorities 'tolerated' this clandestine state, which signified the definite separation of two ethnic communities and absolute exclusion of Albanians as citizens of Serbia. The non-violent approach taken by Albanian elites to resist Serbian policies was the only option, given the tremendous power disparity between Kosovo Albanians and the Serbian authorities. This Ghandian approach attracted a great deal of sympathy in the West, but the West was very slow (if not reluctant) to start pressuring Belgrade to change its policies in the province.

The situation at this moment was clear. The zero-sum issues that divided both sides made compromising very difficult. Thus the early attempts at international involvement in the crisis were faced with the serious challenge of formulating effective approaches in order to create a non-zero-sum outcome.

Despite the apparent pattern of neglect on the part of the international community, the biggest disappointment for Albanians in Kosovo originated with the

Dayton agreements in 1995 that ended the civil war in Bosnia. For several years, the low degree of inter-ethnic friction and the illusion of stability in Kosovo – due to repressive policies that excluded Albanians from participating in the system on one side and shadow state structures established by these very Albanians on the other – indirectly motivated the international community to overlook the real situation on the ground. According to Caplan, it was the absence of war in Kosovo that made foreign countries believe that there was no urgent need to deal with the question (1998, 751). It seemed as if non-violent resistance, which attracted sympathy in the West, was the 'victim of its own success' (Caplan 1998, 751). Despite Western sympathies, the Albanian leadership lacked a strong ally for their cause. In fact, at that time Milošević was identified as the 'stabilizing factor' and collaboration with him was seen as essential to creating and maintaining peace in ex-Yugoslav countries. So, not surprisingly, up until March 1998, both the American administration and its European counterparts were reluctant to accept any claim of independence by the Kosovo Albanian elites.

For Albanians in Kosovo, Dayton provided an obvious signal that ethnic territories have legitimacy (given the fact that the *Republika Srpska* was established) and that international attention can only be garnered through war (Surroi 1996). Disappointment culminated with the increasing support of the Albanian population for the radical separatist Kosovo Liberation Army (UCK). Their militant activities against Serb forces in the province soon brought them control over almost 30% of Kosovo's territory. Gradually, even some members of the political elite started supporting the guerilla warfare of the UCK, claiming that the "path of nonviolence has gotten [them] nowhere ... the Kosovo Liberation Army is fighting for [their] freedom" (Caplan 1998, 752). It was obvious that Dayton represented the turning point for Kosovo Albanians and their future demands. Demands for extended autonomy and a return to the situation prescribed by the constitution from 1974 were now overruled. The only political aim at that point was an independent Kosovo.

Internal characteristics of the conflicting sides

The radicalization of the Kosovo Albanian separatist tendencies was rapidly restricting the space for any compromise-based solution. The international community was resolute that a mutually acceptable compromise solution needed to be found. Given the fact that, in as early as 1991, the overwhelming majority of Kosovo Albanians voted in favor of independence, it was unlikely that the population would settle for the restoration of autonomy that the international community was trying to put forward as a compromise. In fact, after seven years of frozen and intractable conflict, marked by the establishment of a segregation system, Albanians in Kosovo now had less reason to accept any form of political autonomy within Serbia. As a direct consequence of the conflict's intractability, there was no trust in Serbian authorities that they would guarantee Kosovo Albanian autonomy, given the fact that it was the same authorities that had abolished it in the first place.

As the mediation literature suggests (e.g., Bercovitch 2005), in the case of intractable conflicts, one of the main goals of successful mediation is actor transformation. In the case of Kosovo, a stable settlement would seem to be attainable only through the establishment of a truly democratic regime in Belgrade. However, at that time, opposition forces in Serbia were largely silent on the matter of what was happening in Kosovo, while the strongest opposition parties were even defending Milošević's policies in the province (Caplan 1998; Troebst 1998). Even public opinion seemed to reflect complacency. According to a survey done by the Helsinki Committee for the Human Rights Office in Belgrade:

> An independent Kosovo, or the Republic of Kosovo within the FRY, is admissible in the view of only a negligible number of our respondents. Likewise, very few respondents would accept a division of Kosovo. A vast percentage (41.8%) believes that the solution is to be looked for in the forcible or 'peaceful' expulsion of the Albanians. On the other hand, 27.2% of those manifesting 'democratic tolerance' would be willing, at best, to grant the Albanians their cultural autonomy.... In other words, in the case of Kosovo is the Serbian public opinion neither willing to search for a compromise nor even for a minimum democratic solution.
>
> (Troebst 1998, 21–22)

The situation amongst the Kosovo Albanian political elite was also problematic. The non-violent tactics of Rugova and his LDK were losing public support due to the increasing popularity of violent tactics employed by radicals in the UCK. At the same time, other political parties were less inclined to negotiate with Belgrade on the issue of autonomy. The Parliamentary Party of Kosovo (PPK), the biggest opposition party in Priština, headed by Adem Demaci, promoted as a compromise the reconstruction of Yugoslavia as a confederation or association of independent states of Kosovo, Montenegro, and Serbia better known as 'project Balkania.' Less than this was not an option for the PPK. Clearly this option was less palatable to Serbia and thus was not even considered by policy makers in Belgrade.

The deep radicalization of political elites on both sides was a direct obstacle to a long-lasting solution. To rise above the deadlock, the international community – that wanted to resolve the crisis through negotiations – was challenged by two conflicting principles that they had yet to reconcile: the autonomy of Kosovo and sovereignty of Yugoslavia. The latter principle was mirrored in the fact that Belgrade was reluctant to accept any foreign third-party intervention, claiming that the situation in Kosovo was an internal affair. The principle of the inviolability of state sovereignty and territorial integrity was something that the international community was not willing to jeopardize, given new dynamics in the region and globally. There was a fear that recklessness in approaching the situation might serve as a signal for other states to intervene elsewhere according to their own judgment (i.e., there was apprehension that Russia might use this precedent as justification for future intervention in ex-Soviet states) (Caplan 1998). For this reason, any form of direct intervention was put aside, especially the use of force, unless it was to be authorized by the UN Security Council.

The surfacing of the UCK put a great deal of pressure on the LDK leadership to show determination in achieving independence. Since the LDK was insistent on the employment of non-violent methods, it understood UCK's pressure as an additional motive to try to find some compromise with Belgrade, otherwise large-scale violence would be unavoidable. Along with the intra-Albanian power-struggle, the regime in Belgrade was also subjected to internal pressures from the emerging democratically-oriented opposition, headed by Democratic Party (Demokratska stranka, DS) forces in 1996. The DS were compelling Milošević to seek to achieve some progress toward finding a settlement that would pacify the situation in Kosovo. A result of this convergence of interest between Rugova and Milošević was the negotiated settlement of September 1996 on the normalization of the education system facilitated by mediation activities by an international, non-governmental organization, Comunità di Sant'Egidio (Troebst 1998). Having had success in mediating the conflict in Mozambique, the NGO's involvement was accepted because its interests were not suspicious to either side, but were perceived as being a desire to contribute to the de-escalation of the conflict. Clearly, given the fact that there was no true international guarantor ready to exert pressure on both sides to realize the agreement, the sides were unwilling to implement it. In the end, it merely resulted in a demonstration of good will – mainly toward the international community – and an intention to achieve some results in terms of bridging differences, but nothing further as clear incentives were missing. As in all intractable conflicts, the conflicting parties felt that "at best they may reach temporary cessations of violence and that they cannot reach a fundamental and genuine resolution of their issues" (Bercovitch 2005, 100).

Involvement of international actors and their interests in the conflict

During the 1980s, initial steps to encourage dialogue between representatives of Kosovo Albanians and authorities in Belgrade were taken by governmental and non-governmental third parties, but none of them made any significant progress. In fact, while the Serbian officials were resisting any third-party involvement, especially from abroad – both from foreign governments and non-governmental organizations – Albanians were of the opposite opinion. Both sides were well aware of the repercussions of such third-party involvement, namely the internationalization of their conflict.

Western countries: the EC/EU and the United States

During the Cold War period, Western countries were fully aware of the nationalist tensions in Yugoslavia. It was for this reason that they supported Tito's firm regime, which was able to keep ethnic tensions at bay. Soon after Tito's death in

1980, these projections proved to be right, as was shown by the violent clashes between Albanians and Serbs in Kosovo in 1981. With the end of the Cold War, the American and European stance toward issues in Yugoslavia started to change dramatically. The geopolitical relevance of Yugoslavia was fading away and the country became just one of the many communist countries that needed to democratize its system and liberalize its economy. In this respect, the situation in Kosovo appeared to be the perfect lens through which Yugoslavia was viewed.

Severe abuses of human rights in Kosovo represented the main concern for American diplomats at that time. However, this concern was more superficial than what would have been needed for Americans to be more actively engaged in managing the crisis. In fact, the limits of American policy were best described by Zimmerman who assumed an Ambassadorial post in Belgrade in 1989:

> I was to reassert the traditional mantra of US support for Yugoslavia's unity, independence and territorial integrity. But I would add that the United States could only support unity in the context of democracy; it would strongly oppose unity imposed or preserved by force.
>
> (Zimmermann 1995, 3)

At the same time, for the US, the situation in Kosovo represented only one aspect of the greater overall crisis Yugoslavia was experiencing.

American unwillingness to take action was made easier by Western Europe's argument that Europe should be the one dealing with issues in Yugoslavia. The logic behind this claim derived from the fact that almost half of Yugoslav foreign trade was with the countries from the European Community (EC), while only a fraction was with the US. Although there was an apparent motivation to act, Western European countries lacked a common perception of the situation in the country. Touval argues that "their divergent attitudes stemmed largely from cultural-historical preconceptions existing in their respective societies" (1996, 410). Despite the fact that the EC as a whole seemed to send a unified signal on its position on the matter, individual EC member states sent contradictory signals. On the one side, the United Kingdom and France insisted that the primary concern should be the preservation of Yugoslav unity and territorial integrity, while Italy and newly-unified Germany were much more inclined to emphasize the necessity and primacy of promoting human rights and democratic standards, which for them represented euphemisms for respecting the principle of self-determination. Such ambiguity in the European position was further complicated by the fact that Europe's main interest was in the evolving situation in the rich northern republics of Slovenia and Croatia that were looking for allies for their separatist movements. Kosovo was largely ignored.

In fact, the politically powerful European states were willing to act with determination, but only through unofficial channels because they wanted to avoid being criticized for "violating the normative and legal injunction against interference in the internal affairs of a sovereign state" (Touval 1996, 413). Any attempt to become directly involved, including via mediation, would have entailed exhaustive participation in Yugoslavia's internal politics, which Western countries wanted to avoid. However, this had no effect on the crisis in Kosovo. Even when Western countries gave up on their goal of the preservation of Yugoslav unity, the right to secession was recognized only for those entities that had the status of a republic in the federation, which Kosovo never managed to obtain. This happened once the wars in Slovenia and Croatia started and the EC rushed to establish an arbitration commission better known as Badinter Commission (after Robert Badinter, Chief Jurist and President of the French Constitutional Court), which was supposed to resolve disagreements between parties in the Yugoslav crisis. More importantly, this commission issued several crucial opinions that rapidly became pillars around which the international community's future activities revolved. For Kosovo, one finding of the Badinter Commission was essential: in the process of dissolution, the international community in fact recognized the right of secession for those entities that had the status of a federal unit, i.e., republics, but not for the autonomous provinces. Despite the fact that Kosovo requested recognition as a sovereign state, along with other republics, and the results of a clandestine referendum on independence, the EC refused to consider it (Caplan 1998). In a nutshell, by the 1990s, efforts to employ preventive diplomacy in the crisis in Kosovo could only be described as weak and ineffective because of the reluctance of outside actors to become engaged more directly and due to their holistic approach to the situation in Yugoslavia more generally.

Along with the radicalization of Albanians in Kosovo, the international community also gave Milošević a great deal of room to maneuver in the province. Soon after the Dayton agreement was signed, Western countries started lifting previously imposed sanctions from Serbia and Montenegro (then known as the Federal Republic of Yugoslavia, FRY). Initially sanctions were supposed to be lifted only in the event that the FRY implemented a set of laws that would improve minority rights, especially those pertaining to Albanians in Kosovo. This matter was neglected due to Milošević's constructive contribution in Dayton. On 23 February 1998, the US envoy to the region, Richard Gelbard, labeled the UCK as a terrorist group whose activities were strongly condemned by the US (Phillips 2012, 87).[2] Milošević interpreted this as a go ahead to launch several large-scale attacks against the Albanian population in Kosovo under the guise of engaging in anti-terrorist activities.

The upsurge of conflict in Kosovo did not draw synchronized attention from the international community to mediate a settlement until KLA activities posed a serious challenge to Serb dominance in Kosovo, which resulted in a disproportionate retaliation by Serb forces and subsequent humanitarian crisis. As Burg notes,

> it was the onset of fighting between Serbian (formally Yugoslav) military and police units and the KLA, and especially the use of disproportionate force by Serbs against civilians in Kosovo, in early 1998 that prompted US and international efforts to mediate the conflict.
>
> (Burg 2005, 202)

The initial efforts showed signs of 'continual equivocation' (Caplan 1998). The Contact Group, composed of six nations (the US, UK, France, Germany, Italy, and Russia), often threatened to reestablish sanctions unless authorities in Belgrade withdrew their special forces from the province and began a process of dialogue with the Kosovo Albanian leaders. Despite the fact that Milošević was not complying with its demands, the Contact Group was reluctant to impose and strengthen sanctions and chose to be more flexible with deadlines. The hesitance of the international community in this period can be attributed to various factors, but there are two that deserve special attention. First of all, for the first time, a non-Western country was included in the coalition of international actors that was active in managing the conflict, Russia. Emerging from the ashes of the dissolved USSR, Russia was now assuming a much more active role in international politics. Its absence from previous conflict management activities in Yugoslavia would not be indicative of its future behavior. Perceived as a country that had particular influence over authorities in Belgrade, Western countries had a strategic interest in including Russia as a partner in their coalition because it would allow them to create the necessary incentives to encourage Belgrade to collaborate and move toward a negotiated settlement. Nevertheless, as a member of the Contact Group, Russia was the most insistent in refusing to support many of the sanctions suggested by other states. On the other hand, Western countries were much more willing to apply more stringent measures if the fighting in Kosovo continued – especially in light of previous conflicts in Yugoslavia. For Caplan, these divisions prevented the Contact Group "from acting with greater determination" (1998, 754).

The second matter that contributed to the reluctance of the international community to become more involved was the fact that it shared a common interest in preventing the independence of Kosovo, which it believed would create a possible precedent, giving credence to separatist aspirations across the globe. Despite the fact that international actors differed in their opinions on the nature of engagement, they were all reluctant to use measures that would weaken the repressive Serbian regime in Kosovo. Particularly when reports of the growing strength of the UCK were starting to come in, the Contact Group stopped insisting so vociferously that Belgrade should reduce its special forces in the province. The Group started demanding only a suspension of attacks on the civilian population in Kosovo (Caplan 1998; Phillips 2012).

However, the crisis in Kosovo was deteriorating dramatically. By the end of March, Serbian security forces launched large-scale military attacks against civilian communities in Kosovo that resulted in the displacement of approximately 200,000 Albanians from their homes (Phillips 2012, 90). Faced with an alarming humanitarian situation, the UN Security Council immediately responded; on 31 March 1998, it adopted Resolution 1160, which imposed an arms embargo on Yugoslavia on the basis of Chapter VII of the UN Charter. The resolution also called for a substantive and meaningful dialogue on political status issues between Belgrade and Kosovo Albanian authorities and recognized the willingness of the Contact Group to facilitate the talks. The resolution concluded that the outcome of such talks should be founded on the principle of Yugoslav territorial integrity, respect for OSCE standards and the Charter of the UN, and should promote an "enhanced status for Kosovo" which would imply a larger degree of autonomy and "meaningful" self-administration (S/RES/1160 1998). The implications of this resolution were far reaching considering that the document in fact labeled the situation in Kosovo as a threat to international peace and security. Even so, authorities in Belgrade remained reluctant to accept any foreign involvement in the case, claiming that the issue was purely internal in nature.

Despite the reluctance of the authorities in Belgrade to accept third-party involvement while the situation in Kosovo was deteriorating further, the Serbian government gradually faced considerable pressure from abroad. It first started communicating about the issue with US diplomats (Phillips 2012, 91). At that time, as a clear sign of a unipolar power-balance in the world, the American administration demonstrated the greatest determination to manage the conflict and if necessary to resort to the use of force. Despite the fact that the US was orchestrating the whole process, it had to rely on the assistance of other members of the Contact Group. It was Russia who managed to extract a very important concession from authorities in Belgrade who agreed to restart negotiations with Kosovo leaders in June 1998 "to the extent that terrorist activities are halted" (Crawford 2002, 508). This time, Kosovo leaders did not collaborate due to extreme pressure imposed on them by the UCK not to accept anything but full independence for the province. Slowly, US officials, using facilitator strategies, were able to start indirect negotiations with Belgrade and Priština, using a distinct form of shuttle diplomacy mixed with sporadic threats of military intervention, since the two sides did not want to negotiate directly. The lack of direct communication was a sign that compromise was far from attainable, especially since the authorities from both sides were very limited in their bargaining power. This time, both sides had considerably less room to maneuver, just as in 1996 when they signed the (never implemented) agreement on education in Kosovo. It was virtually impossible to reconcile the claims of independence and reaffirmation of Kosovo as an integral part of Serbia. Between June and October, several attempts at shuttle diplomacy by US officials failed because Kosovo leaders could not accept proposals from the international community that maintained that Kosovo was to remain an integral and inalienable part of Serbia (Phillips 2012, 91–94).

Given the futile results, belligerent activities between the UCK and Serbian forces escalated again, resulting in another UN Security Council resolution that condemned all acts of violence in Kosovo, in particular the "indiscriminate use of force by Serb security forces" and again urged both parties to cease fire and seek a political solution (S/RES/1199 1998). It is also noteworthy that by that time, US officials had gradually stopped labeling the UCK strictly as a terrorist group. In fact, in July 1998, James Rubin, the spokesperson of the State Department said "not all activities of UCK should be considered as terrorism." From that moment on, the UCK had more legitimacy in the eyes of the international community (B92 2008). In a short time, the position of the UCK would change from a terrorist group into a partner in the mediation process, enabling the third parties to engage them more directly in the peace process.

During this process, US officials were losing leverage over the LDK and Milošević, and they had no leverage whatsoever over the UCK (Burg 2005, Crawford 2002). After mixing diplomacy with threats of using military force to impose a settlement, an agreement concluded between Richard Holbrooke and Milošević in October 1998 that called for the reduction of Serbian security forces and their withdrawal from Kosovo fell apart because it was used by the UCK to expand its power in the province. Not surprisingly, by the end of 1998, the negotiations had become completely ineffective.

While the futility of negotiation efforts was becoming more and more evident, the situation in Kosovo was becoming even less stable. The level of violence was drastically increasing; the conflict exhibited all the elements of intractability. By the end of 1998, Serbian forces had responded to the UCK's expansion of power in the province with a systematic campaign across all municipalities forcing more than 300,000 ethnic Albanians to leave their homes and leading to countless civilian casualties. Serbia claimed that their actions were legitimate and directed toward terrorists in Kosovo. However, soon the international community would discover that the attacks were directed at the Albanian civil community as a whole, rather than the terrorist cells of the UCK. The turning point was in January 1999, when the foreign press released a story covering the mass murder of 45 ethnic Albanian civilians in Račak, executed at close range by Serbian forces (Weller 1999). Confronted with this unprecedented level of hostility, the Contact Group reacted swiftly.

Since conflict intensity was high, with elevated levels of violence and distrust between the parties, the tactics of communication and formulation were not enough. The Contact Group ministers immediately met in London and assumed a more decisive role using a directive-manipulator strategy. The ministers "unreservedly condemned" what happened in Račak, stressing that the situation in Kosovo "remains a threat to peace and security in the region, [and was] raising the prospect of a humanitarian catastrophe" (Chairman's conclusions 1999). Blaming both the Belgrade authorities and the UCK for perpetuating conflict and violence in the province, they called on them to end their belligerent activities and commit themselves to a process of negotiation that would lead to a political settlement. The negotiations needed to reestablish substantial autonomy of Kosovo in a form agreed to by both sides. Parties were required to gather in Rambouillet by February 6 and proceed with negotiations with the direct involvement of the Contact Group. The statement concluded that

> the Contact Group will hold both sides accountable if they fail to take the opportunity now offered to them, just as the Group stands ready to work with both sides to realize the benefits for them of a peaceful solution.
>
> (Chairman's conclusions 1999)

Russia

Despite the fact that the Rambouillet conference was mainly about the fate of Kosovo, it became an exceptional opportunity to provide an arena in which most of the friction lingering in the post-Cold War transformation process dissipated. According to Weller, it was an excellent opportunity for a "fundamental change in the roles of international actors" (Weller 1999, 212). It was also an undeniable statement against the materialization of a unipolar system dominated by the US.

First of all, the steady emergence of Russia as the new-old global power was most emblematically represented by its membership in the Contact Group and presence at the Rambouillet conference in particular. Moscow developed a firm foreign policy stance that aimed to reject the concept of an imposed settlement upon Yugoslav authorities, especially if it was to be enforced by NATO. In case that would turn out to be unfeasible, Russia's priority was to maintain a managerial role for itself in the future administration of the situation. At that time, the best way to achieve these aspirations was to promote the involvement of collective bodies in the crisis in which Russia could block decisions requiring consensus (Weller 1999). Along with the Contact Group, these bodies were also the OSCE – which provides an additional layer of institutional authority in conflict management and where decisions are made by consensus – and more importantly, the United Nations Security Council where Russia is vested with veto power.

As Levitin (2000) explains, the Russian interest in the situation in Kosovo was marginal during the early 1990s. The first reported talks with Belgrade regarding the crisis took place only in 1996. For far too long, Moscow ignored information about the deployment of Serbian security forces in the province, especially in the period when the intensity of violence was culminating (1997–1998). Such laxity deprived policy makers in Moscow of the possibility of acknowledging the importance of moderate forces in Kosovo – namely the non-violent resistance movement – and thus indirectly contributed to the subsequent upsurge in radical forces in the province. The first contact with leaders from Priština was only established in July 1998. Undoubtedly, by then, Russia had assumed the role of a passive bystander in the crisis settlement. Finally, this lack of interest was best observed in the Russian 'withdrawal' of its veto in discussions on Kosovo, both in the Contact Group and the UN Security Council throughout the years. The first concrete involvement of Russian diplomats took place in the second part of 1998, at which point Moscow exercised its relative leverage over Belgrade, given the traditionally close relations between the two capitals and a shared religious and Slavic heritage. Russia, faced with the imminent NATO bombing campaign in Yugoslavia, managed to pressure Milošević through indirect channels to accept negotiations with Priština, which temporarily suspended the use of coercive force. It was a clear signal to the rest of the international community that Russia could act as a useful biased mediator, as it possessed the necessary leverage to create essential incentives for Serbia to cooperate in solving the conflict. Despite this contribution, it was only in

Rambouillet that the Russians actually got involved in a more constructive discussion in formulating peace plans with the Western countries of the Contact Group, which had already been active in this matter since mid-1998. According to Levitin, "the real reason for Russia's reluctance to join in serious discussions concerning Kosovo's legal status stemmed not from a substantive gap between Russian and Western positions, but from the Russian habit of inertia, delay and fear of decision-making" (2005, 136). This attitude was a consequence of the "lack of clear vision" in Russian geo-political preferences in the Balkans that persisted in Moscow during the 1990s (Levitin 2005). In other words, Russia lacked a clear idea of its interests in the region.

Until mid-1998, Russia had a very rigid position on the issue of Kosovo's legal status. In 1997, when the Contact Group drafted a very vague formulation of Kosovo's autonomy, Russia's traditional historical relations with Serbia prompted Moscow to insist that the principle of self-governance be accepted only if the province remained within Serbia's formal jurisdiction (Levitin 2005, 136). With the outbreak of hostilities in the second half of 1998, Moscow started contemplating the idea of a special status for Kosovo, though always within the Yugoslav federation. Despite this change of attitude, Russia was very slow to adapt to group dynamics within the Contact Group. During the shuttle diplomacy episode conducted by US envoys in late 1998, Russia did not oppose any of the formulations proposed for a settlement in principle. However, lack of vision and inertia in the conduct of foreign affairs made Russia assume a "kind of slack resistance" (Levitin 2005, 136).

France and the United Kingdom

According to Weller (1999), France also aspired to advance its role as a global power and tried to challenge the US position to delegate future decision-making mechanisms to NATO and away from the UN Security Council, where France enjoyed the same leverage as Russia. Germany and Italy were also more inclined to strengthen the role of the UN and initially even indicated that they would not support any use of coercive means by NATO unless it were approved by a Security Council resolution. The choice of Rambouillet for negotiation talks (instead of an American air base, e.g., Dayton, Ohio where the Bosnian war was settled) was an implicit signal to the US that their European partners were resolute that they would approach the crisis in Kosovo with more determination (Weller 1999, 212).

The only European country that deviated from this position was the United Kingdom. In fact, policy makers in London were much more inclined toward US policies in this matter and shared the idea that NATO should maintain a dominant role in the future administration of the conflict. However, both countries were well aware that forceful action by NATO, without a clear mandate from the Security Council, would only increase friction within the Contact Group during the Rambouillet talks. The fact that there was an undeniable humanitarian crisis in the province provided much more room to consider coercive action and promote it to partners in the Contact Group. Even the UN officials backed this vision. The UN Secretary General Kofi Annan, in his visit to NATO headquarters, stressed the importance of "contemplating" the use of force to halt internal conflict, despite the reluctance of the host government, especially bearing in mind the Bosnian experience (Annan 1999).

Multiparty mediation process

The contact group's mediation strategy

In order to get everyone on board and create 'internal coherence,' the US strengthened diplomatic contacts with all members of the Contact Group. Despite their initial differences, all European countries eventually agreed to employ coercive power through NATO as a necessary incentive in the upcoming talks. Then NATO Secretary-General Javier Solana publicly announced full support for a political settlement under mediation of the Contact Group that would reaffirm sovereignty and territorial integrity of Yugoslavia and completely protect human and other rights of all ethnic groups. At the same time, NATO called on both sides to end the violence and pursue their goals through peaceful means. Yugoslav authorities were asked to start reducing the number of security forces in the province, while Kosovo Albanians were told to immediately cease hostilities and provocative actions (Weller 1999, 221). Shortly thereafter, NATO officials directly threatened Yugoslav officials with air strikes, despite the continuous acknowledgement of Yugoslav territorial integrity and sovereignty, in the event that they failed to commit to the achievement of a settlement. They also threatened to take all appropriate measures against Kosovo Albanian leaders in the event that they failed to comply with the demands of the international community. The threat of the use of force was justified as being a humanitarian action (Weller 1999, 223).

At this point, the stage was set for 'mediation with muscle.' By the end of January 1999, the foreign ministers of the US and Russia met and jointly declared that they were determined to "maintain close contact in order to *coordinate* US and Russian support for a resolution of the crisis" (Weller 1999, 221; emphasis added). For the US, the only acceptable strategy for tackling the situation in Kosovo was a combination of "diplomacy with a credible threat of force," for which they already had the support of their allies and it would be promoted through Contact Group (Weller 1999, 221). Even though policy makers in Washington showed the highest level of commitment to resolving the conflict in Kosovo, they were aware that they needed partners in order to make the strong inducements require to get both sides to sit at the negotiation table.

Despite the initial internal struggle for power, the Contact Group managed to find coherence and members shared the idea that the conflict in Kosovo needed to be managed as promptly as possible (Phillips 2012, 101). The Contact Group immediately stepped in with a 'directive-manipulator' strategy and presented a document containing 'non-negotiable principles/basic elements' for a settlement to the parties. These principles were divided into four groups: (a) general elements, including the necessity of an immediate end of violence and respect of ceasefire; peaceful solution through dialogue; an interim agreement – a mechanism for a mutual settlement after an interim period of three years; no unilateral change of the interim status; and international involvement and full cooperation by the parties on implementation; (b) governance in Kosovo, including a high level of self-governance for Kosovo through own institutions; harmonization of Serbian and federal laws with the interim agreement; and members of all national communities to be fairly represented at all levels of administration; (c) protection of human rights including judicial protection of human rights guaranteed by international conventions, establishment of an ombudsman office; and (d) implementation, which included dispute management mechanisms, establishment of joint implementation monitoring commission, and a considerable role for international bodies such as the OSCE (Weller 1999, 225–226). The general principles also included preservation of territorial integrity of the FRY and neighboring countries; protection of rights of the members of all national communities within the FRY; protection of rights for members of all national communities in FRY; free and fair elections in Kosovo; amnesty and release of prisoners (Weller 1999, 225–226).

It was mandatory for the parties to take notice of these non-negotiable principles. The mediators did not require a formal consent on the principles, since they were considering the decision of the parties to participate in negotiations as implicit acceptance of them. Most of the principles were a compilation of proposed suggestions by the US envoys in the shuttle diplomacy period. The crucial addition was the mechanism of an interim agreement that implied a transitional phase of three years, after which a final settlement should be achieved.

Party arithmetic

The Serbian delegation was composed of three groups. First of all, there were prominent political figures from Belgrade that were directly mandated by Milošević. Along with them, the delegation included individuals that acted as representatives of several non-Albanian ethnic groups from Kosovo (Phillips 2012, 102). However, from the beginning, their representativeness was put under serious doubt when numerous communities in Kosovo learned about their presence in Rambouillet. As it turned out during the conference, their role was quite marginal and they were only included by Belgrade authorities as a demonstration of alleged unity of non-Albanian constituencies in Kosovo. Most importantly, the delegation consisted of professional negotiators and experts that assumed leading roles once the process started (Weller 1999, 226). American diplomats viewed the Serbian delegation as 'intentionally unserious,' an indication that Serbian authorities were not interested in a diplomatic solution because no one in their delegation had sufficient authority to make decisions or accept agreements (Phillips 2012, 103).

The Kosovo delegation was also controversial, and deeply divided (Phillips 2012, 103). Members of the leading party, the LDK, comprised only one third of the overall delegation. The rest of the delegation consisted of representatives of opposition parties in Kosovo, whose stances on the issues were far less flexible and more inclined toward the UCK. And more importantly, there were a considerable number of representatives from the UCK itself. The UCK not only became a negotiating partner, but its leader, Hashim Thaci, was also assigned to head the tripartite presidency of the Kosovo delegation. The delegation was primarily broadened due to extreme pressure coming from Kosovo (Weller 1999, 227). This was viewed as acceptable by the mediators because they realized that in excluding the UCK (and other opposition parties) from all previous negotiations, they had only lost leverage over them. Considering that the UCK had become an important actor in the conflict, mediators used a particular form of party arithmetic. It implied inclusion of additional players that might be constructive to the implementation phase once the settlement had been achieved.

The mediation was conducted by three key negotiators – Christopher Hill (US), Wolfgang Petritsch (representing the European Union), and Boris Mayorski (Russian Federation) – all appointed by the Contact Group who were expected to represent the interest of the entire coalition and not of their state of origin. Since the Contact Group had, on previous occasions, declared a shared commitment to resolving the conflict, had 'muscle' at its disposal, and support from very relevant international organizations (such as the UN and the OSCE), the mediators immediately assumed both formulator and manipulator strategies.

The mediation process

At the beginning of the conference, both sides received a draft version of the political settlement, which consisted of a framework agreement and three annexes (on the constitution of Kosovo, elections, and an ombudsman). The mediators also formulated a very strict procedure for the process of negotiations. The parties were not expected to engage in direct talks, but rather they were to submit comments on the drafts. In the event that both sides agreed on a modification of the text, that change would immediately be included; if there was no consensus, alteration of the text would not take place and the draft would remain unchanged. Modifications were not allowed to diverge from the non-negotiable principles (Weller 1999, 228).

From the beginning, the Kosovo delegation assumed a very constructive strategy and immediately submitted written comments on the draft, claiming that the document was acceptable in principle and that they would suggest some changes in order to improve it. The Serbian delegation, on the other hand, was much less constructive, as it did not produce any comments for quite some time and engaged in several attempts to downplay the position of the Kosovo delegation, to no avail (Weller 1999, 228).

The Kosovo delegation hoped that its constructive role would be rewarded by the mediators, but that never happened. In fact, the mediators were much more occupied with urging the Serbian delegation to submit some comments and suggestions on the first draft. The first proposal from the Serbian block was challenging the non-negotiable principles, so the mediators "then proceeded to engage the FRY/Serb delegation in an intensive dialogue, so as to whittle down the wide-raging comments in to a more limited number of submissions which might be discussed" (Weller 1999, 229). Under these circumstances, the Kosovo delegation and its comments were largely ignored by the mediators until some progress was made with the other side. The mediators' revised draft came as a shock to the Kosovo delegation because it included almost all demands from the Serbian side (such as codifying the legal status of Kosovo in the constitutional settlement, the establishment veto powers for all community leaders in Kosovo, and a limiting of the authority of Kosovar institutions), while suggestions from the Kosovo delegation were largely ignored and only a few were included (Weller 1999, 231).

Once the revised draft was presented, mediators suggested that both parties consider it to be a final version of the political settlement. Both sides declined to do so. The Kosovo delegation refused to receive the document, considering it to be a direct result of talks between mediators and the Serbian delegation, which represented a breach of the faith that they had had in the process. In other words, the presentation of the draft led to the development of a feeling of distrust and betrayal that seriously jeopardized further constructive participation of the Kosovo delegation. However, the mediators were insistent on the matter. Since there was no going back to the original draft, the Kosovo delegation presented a statement containing a list of necessary changes that needed to be considered if negotiations were to succeed. The Serbian delegation also insisted on further changes. Realizing that neither side was willing to accept the document, mediators extended the deadline and took the positions of both sides into consideration.

This time the procedure was somewhat different. Negotiations were actually conducted in a form of genuine proximity talks (Weller 1999, 232). This meant that substantive suggestions from one side were channeled through a body of legal experts to the other side. In the event that the other side refused to accept suggested changes, the mediators would aim to reduce the scope of alterations and refine them through negotiations with both sides until they agreed. Using this method, in a very short span of time, mediators were able to produce a new draft that merged all previous annexes into a comprehensive document that was entitled the Interim Agreement for Peace and Self-Government in Kosovo (S/1999/648 1999). In sum, the agreement prescribed that Kosovo would not be an independent state, but a component part of Yugoslavia with a status some-where between an autonomous province and a federal unit. Federal laws were supposed to remain in force in Kosovo as long as they were compatible with the agreement. The proposed constitution of Kosovo was deeply rooted in the Yugo-slav federal tradition and prescribed "sovereign rights at the level of the auto-nomous sub-state entities" (Stahn 2001a, 538). The status of Kosovo within Yugoslavia was to be safeguarded by an international supervisory institution with binding decision-making powers. This meant that Kosovo would become a sub-state entity protected by international guarantees and supervision, without assuming characteristics of an international protectorate or international territory. Despite the international military presence of Kosovo Force (KFOR), Kosovo still remained under the overall external protection of Belgrade (Stahn 2001a, 538).

In the meantime, the mediators also had to put additional pressure on both sides, especially on the UCK, which was still reluctant to accept anything less than independence and was very reluctant to accept the process of demilitarization, given the high level of distrust and animosity towards Serbian security forces. Thus through a coordinated activity, representatives of militaries from all Western countries in the Contact Group discussed issues of demilitarization in practice and mechanisms of international guarantees that the security in the province would be under strict control. From that moment, it was implicit that KFOR would be a NATO-led mission. Ultimately, a very important concession was made to the Kosovo delegation in the form of the inclusion of the phrase "will of the people" in the part referring to the interim period of three years. It meant, implicitly, that the people of Kosovo were granted a mechanism and a possibility to achieve independence after this period. At this point, the Kosovo delegation was persuaded by mediators (especially the representative from the US) to accept the agreement. The initial response was that the delegation needed time to consult the constituencies in Kosovo, but after a short while, the Kosovo delegation issued a declaration that "noted that in order to facilitate such consultations, the delegation had voted in favor of the agreement as presented in the negotiations on 23 February" (Stahn 2001a, 233). According to Ker-Lindsay, they were aware that unless they accepted the proposed agreement, they would inevitably lose any form of international support (Ker-Lindsay 2009, 14).

The position of the Serbian delegation was somewhat more confusing. While it was evident that the opposite side was not willing to accept the agreement, Serbs were issuing statements demanding further concessions. However, once it was clear that the Kosovo delegation was going to sign the document, the Serbian delegation stepped forward with a declaration that emphasized the considerable progress towards commonly acceptable solutions that was made during the negotiations. At the same time, it asked for further clarification on the issues of Kosovo's self-government and on international presence in Kosovo during the implementation of the agreement. Thus, for the Serbian delegation, the issues that had made the talks necessary had not all been dealt with and negotiations were far from being concluded (Weller 1999, 223).

The Contact Group, faced with firm stances on both sides, issued a joint statement that was clearly the product of a directive strategy. The statement put forward an ultimatum for both sides. The statement noted that "important efforts of the parties and the unstinting commitment of our negotiators Ambassadors Hill, Petritsch and Mayorsky, have led to a *consensus*" on substantial issues regarding self-governance and autonomy of Kosovo and established a "political framework ... and groundwork ... for finalizing the implementation ... including" (Contact Group Statement, 1999; emphasis added). The mediators indicated that the document needed to be completed and signed as a whole by both sides at the upcoming conference on March 15 in Paris that would cover all aspects of implementation. The future conference was not intended to be a place at which talks on the political settlement could be reopened. Only discussions on the issues of implementation of the agreement were to be discussed.

In Paris, the Kosovo delegation submitted a letter immediately in which it indicated its full acceptance of the interim agreement from February 23. The mediators were reluctant to pressure the Kosovo delegation to sign right away and advised them to postpone this act until the Serbian delegation was on board. The Serbian side still had its reservations about the document. In direct communication with Serbian delegates, the mediators indicated "the *unanimous view* of the Contact Group that only technical adjustments can be considered which, of course, must be accepted as such and approved by the other delegation" (Weller 1999, 234; emphasis added). It was a clear signal to the Serbian delegation that possibilities for further concessions were completely exhausted at this point. However, the Serbs did not accept this and instead issued a counter-draft that was undoubtedly aimed at reopening discussions on the political settlement from the beginning. The draft requested a formal subordination of Kosovo to the federal and republican system and complete marginalization of provincial institutions. According to some observers, this proposal sought to formalize an "institutional system of apartheid" (Weller 1999, 235). Ultimately, the draft completely removed the part regarding outside military and civilian presence for the implementation phase. For the Serbian delegation, it was absolutely unacceptable that NATO forces assume any control in Kosovo (Black 1999). Around this time, Milošević, in the presence of Russian officials, stepped out and determinedly announced that Serbia would never accept a requirement to withdraw its forces from Kosovo and allow the presence of foreign troops on its own soil (B92 2008). On March 18, the Kosovo delegation signed the agreement in a formal ceremony that was not attended by the Russian delegate Mayorski. This demonstrated that coherence and coordination within the Contact Group was falling short. For the first time, one of the mediators was not acting as a representative of the entire coalition, but rather of a particular country.

Emergence of diverging interests between third parties

According to Levitin (2000), Serbia insisted on the matter of not accepting a NATO-led international military presence in Kosovo, believing that it would have support from the Russian delegation. During the conference, Russian officials tried to find reasons to cast doubt on the Kosovo delegation, labeling it as 'illegitimate' and inappropriately composed due to the presence of the UCK. However, these were not real concerns, but rather tactical feints, without any strategic purpose, that sent false signals to the Serbian delegation. Russian officials were well aware that the agreement was not feasible without an outside military that would implement it. Yet they avoided discussing a mutually acceptable arrangement and declined to offer any sensible alternative to Western plans to use NATO forces. This contributed to the lack of coordination among the mediators. As Levitin claims, "the Russian habit of procrastination, especially with regard to the military annex of the agreement, contributed to Rambouillet's collapse" (Levitin 2000, 137). Notwithstanding these harsh accusations, it was obvious that Russia did not have the same vision of a common solution to the conflict anymore. Its interests were now diverging from the rest of the coalition. It meant that the mediators were unable to coordinate their leverage on both sides: while one group was exerting pressure, creating the required incentives to push the Kosovo delegation to accept the agreement, the Russians abstained from exercising indispensable leverage on the Serbian delegation to do the same. As a consequence, the Serbian delegation perceived these mixed signals as an inducement to assume a much more unyielding position that eventually prevented them from signing the agreement.

The emerging division within the Contact Group did not reveal itself immediately. In fact, the mediators tried once more to convince the Serbian delegation to accept the agreement, reminding them that they were mediating with muscle. Once this attempt failed, the Contact Group issued a statement in which it indicated that the Rambouillet Accords were the only peaceful solution to the crisis in Kosovo. They acknowledged the opportunity taken by the Kosovo delegation to accept the Interim Agreement and blamed the Serbian delegation for its attempt to unravel the conference. For all members of the Contact Group, there was no point in extending the talks. Negotiations were adjourned until such time as the Serbs expressed their acceptance of the final document. The Contact Group resolved to engage in consultations with other international partners that may be ready to act. They warned authorities in Belgrade not to continue any military activity in Kosovo because "such violations would have the gravest consequences" (Weller 1999, 236). Russian lack of cooperation with the rest of the Contact Group guided the process directly into a deadlock.

Despite these warnings, Serbian authorities continued their initial strategy of deploying troops to Kosovo. At the same time, when the Contact Group issued the last statement, Serbian security forces tightened their grip on Kosovo. Using extremely violent measures, they managed to displace around 200,000 ethnic Albanians outside of the province. This was a crucial error in their strategy (Posen 2000). Violent measures taken in Kosovo accompanied by an open refusal to accept the agreement (the final attempt by Holbrooke on March 23 to persuade Milošević ended in failure) were a signal to the Western countries that the 'muscle' at their disposal (i.e., NATO) needed to be deployed. On March 24, 1999, NATO air forces started an 11-week-long bombing campaign of Serbia that led to numerous civilian and military casualties and extreme material damage.

The start of the NATO campaign provoked particularly harsh rhetoric from Russia. Officials in Moscow immediately condemned the use of force without the authorization of the UN Security Council and took symbolic action to cease cooperation with NATO (Smith and Plater-Zyberk, 1999). According to Antonenko (2000), Russia's reaction to the bombing campaign had little to do with the Kosovo situation, but was rather the materialization of a greater anti-NATO sentiment and an avenue for venting post-Soviet frustrations. For Levitin, "the deterioration has to be understood in the context of more general and long standing trends in Russian foreign policy" (Levitin 2000, 138). Moscow was also continuing to send very mixed signals. For instance, on March 25, the Russian Foreign Minister Ivanov emphasized that Belgrade should be aware of its responsibility to resolve the problem in Kosovo and opt to accept the political settlement drafted in Rambouillet. The day after, he declared that the Rambouillet peace documents are "practically null and void" (Smith and Plater-Zyberk 1999, 4). Nevertheless, in his speech at the *Duma*, Russian President Yeltzin highlighted that "the tragic mistake of the American leadership should not result in a prolonged crisis of US–Russian partnership" (Smith and Plater-Zyberk 1999, 4). Such mixed signals reflected Russia's persistent inability to formulate a clear set of preferences regarding the issue. On the one side, it wanted to maintain its influence in Serbia, while on the other, it was eager to improve its relations with the rest of the Contact Group.

Looking back at the model, despite initial confidence that the mediators were able to find internal coherence within the Contact Group and aimed at successfully coordinating the multiparty mediation efforts, the process never moved from point (b). Initial readiness on the part of Russia to work together with the rest of the Contact Group initially guided both sides to accept a peace conference and negotiate together, which represented an important step toward success. On the other hand, Russia's initial readiness proved to be a façade as it was unwilling to employ the necessary leverage to induce its partners in conflict (in this case the Serbian government) to accept the compromise solution that was drafted in Rambouillet. While the Western states were able to induce the Kosovo delegation to compromise, the Russians were unwilling to exercise the requisite leverage to 'deliver' the Serbian government to an agreement. Finally, the lack of success could be associated with the absence of clearly formulated preferences on Russia's part, which prevented adequate coordination of mediators and their leverage.

Inclusion of the UN in the process

Russian hope to be still treated like a partner by the West was best demonstrated in June 1999, when the NATO campaign was about to turn into a ground operation[3] (Phillips 2012, 113). Despite their open opposition to NATO intervention, Russia managed to extract a very important concession from Belgrade. Using the necessary leverage through informal channels and backdoor communication, Russian officials persuaded Milošević to accept a cease-fire that would allow for an international, NATO-led military presence in Kosovo. Russians acted in the name of the entire Contact Group, offering Milošević the option to have the international military presence be under the UN flag, thus reducing the likelihood that Serbia would lose face domestically and abroad (NY Times 1999). More importantly, Serbia and Russia had converging interests in including the UN as a new actor in future conflict management activities. In Serbia, Milošević publicly stated that by transferring future management of the problems in Kosovo to the UN, Serbia would preserve its sovereignty and territorial integrity that were guaranteed by the UN Charter. He claimed that the problems in Kosovo would finally be dealt within the body whose responsibility it is to preserve global peace and security and thus reduce the impact of the coalition that used muscle to manage the conflict. This was a direct indication that for Serbian authorities, the UN would act as a new player that was vested with the requisite legitimacy derived from norms and values that were inherent to the organization. On the other side, Russia managed to transfer future conflict management activities to a body in which it had more mechanisms of control.

In order to create the necessary legitimacy for this move, Russia assured officials in Belgrade that the UN Security Council would pass a resolution that would formalize its presence. Given the fact that, for Serbia, UN involvement was crucial at this point, the official presentation of the document was done by Special Envoy Martti Ahtisaari and the document was adopted by the Serb parliament on June 3. This meant that the mediation process had now been joined by a new actor, this time an international organization. Until then, UN involvement was somewhat sporadic and largely conditioned by power politics at the international level. It was mostly based on the occasional issuing of resolutions, but fell short of direct involvement in the process.

The new reality in Kosovo

The Kumanovo Agreement and UN Security Council Resolution 1244

The ceasefire was signed on June 9 in Kumanovo, a Macedonian town on the border with Serbia. The Kumanovo Agreement reaffirmed the document presented by Ahtisaari to include the deployment in Kosovo of effective international civil and security presences under the auspices of the UN. It was noted that the UN Security Council was set to adopt a resolution regarding the deployment of an international security force (KFOR) that would "operate without hindrance within Kosovo and with the authority to take all necessary action to establish and maintain a secure environment for all citizens of Kosovo and otherwise carry out its mission" (Kumanovo Agreement 1999). The following day, the UN Security Council passed Resolution 1244, which lay the foundation for a new reality in Kosovo. The resolution was proof of the compromise that had been reached within the Contact Group and was transposed in the Security Council. Undeniably, it refrained from recognizing Kosovo as an independent state, reflecting the Russian stance, but it also abstained from delivering any binding statements regarding Kosovo's final status, which was in line with the Western countries' position. The conciliatory formula endorsed the sovereignty and territorial integrity of the FRY, while assigning the interim UN Mission in Kosovo (UNMIK) with the task of "facilitating a political process designed to determine Kosovo's future status, taking into account the Rambouillet accords" (S/RES/1244 cl.11, 1999). As Stahn (2001a) noted, this vague formulation allowed for a variety of scenarios. Evidently, the allusion to the sovereignty of the FRY seemed to signify that in any potential future scenario regarding Kosovo, the province would remain part of the FRY. Nevertheless, by mentioning the Rambouillet Agreement, which stated that the future status would be determined by the 'will of people,' the resolution seemed to be somewhat open to interpretation with regard to Kosovo's final status.

Pending the final settlement of Kosovo's status, the resolution charged UNMIK (headed by a special representative of the Secretary-General) with the administration of the province. Its mandate was: to promote the establishment of substantial autonomy and self-government in Kosovo; perform basic civilian administrative functions; organize elections; and maintain law and order using all necessary means (Stahn 2001a). Despite the fact that the resolution did not specify a strict deadline for the establishment of necessary institutions, once they were established, they were required to be transferred to the people of Kosovo in anticipation of a final settlement (Stahn 2001a). In practice, the mission was bestowed with powers traditionally only enjoyed states: the mission introduced a different currency; established its own legal system; and signed international agreements on behalf of the province. In other words, in practice, from the beginning, the FRY was dispossessed of its sovereign rights over Kosovo under the United Nations' interim administration (Stahn 2001a). As the Secretary-General pointed out, UNMIK became "the only legitimate authority in Kosovo" (S/1999/1250 1999, par.35). According to several authors (Stahn 2001a, 2001b; Ruffert 2001; Kreilkamp 2003; Perritt 2005; Knoll 2005, 2006; Willigen 2009), Kosovo was transformed into an 'internationalized territory.' This neutral term indicates that the FRY was prohibited from exercising any form of power in Kosovo, while the UN administration was "pre-empted from disposing over the territory" (Stahn 2001a, 540). In legal terms, the UN sought to act as a *trustee* that had absolute administering power over the province for a *limited time* without acting as a new sovereign (Ruffert 2001, Stahn 2001a). Once the task of preparing the province for self-governance was complete, UNMIK was to transfer its authority to a different entity that the nature of which, according to the resolution, should be determined in the context of a political settlement (Stahn 2001b).

UNMIK regulations and the constitutional framework for provisional self-government

From the beginning of its mission, the Special Representative issued various regulations that contained basic 'constitutional' rules. According to these regulations, all powers (legislative, executive, and judiciary) were vested in UNMIK and had to be exercised by the Special Representative. Institutions that were gradually being established (the Banking and Payments Authority of Kosovo, the Independent Media Commission, the Housing and Property Directorate, the Housing Claims Commission, etc.) were characterized by joint administration – one Kosovar and one UNMIK representative – and were based on the idea of good governance and other democratic principles. As Ruffert noted, the UN was "furnishing Kosovo ... with governmental and administrative institutions to bestow upon the respective populations the opportunity to exercise their rights of self-determination" (2001, 626).

In May 2001, the Special Representative promulgated the Constitutional Framework for Provisional Self-Government (Constitutional Framework) which was intended to be a major step toward the establishment of provisional self-government in Kosovo, beginning with the election of a constituent assembly in November 2001 (Regulation 2001/9; Kreilkamp 2003). According to this document, the Provisional Institutions of Self-Government (PISG) were to be: the Kosovo Assembly, the President of Kosovo, the Kosovo Government, and the Kosovo courts – institutions that would "normally be associated with a state of the sub-entities of federation" (Stahn 2001b, 151). It is very important to note the latter because such a scenario – Kosovo enjoying the status of a de facto equal federal entity in Yugoslavia while *de jure* still part of Serbia – was prescribed by the Rambouillet Accords, which were turned down by the FRY at that time.

Again the document was a result of a political compromise which was reflected (again) in its ambiguous language. Despite the fact that the term 'constitutional' might have created high expectations amongst Kosovo Albanians, the document did not make any direct reference to the achievement of independence for the province and, in fact, deliberately avoided any term directly associated with it. At the same time, the FRY was not mentioned at all in the entire document. Put simply, Kosovo was not explicitly made a part of either the FRY or Serbia, which implicitly meant total suspension of their administrative control in Kosovo. This document initiated a slow devolution of power from UNMIK to local authorities. Significant aspects of legislative, executive, and judicial power were to be transferred to local institutions (both of the central and municipal administration). Soon after the adoption of the Constitutional Framework, both the Special Representative and UNMIK faced severe criticism: internally, from Belgrade and from the international community. According to the report by the Independent International Commission on Kosovo, "under UNMIK constitutional provisions ... the UN administration retains ... vice regal powers, appropriate to colonial dependency, rather than to a self-governing people" (Kreilkamp 2003, 648). The report emphasized that the international administrators had "pervasive distrust of the administrative and political capacity of the population" which seems to explain the constitutional provisions adopted in the Framework (Kreilkamp 2003, 648). The report that was published in 2001 called upon the international community to grant Kosovo "conditional independence" which is "quite distinct from limited self-rule under UNMIK" (Kreilkamp 2003, 651).

Serbian authorities in Belgrade were not pleased with the framework, claiming that it violated the spirit of Resolution 1244 that "enshrine[d] their right to carry out certain state functions in what they still view as Serbian province" (Knoll 2005, fn. 16). Based on this position, the Serbian government encouraged the Serbian minority living in Kosovo to boycott the provisional institutions and, for this reason, established parallel structures of government, especially in the areas of education, justice, and health care, in municipalities in which Serbs were the majority. By not participating in provisional institutions, the Serbian side implicitly acknowledged the fact that provisional institutions that were being established were to be exclusively Kosovar and out of Belgrade's control. This made it possible for the Kosovo Albanians to feel absolutely detached from the Serbian presence in the province. Given the fact that UNMIK was mandated with an interim assignment, it was part of its task to strengthen the established institutions in order to accomplish "the setting-up and development of meaningful self-government in Kosovo pending a final settlement" (Regulation 2001/9, par. 2). Gradually, Kosovo established all the institutions that were necessary to have a functioning independent state.

In this environment, the province awaited the signal from the Security Council that the talks on Kosovo's future status might begin. On May 23, 2005, the UN Secretary General appointed Ambassador Kai Eide to carry out a comprehensive assessment of the situation in Kosovo in order to determine whether or not the conditions were suitable to permit political discussion on final status. On October 7, 2005, Eide concluded that "while the standards implementation in Kosovo had been uneven, the time was ripe to enter the final-status negotiation process" (D'Aspremont 2007, 650). His remarks met with approval at the UN Security Council, which a few days later decided to initiate "a political process designed to determine Kosovo's future status" (S/PRST/2005/51). The Council appointed Martti Ahtisaari as a Secretary General's Special Envoy for Kosovo (UNOSEK), who officially began consultations and talks with Kosovo Albanians and Serbian authorities on November 14, 2005.

Multiparty mediation by the UN

The initial coherence in the contact group

From the beginning, Ahtisaari had been given "considerable room to maneuver" by the Contact Group (ICG 2006a). The Contact Group provided him with a working framework in ten guiding principles. He was instructed that once started, the process could not be blocked and must be brought to conclusion and that the result may be determined by who leaves the table first rather than by compromise (ICG 2006a, 1). The settlement needed to include and promote elements such as regional stability, sustainable multi-ethnicity, preservation of international civil presence in the province, dismissal of partitioning Kosovo, and highlight that any unilateral moves or acts of violence would not be tolerated. From that moment it was evident that the new process of mediation was a particular combination of 'formulator and directive' strategies. On the one hand, the Contact Group again prescribed non-negotiable principles and made the expected spirit of the agreement clear, while Ahtisaari, on the other hand, was supposed to explore, formulate, and offer best solutions to both sides. Despite the fact that the ten principles were non-negotiable, it was already questionable whether or not they prescribed a very clear mandate for Ahtisaari as to where the process should lead. Ahtisaari made it clear that independence was the only possible outcome. He argued: "You need to look at history. Milosevic lost the right to govern by acting as he did. If you misbehave you will lose your right to govern and may also be held personally responsible" (Ahtisaari quoted in Phillips 2012, 160). Moreover, at a meeting in London on January 31, 2006 Ahtisaari informed all of the members of the Contact Group (including Russia) of the final outcome and asked each state to individually and in secret deliver an eight-point message to both sides. The first point was a clear signal of what kind of outcome the Ahtisaari-led mediation aims to yield:

> The unconstitutional abolition of Kosovo's autonomy in 1989 and the ensuing tragic events resulting in the international administration of Kosovo have led to a situation in which a return of Kosovo to Belgrade's rule is not a viable option.
>
> (Ahtisaari 2007)

Ahtisaari justified his diagnosis by resorting to the principle of Responsibility to Protect;[4] at an interview following his Nobel Prize acceptance speech he claimed: "if a dictatorial leadership in any country behaves the way as Milošević and company did vis-à-vis the Albanians in Kosovo, they lose the right to control them anymore" (CNN 2008).

All but the Russian Federation delivered these private messages in the course of February and March 2006 to Belgrade, Priština and Kosovo Serbs (Ahtisaari 2007). Ahtisaari was confident that "everyone knew that independence was coming" (CNN 2008). Privately, all Contact Group countries saw monitored, conditional independence as the only viable outcome. According to a British diplomat, during the December 2005 meeting in Paris, "the taboo on the outcome had completely gone ... everyone was talking about independence, and in front of Russians ... they did not object" (ICG 2006a, 11). Indeed, on several occasions, Russian diplomats had indicated their acceptance that full independence was the only viable outcome (ICG 2006b, 2). It appeared that Russia perceived the new reality in Kosovo in the same way as other members of the Contact Group, but was reluctant to stress it explicitly in public. In London, in January 2006, the developing consensus in the Contact Group was translated into the joint Ministerial Statement which indicated that the settlement had to be "acceptable to the people of Kosovo" and that there was no going back to the status prior to 1999 (Contact Group London Statement 2006). However, the real concern of whether and when to publicly announce the Contact Group's view of the outcome remained. There was a fear that in expressing their support for the independence of Kosovo too soon, Priština – satisfied with the outcome – might not be willing to make any concessions afterwards, while a dissatisfied Serbia would simply leave the negotiations. The Contact Group's goal was "to get sufficient acquiescence from both sides so a settlement can be written into a new Security Council resolution to supersede 1244" (ICG 2006a, 13). Indeed, none of the Contact Group's members was inclined to impose a solution without at least Belgrade's implicit consent. For this reason, the Contact Group and Ahtisaari's team insisted that Kosovo Albanians would need to earn their independence through tangible initiatives and concessions in order to accommodate Serbian requests. As Ahtisaari's deputy Rohan indicated, "their aspirations and status will not come automatically ... much work has to be done" (Rohan 2005).

Actor transformation and UN legitimacy

From the beginning of his mandate, Ahtisaari assumed a very constructive 'procedural-formulator' strategy. He first explored the positions of both sides for a period of three months through informal talks in Belgrade and Priština. It is noteworthy that in the interim period, the two sides went through a phase of actor transformation, which is commonly identified as a very valuable occurrence in terms of managing intractable conflicts (Bercovitch 2005). In Serbia, Milošević was ousted by a more democratic government. In Kosovo, Rugova died in January 2006 (just before the first official round of talks had begun) and the political party of the demilitarized UCK took over. Despite the fact that there were new actors on both sides, neither one changed its previous position. In Belgrade, the new government was ready to negotiate with Priština, thereby indicating its detachment from the pre-1999 politics of stubbornness; but it remained resolute that Kosovo was an integral part of Serbia, as Resolution 1244 prescribed. For the Serbian authorities, the UN-led mediation process was supposed to provide sufficient assurances that Kosovo could not secede from Serbia, because it would violate Resolution 1244, which directly identified Kosovo as an integral part of Serbia. They also warned that any decision made by the UN envoy had to be in line with the UN Charter that unquestionably guaranteed the inviolability of the borders of a sovereign state. Thus for the Serbian side, the UN was vested with the essential level of legitimacy required to prescribe future behavior deriving from norms (i.e., the UN Charter and the Resolution 1244) that officials in Belgrade viewed as necessary in the upcoming process.

On the other side, transformed UCK leaders expected formalization of the actual situation on the ground, in which Kosovo was already developing all necessary institutions for a functioning independent state and Serbia had not had any influence since 1999. Thus authorities in Kosovo also perceived UN involvement to be a mechanism through which the mediation process would gain more legitimacy because the new contextual factors that were conditioning the ongoing mediation process were a direct normative product of the UN and its specialized bodies. They assumed that the UN would not neglect the reality on the ground which itself had been set up by the UN administration of the province. It was clear that both sides maintained the unyielding positions of their previous administrations that, again, were extremely difficult to reconcile.

The mediation process

Ahtisaari realized that the only way to reduce the gap between the two sides was if he could structure the negotiations in such a way that 'technical' issues, which were causing less friction, were tackled first. This way both sides would provide concessions, which would later pave the way to finding a solution to the last remaining question regarding final status. He set up a timeframe for talks and stressed his expectation that negotiations would be concluded in 2006. The technical issues that were to be tackled were: decentralization; community rights; protection of the Serbian Orthodox Church; state property claims; and debt. The official talks started on February 20, 2006 in Vienna, where Ahtisaari and his team (UNOSEK) had their headquarters. Once again, the selection of the location of the talks was an indication that the issue was of primary concern to the European members of the Contact Group and that it was expected that, through the EU, they would be able to create incentives for both sides to agree on a negotiated settlement. The EU policies were perceived as the main carrot in the process, as both Serbia and Kosovo declared their commitment to the EU integration process.

The talks were conducted less expediently than was initially expected. In five rounds of talks, substantial differences between the two sides surfaced. The Kosovo delegation was initially extremely reluctant to talk about decentralization, unless the issue of status was addressed first. On the other side, the Serbian delegation, which was getting signals from the Contact Group that Kosovo was going to be granted conditional and monitored independence, wanted to stall the talks as much as possible and use that time to lobby within the Contact Group, especially with the Russian officials, emphasizing their legalistic approach towards the issue. Nevertheless, signals that were coming from Western capitals and Moscow were not encouraging. France was the first member of the Contact Group that indirectly warned Serbia that its legalistic approach toward Kosovo's independence would not find support and that it needed to face reality (ICG, 2006a). Soon after that, Italy advised Serbia to realize that conditional independence would be the main topic of the talks in Vienna. Finally, in late 2005, Russia made it clear to Serbia that Moscow would not be drawn "into confrontation with the West over Kosovo" and that they would not veto a new Security Council resolution that would promote independence, given that might be the outcome of the negotiation process (ICG 2006a, 11).

Under considerable pressure from the outside, the Kosovo delegation started making concessions regarding decentralization, protection of minority rights, and the Serbian Orthodox Church. These concessions, however, were met with increased signaling from the Contact Group – on several occasions it was unofficially announced that there was consensus within the Contact Group on the final status and that the people of Kosovo should be prepared for independence (B92 2006). And while the Kosovo delegation was complimented for its efforts to find a compromise, the Serbian delegation was warned for its inflexibility in negotiations. The fact was that the Serbian delegation did not even have a platform for negotiations until the end of March, so despite the fact that their procrastination might have appeared tactical, it was primarily unintentional. However, once the platform was presented, the Serbian delegation demonstrated a certain desire to compromise by offering a formula, "less than independence more than autonomy" for Kosovo as part of Serbia. According to Serbian Foreign Minister Drašković, in light of the new reality on the ground and the change of political elites in Belgrade, the Serbian government was ready to accept that it did not have authority over Kosovo and that Kosovo would be able to retain 95% of its own control and administration, while only issues of foreign affairs and the military would be in the domain of Serbia, or as he put it: "Kosovo can get everything apart from a separate seat in the UN" (Drašković 2006). Ironically, the Serbian delegation was now offering the same platform that the Rambouillet accords prescribed, which was callously rejected by Milošević.

As the time for negotiations was running out, the mediators were becoming well aware that it was highly unlikely that they would achieve a negotiated settlement on Kosovo's final status. It was clear that once Kosovo officials were aware of the fact that independence was imminent, they would become impatient, less disposed to negotiate, and would start to urge the international community to formalize their new status. On the other hand, high officials from Serbia, also realizing the inevitability of independence for Kosovo, stated that recognizing Kosovo was not an option, was equal to political and national suicide for every politician in the country, and that no one was likely to assume that responsibility (Jeremić 2006).

Emergence of diverging interests within the contact group

Once the mediators realized that all opportunities to achieve a mutually acceptable settlement were exhausted, they decided to delegate the issue to the UN Security Council to "impose independence" (ICG 2006b) through a superseding resolution. At that moment, within the Contact Group, initial fractions were emerging. The Quint (the informal group of Western members of the Contact Group) was well aware that the Serbian side was correct in its reassertions that the Security Council could not declare Kosovo independent because it was against the UN Charter to violate a member state's sovereignty and territorial integrity. For this reason, they tried to establish a method through which using a new Security Council resolution, the settlement might be imposed. The most uncertain factor at that moment was Russia's stance. Russian tacit consent for Kosovo's independence was challenged when the Financial Times ran a story that Russia and China would not block the independence of Kosovo (Financial Times 2006). According to Ahtissari, "the leak forced Russia to take a more principled stand" (Ahtisaari quoted in Phillips 2012, 163). Russia started claiming that it would not support any settlement that would be imposed on Serbia and that the outcome should be acceptable to both sides. Despite the fact that Russia signed the London Ministerial Statement, this dissent derived from Moscow's newly formulated foreign policy interests, which once again sent very confusing signals to both Serbia and the rest of the Contact Group. The Contact Group members were confident that Russia was inclined to benefit from the precedent established by Kosovo's independence by securing international recognition of 'friendly mini-states' – Abkhazia, South Ossetia and Transdniestria – which would break away from Georgia and Moldova using Kosovo as a model (ICG 2006b). Despite the fact that Russia had a significant interest in having Kosovo be a negative precedent, publicly it renounced it, stating that "if Kosovo's independence is recognized despite Serbia's will, this will create a very negative precedent in international relations" and that it was ready to use its veto power in the event that the Kosovo solution did not conform to Russia's interests (Lavrov quoted in ICG 2006b, 2). Obviously, Serbia understood this as explicit support for its position and consequently hardened its stance.

Given the new developments, the rest of the Contact Group aimed to reduce friction and prevent a potential domino effect, by arguing that the Kosovo case was unique and that it could not provide a blueprint for other secessions and self-determination claims (ICG 2006b, 2). The first compromise within the group was formulated in the New York Statement, in which ministers looked forward to a "durable solution to the last major issue related to the break-up of Yugoslavia" (Contact Group New York Statement 2006). Following this statement, and recognizing that the opportunities for negotiations had been exhausted, Ahtisaari decided to present a comprehensive settlement package to the Contact Group. Given the potential discomfort of Russians with the term independence, he opted for a document that would imply independence only in substance, while refraining from using the actual word. The settlement's lack of direct reference to independence was intended to curtail resistance and improve the chances of its acceptance by all members of the Contact Group and by both conflicting sides, and "postpone any discord until a later point in the process" (ICG 2006b, 3).

The presentation of the document was scheduled for September 2006, but it was postponed until February 2007 due to parliamentary elections in Serbia and the Contact Group's fear that even implicit consideration of Kosovo's independence would result in yet another actor transformation in Serbia, but this time a less constructive one. Serbia interpreted statements coming from Russia as an indicator of a lack of consensus within the coalition. As such, it represented an opportunity to stall the process and delay the formation of government as long as possible until May 2007, in order to avoid being blamed for 'losing' Kosovo, with the expectation that the Contact Group would be less inclined to impose a resolution without an executive authority in Serbia (ICG 2007a, 7). Ahtisaari presented two documents to the Secretary General: the Proposal – an outline for state formation that harmonized the idea of an internationally supervised entity and an independent state – and the report on the reasons behind the proposal. He explained his position as follows:

> For the past eight years, Kosovo and Serbia have been governed in complete separation. The establishment of the United Nations Mission in Kosovo (UNMIK) pursuant to resolution 1244 (1999), and its assumption of all

legislative, executive and judicial authority throughout Kosovo, has created a situation in which Serbia has not exercised any governing authority over Kosovo. This is a reality one cannot deny; it is irreversible. A return of Serbian rule over Kosovo would not be acceptable to the overwhelming majority of the people of Kosovo. Belgrade could not regain its authority without provoking violent opposition. Autonomy of Kosovo within the borders of Serbia – however notional such autonomy may be – is simply not tenable.... Upon careful consideration of Kosovo's recent history, the realities of Kosovo today and taking into account the negotiations with the parties, I have come to the conclusion that the only viable option for Kosovo is independence, to be supervised for an initial period by the international community.

(S/2007/168 2007)

The UN Security Council held a closed meeting on March 19, 2007, at which all the diverging interests and perceptions were brought to light. For the Western countries of the Contact Group, both the proposal and the report were supposed to be accepted because Kosovo urgently needed a sustainable solution to its status and any delay would lead to instability. The Russian delegation, however, proposed the retention of Resolution 1244 with selective implementation of parts of the proposal. It also rejected any notion of time running out for Kosovo and objected to making a rushed decision. Most importantly, Russia accused Ahtisaari of conducting shallow and abbreviated negotiations (ICG 2007a, 6).

Russian refusal to accept the proposal formulated by Ahtisaari suggests that in the event that mediation efforts conducted (and coordinated) by an international organization are not compatible with a powerful state's interest, the mediation effort is less likely to be successful. At the same time, the lack of success can be attributed to a lack of convergence of interests between Russia and the rest of the Contact Group, which conferred the necessary level of legitimacy to the UN envoy to formulate and, if needed, impose a solution on their behalf as well. Ahtisaari, argued that the general deterioration of relations between Russia and the US, on the global level, led to the Russian resistance to accept his proposal in the Security Council. Thus, the deadlock was less related to the negotiation process and more to the bilateral relations between these two states (Vesti 2012). Lack of convergence of interests once again led the process to a deadlock. Finally, while initial indications of a convergence of interests within the Contact Group induced Serbia to start realizing that Kosovo's independence was imminent; eventual Russian defection from the rest of the Contact Group induced the Serbian government not to accept Ahtisaari's proposal and to start stalling the process.

The additional attempt to mediate by the Troika

Diverging ideas on the process between mediators

Faced with Russian dissent, the US, UK, and France decided to stop drafting a new Security Council resolution. French president Sarkozy proposed another round of talks, this time conducted by the Troika – US, Russia, and the EU – in order to accommodate Russian demands that negotiations needed to continue until both sides found a mutually acceptable solution. For the first time in the Kosovo conflict, the EU assumed the role of the actor with the most responsibility for the process. The talks took place in Brussels. The role of the EU was to balance the opposing stances of the US and Russia, and using a 'formulator' role, thereby trying to ensure that every conceivable solution would be taken into consideration. Just as Ahtisaari had, the Troika avoided talking about status issues, but rather focused on cooperation and future relations between Serbia and Kosovo. A 14-point document was proposed which outlined that special relations between the two sides were based on the principles that: (a) Belgrade will not govern nor re-establish a physical presence in Kosovo; (b) it will not interfere in Priština's relations with international financial institutions nor hamper Kosovo's EU stabilization and association process; and finally, (c) that it accepts Kosovo's complete integration in regional bodies, especially economic institutions (Troika Proposal 2007). Once again, the mediators were confronted with unyielding positions on both sides. While Belgrade insisted that negotiations should focus on substantial autonomy for Kosovo, Priština considered independence to be non-negotiable and wanted to negotiate its post-status relations.

However, the lack of consensus on how the negotiations should be conducted was not just between Belgrade and Priština any longer. This time, mediators had highly opposing views on the format of talks. The EU representative, Wolfgang Ischinger, who proposed the 14 points, assumed a much more formal role, using the 'formulator' strategy. His idea was that the Troika talks should leave 'no stone unturned' in the search for a compromise agreement "which even if only partial could have shifted some responsibility from Western capitals to Belgrade and Priština" (ICG 2007b). On the other hand, the Russian diplomat Aleksandr Botsan-Kharchenko translated his country's position of "not imposing a settlement" into a 'communicator' strategy, claiming that the two sides needed to find a compromise on their own and that the mediators should only facilitate the talks. The differences in positions on the format of talks undoubtedly reflected the diverging interests between the mediators, who obviously did not share the same idea of a solution to the conflict. The lack of shared ideas between mediators directly affected their coordination. During the negotiations, mediators rarely offered joint proposals; more often individual suggestions were made that were openly rejected during official talks by other mediators.

Lack of cooperation between mediators

Initially, mediators agreed to 'suggest' an 'Ahtisaari-plus plan' to both parties, implying a loose association or union between Serbia and Kosovo, which aimed to complement the plan for internal governance contained in Ahtisaari's proposal. The 'suggestion' was made informally at first, in order to explore the positions on both sides regarding the proposed 'association of states' model. For Priština, this represented an 'Ahtisaari minus plan,' since it shrunk political independence in exchange for an extremely 'interdependent' relationship with Belgrade and access to global financial institutions. For Serbian officials, the association of states model was absolutely unacceptable as it formulated 'independence by another name' (ICG 2007b, 4). Despite such positions, all Western capitals urged Ischinger to present this model officially because, apparently, there was little hope for compromise and mediators needed to assume a much more directive role. However, Russia blocked the official presentation and the Troika had to compromise for a vaguer 'neutral status' proposal, according to which Serbia and Kosovo would concur on instruments for stabilizing their relations "prior to and regardless of the ultimate status decision" (ICG 2007b, 4). It was obvious that mediation was not going forward at all. Under these conditions, the mediation process became not only a reconciliation process between Belgrade and Priština, but also a process of appeasement between the three mediators. The difficulty of reconciling US, Russian, and European positions was evident until the end of talks, which directly hampered the Contact Group from issuing any clear recommendation to the UN Secretary-General. On December 10th, after two years of negotiations and eight years after the first international involvement, the Troika officially declared negotiations exhausted without reaching a compromise.

The failure of the Contact Group to formulate a common platform was a direct result of the fact that its member states did not share a common interest in reaching a solution to the Kosovo problem. As a consequence, their inability to negotiate an agreement amongst themselves led the peace process to a deadlock, as neither party in the conflict was willing to compromise any further.

Notes

1 An earlier version of this chapter was published as a case study in Vuković (2012).
2 According to Phillips,

> The U.S. government had not formally designated the KLA as a foreign terrorist organization (FTO). Therefore, the State Department was taken by surprise when Gelbard called KLA a terrorist organization at his Belgrade press conference. According to his senior adviser, Stuart Seldowitz, "Gelbard just slipped. He said what he taught. Bob never said he was wrong about this – or anything." Sonja Biserko, head of the Helsinki Committee for Human Rights in Serbia, confronted Gelbard at a meeting of Serbian civil society leaders on the afternoon of his press conference. "If you call them terrorists, what do you call then Belgrade's state terror?" Gelbard later pronounced, "I know a terrorist when I see one, and these men are terrorists." Gelbard went as far to call the KLA an Islamic terrorist organization after the U.S. embassies in Kenya and Tanzania were bombed.
>
> (Phillips 2012, 87)

3 When Milosevic tried to alter the proposed offer, Chernomyrdin made it clear that the deal was non-negotiable, while Ahtisaari emphasized that Blair was prepared to issue an ultimatum and request a UNSC approval for a ground invasion (Ker-Lindsay 2009, 15; Phillips 2012, 113).
4 For a discussion on Responsibility to Protect see Bellamy (2006) and Evans (2008).

7 Sri Lanka[1]

One of the most violent and intractable conflicts in Asia, fought for decades between Sri Lankan Tamil rebel forces and the government of Sri Lanka,[2] ended on the battlefield. On May 18, 2009, following the killing of Velupillai Prabhakaram, the leader of Liberation Tigers of Tamil Eelam (LTTE), the government officially declared that "the war against the terrorists is now over" (statement taken from Goodhand and Korf 2011, 1). The conflict, which officially started in 1983 following pogroms against Tamil civilians, had resulted in more than 70,000 casualties and hundreds of thousands displaced persons as of 2006 (ICG 2006a). Early peace initiatives – including the Thimpu talks in 1985, the Indo-Lanka Accord in 1987,[3] the Premadasa/LTTE talks in 1989–1990, the Kumaratunga/LTTE talks in 1994–1995 – yielded only modest advances and failed to lead to a significant breakthrough in bridging the differences between the parties and brokering a peaceful solution to the conflict. The fifth and final peace process, the focus of this chapter, the Wickremesinghe/LTTE–Rajapaksa/LTTE talks, which consisted of six rounds of talks in 2003 and two in 2006, managed to generate a cease-fire agreement (CFA), but became obsolete in 2006 when both parties resumed military activities. According to a UN report, in the tragic events that followed, 40.000 civilians lost their lives (UN Report on Sri Lanka 2012, 14).

The final peacemaking efforts were highly internationalized. They included numerous external actors in possession of both tactical and strategic means. Each actor had particular leverage at its disposal and a set of alliances within Sri Lankan society, allowing for the possibility of strategic complementarity among them (Goodhand 2006a, 39–40). However, as the following chapter will illustrate, the absence of strategic interests on the part of external actors that would motivate the parties to conduct a coordinated peacemaking effort contributed to its failure. This was certainly not the only reason for failure; many other studies have emphasized the lack of actual ripeness and the conflicting parties' unwillingness to compromise as the main sources of failure (Sisk 2009, Goodhand *et al.* 2011, Svensson 2014). Nevertheless, the following chapter explores the relevance of the interests of external actors with respect to the coordination of their activities and the application of the required leverage in order to guide the conflicting parties toward a mutually acceptable solution. The mediation process was formally led by Norway and was backed by a coalition of donor states. The supporting states were able to generate important financial incentives, but were unable to balance those rewards with meaningful 'sticks.' Given the conflicting parties' intransigent attitudes throughout the process, mediation required external states to 'play heavy.' Although the external actors indicated their willingness to work together, the requisite convergence of interests between them was never achieved during the process because the conflict was not strategically significant enough to induce them to apply all the (most costly) leverage at their disposal.

Nature of the conflict

Sources of intractability and the employment of repressive measures

In the context of the end of British colonial rule and rapidly growing Sinhala nationalism, the intensification of the Sri Lankan conflict commenced with the new constitution of 1948. Rotberg notes that the constitution "lacked a bill of rights like India's," or anything that could provide "effective formal protection for minorities" (1999, 5). The state's discriminatory policies, like the 'Sinhala Only Bill' that replaced English with Sinhalese as the only official language, led to anti-Tamil riots in 1956, followed by more violent riots in 1958. As a reaction, various Tamil militant groups became active, most notably the LTTE, founded in 1976 and led by Velupillai Prabhakaran. They were created in reaction to the 1972 constitutional changes, which prescribed Buddhism as the country's primary religion and Sinhalese as the official national language (Sisk 2009; see Stewart 2002 on the socio-economic consequences of these policies). The LTTE was able to successfully formulate the nationalistic ideology of the Tamils and develop a parallel economic system within the territories it controlled. The central goal of the LTTE was the establishment of an independent country, the Tamil homeland called Eelam. Rotberg argues that "by the time the war begun the Sri Lankan society had become irredeemably polarized" (1999, 7). As Tamil frustrations grew, periodic episodes of violence, such as the riots of 1977 and 1981, aggravated the already strained relations between the two communities. By 1983, violence had spread to Colombo, where hundreds of Tamils were killed by Sinhala mobs "with the tacit tolerance of security forces" (Sisk 2009, 152). The riots were provoked by ambiguous reports that the LTTE had killed 13 Sri Lankan army personnel in the area of Jaffna, inducing retaliation by the army, which resulted in 44 Tamils being killed (Sisk 2009, 152). Human Rights Watch argued that the events were orchestrated, as "the police and soldiers stood by and watched as Tamils were attacked ... in some cases they perpetrated the acts themselves ... the violence was well organized and politically supported ... high ranking officials, including government ministers were accused of orchestrating the violence" (1995, 88). The notorious 1983 riots prompted thousands of Tamils to flee Sri Lanka and find refuge in India and Western countries. Tamil refugees established a large and vibrant diaspora, which soon became a crucial to supporting and financing LTTE anti-government activities (DeVotta 2007, 77). The epilogue of the 1983 riots was full-fledged warfare between the Sinhalese dominated government and the Tamil community.

Failed peace processes

According to Sisk, a history of failed peace processes[4] contributed to the conflict's intractability (Sisk 2009, 153). The core political issues were largely marginalized by humanitarian, logistical and military issues (Rupesinghe 2006c). The conflicting parties used the negotiations for their own purposes like buying time to rearm themselves and "reconstitute the conflict," while making sure to "discover new differences" through negotiations (Uyangoda 2007, viii). Even in instances in which the government showed modest signs of a willingness to compromise, the opposition parties led by the Buddhist clergy played a crucial role in preventing them from formulating concrete proposals (Biswas 2006, 54). The LLTE, for its part, continued rearming itself and refused to rely solely on negotiations in their dealings with the government. As Biswas observes, the fact that the government was unable or unwilling to articulate tangible incentives to Tamils, along with the LTTE's lack of commitment to the peace process, resulted in an environment where "facilitative intervention does create room for talks but no agreement is reached" (Biswas 2006, 59).

A number of pivotal developments ripened the overall situation and led to the 2002–2006 peace process. At the international level, the post-9/11 environment significantly affected the LTTE's calculations. Before the terrorist attacks on the Twin Towers in New York, thanks to powerful lobbying support from the Tamil diaspora, the LTTE managed to promote itself as a freedom fighting organization created to protect the Tamil minority from the systemic harassment that the Sri Lankan government had been perpetuating for decades. Even though the LTTE's tactics prompted some powerful states with large Tamil diasporas to list it as a terrorist organization prior to 9/11 – India placed it on the terrorist list in 1992, the United States did the same in 1997 and the UK followed suit in February 2001 – the full weight of the label was brought to bear after 9/11, as the LTTE started "fighting a losing struggle to be recognized as a legitimate actor in the international community" (Höglund and Svensson 2007, 107). As Paikiasothy Saravanamuttu, head of the local non-governmental organization (NGO) Centre for Policy Alternatives, points out, "11 September impacted the LTTE's political psyche and its room for manoeuvre internationally in respect of funds, legitimacy and acquisition of weapons" (Saravanamuttu 2003, 132). The shifting international conditions became increasingly burdensome for the LTTE and it struggled to maintain its image of being a group of freedom fighters and to secure a steady influx of financial support from its diaspora and NGOs in Western countries. These new realities prompted the LTTE to amend its approach and explore the possibility of reaching a negotiated solution.[5]

Domestically, the country was suffering from an economic recession, further aggravated by the escalation of belligerent activities in 1999–2001. The population was becoming increasingly exhausted and dejected as a result of the prolonged conflict. By the end of 2001, the economic hardship and escalating conflict contributed to the government's fall. The December 2001 elections were won by a coalition of parties called United National Front (UNF), headed by Ranil Wickremesinghe and his United National Party (UNP). Wickremesinghe, who became the Prime Minister and stayed in that position from 2001 until 2004, is often credited as the architect of the peace process. Chandrika Bandaranaike Kumaratunga, whose Sri Lanka Freedom Party (SLFP) lost the elections and the control over the government, remained president, setting the groundwork for an uneasy partnership.

Multiparty mediation process

Upon taking office, Wickremesinghe and his UNF government set their three main priorities: (1) reviving the country's economy with the help of external donors; (2) signing a cease-fire agreement that recognizes that there are two armies in the country controlling different parts of the territory; and (3) opening negotiations with the LTTE through a peace process that would have an institutionalized role for external actors (Bastian 2008, 84). A cease-fire agreement was reached in February 2002. To ensure the end of hostilities, the agreement established the Sri Lankan Monitoring Mission (SLMM) – composed of five Nordic countries: Norway, Sweden, Finland, Denmark, and Iceland – which was assigned a mandate to monitor the implementation of the cease-fire between the parties and, if needed, to assist the parties by facilitating the resolution of disputes over its implementation.[6] With a cease-fire in place, the LTTE and the government held six rounds of direct negotiations between September 2002 and March 2003.

Even prior to the signing of the CFA, the international community was making efforts to link aid to the peace process (Shanmugaratnam and Stokke, 2004: 14; see also Goodhand and Klem 2005; Bastian 2006). Initially, the most active donors were Japan, the World Bank and the Asian Development Bank. When Wickremesinghe took office, he made it clear that the fragile peace in Sri Lanka could be preserved and advanced only with the international community's support. Although his UNF government insisted on international involvement prior to the signing of the CFA, the end of hostilities bolstered the willingness of very important external actors to take a more active role in the donor community. Based on the UNF's political strategy, the United States, Japan and the EU joined the Norwegian-led peace process in a more institutionalized manner as donor co-chairs. As Bastian noted, the process was now supported by a 'superpower,' Sri Lanka's major trading partners, and its largest donor (Bastian 2006, 247).

The rapid developments in the peace process provided enough reason for the external actors to perceive the Sri Lankan case as an 'easy win' (Goodhand 2006b). Following the signing of the cease-fire agreement, there was noticeable progress toward peace. As reported by Sisk, the six rounds of talks "were initially encouraging: they covered the principal issues of power sharing, federalism and devolution (i.e., the terms of autonomy), development finance and aid, child soldiers, and in Japan in March 2003 a possible joint character of human rights" (Sisk 2009, 159). In fact, with the CFA in place, the parties managed to create considerable momentum. Through a series of unprecedented compromises, they agreed (albeit only nominally) to a decommissioning of weapons, opening of roads and civilian air traffic in conflict-affected areas, the exchange of prisoners and the end of a governmental ban on the LTTE (Sisk 2009, 159). The last concession, which satisfied the rebel group's key demand, prompted the LTTE to assume a more compromising approach. A major breakthrough was achieved in December 2002, following a conference in Oslo, when the two sides announced an important rapprochement by declaring a mutual willingness to explore the federal option as a solution to their ongoing conflict. The statement expressed the parties' readiness to "to explore a solution founded on the principle of internal self-determination in areas of historical habitation of the Tamils peaking people based on a federal structure within a united Sri Lanka" (*Daily Mirror* 2002). For the first time, a federal solution became acceptable to both sides, indicating the LTTE's abandonment of its earlier separatist aspirations (Höglund and Svensson 2006).

The gradually emerging rapprochement between the two conflicting sides in 2002 provided sufficient reason for external actors to "prioritize peacebuilding because it appeared to be a low risk-high opportunity situation" (Goodhand 2006a, 15). The perception of the conflict as being an 'easy win' may have conditioned the external actors to focus primarily on achieving short-term success. Uyangoda noted that it appeared as if the international community was approaching the peacemaking process "as an exercise that should produce an early peace deal" (Uyangoda 2006, 4). Initially, all the external actors involved in the peacemaking process (Norway, the EU and Japan) with the exception of the United States were willing to engage with the LTTE. Nevertheless, even the United States, formally constrained by its rigid post-9/11 anti-terrorist foreign policy objectives, still praised the LTTE's commitment to the peace process and signalled "that a change in LTTE behaviour could lead to a change in the U.S. approach" (Lunstead 2007, 16).[7]

Involvement of international actors and their interests in the conflict

Norway

Norway was first country approached to facilitate the talks in September 1999 (Bullion 2001, 76). Its political and economic stability, absence of a colonial heritage and its lack of specific geopolitical interests in Sri Lanka, made Norway a suitable candidate in the eyes of the conflicting parties (Ram 2001). These characteristics also helped Norway become accepted by important regional actors: India for instance, did not perceive Norwegian involvement as a threat to its own strategic interests in the region (Moolakkattu 2005). Norway is also a country that is home to a sizable Tamil diaspora and one whose prior presence in

Sri Lanka amounted to a number of development and social service projects (Bullion 2001, 77). These long-term development projects helped Norway to establish personal contacts with relevant actors on the ground, cultivating Norwegian interest in engaging in the peacemaking process (Rupesinghe 2006b). Moreover, Norway has a strong track record based on its significant contribution to some of the most complex mediation processes around the globe in the 1990s, including the Oslo Accords (1993); Guatemala (1996); Haiti, Sudan, Cyprus and Kosovo (1999); and Colombia (2000) (Bullion 2001, 76). Maintaining its reputation as a peacemaking and 'great moral' power has been very important to Norway's self-perception (Höglund and Svensson 2009, 179). For a relatively small and distant Nordic country, peacemaking offers the opportunity to assume a more significant role in international affairs (Moolakkattu 2005; Höglund and Svensson 2009). While reputational concerns may explain the Norwegian intent to maintain a presence in Sri Lanka even after the peace process collapsed, these were certainly not the only motivations behind Norway's initial involvement in 1999. In fact, at that time, it was difficult to predict that a regime change and a subsequent successful start of the peace process would take place that would also attract the involvement of other players.

In the context of previous mediation activities, Norway preferred to sustain an approach characterized by the creation of back channels for secret negotiations where the responsibility for success of the facilitated talks remained with the conflicting parties themselves (Joenniemi 2014, 127). As a lead mediator in Sri Lanka, Norway departed from its traditional inclination to maintain a supportive and low-profile role away from public scrutiny (Kelleher and Taulbee 2005, 80). Officially, Norwegian mediators maintained that their role was primarily to facilitate the talks. In reality, they did much more: their activities ranged from facilitating communication between the two sides, to playing a more assertive role in formulating the cease-fire agreement and the Oslo Declaration and a manipulator role by creating positive incentives through financial aid. Nevertheless, from the onset of the peace process, Norway preferred to present itself as a 'postman,' employed to convey crucial information necessary to finding common ground between the parties (Economist 2001). This also meant that the responsibility for the outcome was with the conflicting parties and not with the Norwegian mediators. Erik Slheim, who was appointed as a special adviser to the Norwegian Department of Foreign Affairs in March 2000 and assumed the facilitator role once the UNF government took office in December 2001, pointed out that "it has to be remembered that at the end of the day President Mahinda Rajapaksha and the LTTE leader Prabhakaran will decide. If they want peace, we are here to assist. If they want war, there is nothing we can do" (Rupesinghe 2006b, 344–345; Bullion 2001). The Sri Lankan government also supported this approach. Sri Lanka Foreign Minister Lakshman Kadirgamar explained their expectations:

> But when it comes to substantive negotiation, the Norwegians will have no particular role at all. They will have no mandate to propose solutions. They

will certainly have no mandate to make any judgmental decisions. In that sense, they're not arbitrators, they're not judges, they're not mediators.

(Ram 2001)

The strategy of delegating ownership of the peace process to the conflicting parties was later criticized as a source of Norway's decreased legitimacy and leverage which might have prevented the conflict from escalating once the talks reached a deadlock (Höglund and Svensson 2009). Another criticism of this approach speaks to an incompatibility between the process conducted by a neutral, low-key facilitator and the collectivist culture of Asia, which caused confusion for the parties involved (Moolakkattu 2005).

Norway also aimed to establish a 'joint work principle' or *dugnad* with other relevant international actors (Joenniemi 2014, 128). This strategy was first transformed into the UNF government platform. As a result, the Unites States as a global power, the EU as Sri Lanka's biggest trading partner and Japan as its biggest donor became the co-chairs of the process. While India was not participating in an official capacity, Norway was careful to obtain India's consent for the various steps taken throughout the process. For this reason, the two countries maintained regular consultations on the progress of the peacemaking process. Norway was also very keen to maintain its image of being an impartial third party, able to maintain an equidistant relationship with both conflicting sides. However, upholding the image of an impartial third party in asymmetric conflicts is a very challenging task (Höglund and Svensson 2009). By treating both parties equally, Norway granted legitimacy to the LTTE, something that was never welcomed by the Sinhala nationalists. At the same time, this meant dealing with a rebel group with whom a majority of Norwegian allies would never have wanted to engage, at least not formally (Martin 2006, 126). Throughout the process, Norway was often criticized for being in favor of the LTTE. This was most certainly exacerbated by the LTTE's enthusiastic comments, calling them 'the white tigers' (Martin 2006, 113).

Despite mounting criticism, Norway remained patient with the conflicting parties, an attitude that was characteristic of its previous mediation endeavors. The Norwegian delegation was well aware that criticism was inevitable. As one of the delegates put it: "If you want to get involved in this process, you should not expect not to get your fingers burned, you should expect to get them electrocuted" (Martin 2006, 116). Norwegians resisted the pressure coming from the Sinhala nationalists and local media, even when their embassy in Colombo was besieged by protesters carrying coffins with dead bodies inside and burning the Norwegian flag (ICG 2006a). Norwegian resolve in the process was mainly exhibited in its use of low-key, non-intrusive tactical power. However, it became clear that under such intractable conditions, in order to keep the parties committed, the process required a significant degree of strategic strength. Since Norway was unable to muster the necessary carrots and sticks on its own, it brought in other external players capable of lending the necessary leverage.

United States

The track record of US involvement in peacemaking processes unequivocally demonstrates that it is both willing and able to employ its manipulative strength. American assertiveness in various conflicts has bolstered the perception that if and when the US is involved, it is most likely to due to a veiled interest it has in that specific area. Moreover, this strategically-driven involvement also compounds the expectation that the US will put its strategic leverage to use. However, in the case of Sri Lanka, the US did not have any "significant strategic interests" (Lunstead 2007, 11). First of all, the two countries had neither a historical legacy nor particularly well-developed economic relations. US development assistance had been gradually decreasing since the early 1990s and was expected to decline significantly from around US$5 million annually in 2001–2004, to US$2 million in 2005 (USAID 2000). Second, the Tamil diaspora in the US, which amounted to approximately 35.000 people, was not large enough to have significant sway over US foreign policy priorities (Bandarage 2009, 21). Third, given its proximity to hotspots in central Asia and its geostrategic position in the Indian Ocean, there was speculation that the US might have a military interest in using Trincomalee Harbor and related runway facilities in Sri Lanka (Noyahr 2006). However, as Jeffrey Lunstead, the US ambassador to Sri Lanka in 2003–2006, stated when comparing Trincomalee to Singapore, where the US Navy had already established its presence: "Singapore is ideal because of its internal stability, its superb facilities and infrastructure, and its position. Trincomalee currently lacks all of these, and is unlikely to gain any of them in the foreseeable future" (Lunstead 2007, 11). Furthermore, even within South Asia, US strategic interests are focused on two nuclear powers – India and Pakistan – and on Afghanistan in relation to the fight against al-Qaeda (Kronstadt 2004, Lunstead 2007). As economic and military relations with India had been improving, the US was careful enough not to challenge Indian requests to preserve regional primacy. The two countries held routine meetings at which they discussed the situation in Sri Lanka. According to Lunstead, this spirit of consultation was strengthened because they viewed the conflict in a similar fashion: Sri Lanka's unity and territorial integrity should be preserved, the Tamil community in Sri Lanka had legitimate grievances that the government had to address and the LTTE had to renounce terrorism and enter into a political process (Lunstead 2007, 25). Nevertheless, Lunstead also emphasized:

> This atmosphere of consultation and cooperation should not be misunderstood. It was much more consultation than cooperation. The two countries discussed their understanding of the situation in Sri Lanka and their policies. They did not attempt to develop joint policies or operations. This was not some type of U.S.–India condominium with regard to Sri Lanka. It was in many ways a "non-confliction" exercise to ensure the two sides did not work at cross purposes.
>
> (Lunstead 2007, 25–26)

Finally, despite the fact that in the post-9/11 period, US foreign policy interests were strongly shaped by the ongoing 'war on terror,' the LTTE was seen as a *local* terrorist organization, whose relations with global terrorist groups was either insignificant or non-existent and, as such, its ability to endanger US interests was marginal (Lunstead 2007).

In light of the evident absence of strategic interests, Lunstead explains American involvement as the result of two parallel developments: Sri Lanka's new government was openly pro-Western (and pro-free market) and the US Deputy Secretary of State Richard Armitage had a personal interest in participating in the peace process (Lunstead 2007, 13). In a speech delivered in Washington in February 2003, Armitage asked a rhetorical question, "Why should the United States invest significant attention and resources to Sri Lanka, especially at a time when we have such overwhelming competing interests?" (Armitage 2003, 89). While noting that "it would be tough to make a truly convincing case by sticking to the terms of strict self-interest," his answer was quite unambiguous: "because it can be done. And because it is the right thing to do. Because the parties to the conflict appear to be ready to reach a resolution, more so than at any other time in the past twenty years" (Armitage 2003, 89). The notion that 'it can be done' was reiterated by another participant at that conference, the former US ambassador to Sri Lanka, Teresita Schaffer, who promoted the view that "there was the real possibility of success" (Noyahr 2006, 373). Evidently, in the eyes of US policy makers, the situation in Sri Lanka was ripe for resolution. The perception of an 'easy win' had a dual effect. On the one hand, it prompted the US and other international actors to participate in the peace process (Goodhand 2006a, 2006b). On the other, however, as the process became more difficult to manage, the elusiveness of the 'easy win' contributed to more reluctant participation by external actors.

According to Frerks and Klem, the US endorsed a threefold approach: "pressuring the LTTE, engaging with the government and supporting activities aimed at peaceful transformation" (2006, 43). The US had very limited engagement with the LTTE. Ever since the LTTE was designated a foreign terrorist organization in 1997, the US was unable to provide it with any tangible assistance. Furthermore, in the post-9/11 environment, it was politically unimaginable to meet directly with representatives of a terrorist organization. For this reason, the US never held direct talks with the LTTE. At the same time, the US maintained its support of the government of Sri Lanka. It was the only co-chair that provided military assistance to the government. Even though this assistance never achieved a significant level, for the LTTE, it was still a factor that diminished the possibility of a compromise (Lunstead 2007). Initially, the lack of US engagement with the LTTE still contributed to the 'good cop–bad cop' approach: while the US maintained the role of a 'bad cop,' the EU – still willing to engage directly with the LTTE – played the role of a 'good cop' (Höglund and Svensson 2011). However, this coordination did not last long. The US decision not to allow LTTE officials to attend the Washington Development Conference in April 2003 was a pivotal moment in the peace process. This conference was a preparatory one for a much larger meeting of donors planned for June 2003 in Tokyo. The LTTE reacted by announcing their withdrawal from future direct negotiations. Although there were some claims that this incident was not a reason, but an excuse for the LTTE to walk away from the peace process, the US decision still provided that push. In its response, the US maintained that the LTTE's reasons for withdrawal were "not convincing" and "called on the Tigers to reconsider and to return to the negotiating track" (Asian Tribune 2003).

If the deterioration of the peace process was the first sign of limited (and steadily waning) US strategic interest, the second one came in January 2005 when the new Bush administration replaced Deputy Secretary Armitage with Robert Zoellick, who subsequently passed the Sri Lanka issue to Under Secretary for Political Affairs, R. Nicolas Burns. According to Lunstead, "perhaps the decline in interest was only natural; it could hardly be expected that the same degree of highly personal interest would be sustained in a new administration" (Lunstead 2007, 33). While the US was conducting two highly publicized military operations in Iraq and Afghanistan, the fact that a peace process in a small and distant country "with minimal strategic interests for the US, with a deteriorating security situation based in part on the inability of Sri Lankan political elements to cooperate," reached a deadlock was not a priority for the United States (Lunstead 2007, 33). The US maintained its presence in the peace process through the co-chairs framework, but its visible involvement did not go beyond statements of condemnation regarding the escalation of hostilities and human rights and humanitarian concerns.

The European Union

Similar to the US, The European Union was also seen as a 'reluctant co-chair' due to its unassertive engagement in Sri Lanka before and at the beginning of the peace process (Noyahr 2006, 387). Before 2002, the EU's involvement in Sri Lanka was quite minimal. By 2001, the EU Commission downgraded its delegation in Colombo to one diplomat, with a non-resident head of delegation based in Delhi. A reluctant EU delegation got involved as a co-chair only after intense lobbying on the part of the Sri Lankan government (Noyahr 2006). The "absence of major direct interests" drove the EU to "stick with the Norwegians" and keep a low profile through the peace process (Frerks and Klem 2006, 46). The lack of strong interests was also evident due to the fact that only seven out of 27 EU member states had a diplomatic mission in Sri Lanka: the UK, Sweden, the Netherlands, France, Italy, Germany and Romania. Of these countries, Sri Lanka had closest relations with its former colonizer, the UK, where 300,000 Sri Lankans lived. Other EU member states had rather small Tamil diasporas: in France there were around 100,000 Sri Lankan Tamils, 60,000 in Germany, 24,000 in Italy, 7,000 in the Netherlands, 6,000 in Sweden and 600 in Finland (Bandarage 2009, 21).

The 'good cop' role motivated the EU Commissioner on External Relations, Chris Patten, to meet with the LTTE leader, Prabhakaran (European Commission 2003). The decision did not meet with much praise: the Sri Lankan media strongly condemned the EU for the visit; the local newspapers displayed headlines such as "Keep Patten out of the country," accusing him of "bloody European gumption and insolence of the highest order" (Martin 2006, 116). The EU decision to meet with the LTTE was a direct result of its 'stick with the Norwegians' approach: prior to the visit, the Norwegian delegation issued a statement to the rest of the diplomatic community in Colombo that in order for the LTTE to become a constructive partner, it had to meet with other actors. Nevertheless, following the visit, the EU issued a denunciatory statement regarding the LTTE's human rights record and warned the group that it must comply with international human rights standards if it wished to enjoy "recognition as a political player in Sri Lanka" (Martin 2006, 128).

The 'good cop' role lost its relevance in May 2006, when the EU decided to employ one of its sticks by listing the LTTE as a terrorist organization. Officially, the decision was a response to the August 2005 assassination of Sri Lankan Foreign Minister, Kadirgamar, and other LTTE human rights violations. The Council of the EU's declaration stated that the decision should not come as a surprise to anybody and emphasized that "several warnings have already been provided to the LTTE, which the LTTE has systematically ignored" (Council of the European Union 2006). While the EU was willing to formally engage in talks with the LTTE, and despite the organization's reputation within the global 'war on terror,' it was the LTTE's specific terror tactics and methods – such as child recruitment and political killings – that resulted in grave human rights violations, that prompted the EU to assume a less accommodating attitude toward the LTTE (Ferks and Klem 2006). The actual impact of this 'stick' was quite limited. While the EU remained committed to the peace process, it focused most of its attention on issuing condemnation – both alone and in cooperation with other co-chairs – regarding humanitarian and human rights issues. It appeared as if the conflict never received much attention in Brussels. In one of its reports, the ICG argued that this was due to a 'limited geopolitical impact' of Sri Lanka's conflict, and noted how "while fighting raged in August 2006, the situation did not even reach the agenda of EU foreign ministers meeting in Brussels" (ICG 2006a, 19).

Japan

Japan, while certainly a global economic superpower, rarely took a very assertive role in global politics. In the case of Sri Lanka, it seemed as though Japan was quite content with its role as a passive donor. Nevertheless, a gradual alteration in its international positioning, prompted by increasing Chinese influence, saw Japan resort to non-economic forms of influence, such as military and diplomatic measures (Laurence 2007). Japan assumed a more conspicuous role soon after the peace talks had begun: Yasushi Akashi, a former UN undersecretary for humanitarian affairs, was appointed by the Japanese government to be a special envoy to the Sri Lankan peace process. His official title was the Representative of the Government of Japan on Peace-Building, Rehabilitation and Reconstruction of Sri Lanka. Evidently, for the Japanese, government aid was perceived as the most fundamental impetus of peaceful change. For this reason, in June 2003, Japan hosted a donors' conference at which the participants discussed ways of linking peace negotiations and international assistance for development and reconstruction in Sri Lanka (Noyahr 2006). However, as Japanese relations with Sri Lanka were mostly government oriented, this relationship had a significant impact on the peace process. Japanese aid was largely delivered through government channels and in some exceptional cases through UN agencies. As a consequence, despite the fact that Japan never banned the LTTE, the decision to channel aid through the government led Japan to refrain from directly providing any funds to the LTTE (Frerks and Klem 2006).

India

The only country with unequivocally strong strategic interests in Sri Lanka was India. For a long time, India had preferred to position itself as a regional power with the intention of limiting the influence of other external actors in South Asia (Rao 1988). Phillipson and Thangarajah note that "India has always had substantial intelligence resources in Sri Lanka, including being involved in counterinsurgency initiatives against the LTTE, whose autonomous power India seeks to crush" (Philipson and Thangarajah 2005, 47). The conflict in Sri Lanka had been affecting the political situation in India since the 1980s. Following the anti-Tamil riots in 1983, many Sri Lankan Tamils found refuge in the Indian State of Tamil Nadu, where Tamil guerrilla groups started organizing (Samaranayake 2006). In 1987, the governments of India and Sri Lanka signed the Indo-Sri Lanka Peace Accord. The agreement established the Indian Peacekeeping Force (IPKF) in Sri Lanka, which was mandated to disarm the militant groups. The mission, however, proved to be a failure, as the Indian armed forces failed to disarm the LTTE and suffered losses amounting to some 1,300 troops (Bullion 2001). This was an upsetting outcome for India: it was a clear indication of India's limited ability to apply strategic strength and perform the role of security manager in South Asia. However, it was after the LTTE-orchestrated assassination of the former Prime Minister of India Rajiv Gandhi in 1991 that India made a firm decision not to further its formal engagement in Sri Lanka's peace process. Soon after, the LTTE was declared to be a terrorist organization by Indian authorities, who issued a warrant for Prabhakaran. At the onset of the fifth peace process, Indian Foreign Secretary, Kanwal Sibal, visited Sri Lanka and admitted that though "logically we should be involved," the "legal complexities" were such that "our options are certainly limited" (Sambandan 2002). For its part, India reluctantly granted its acceptance of the Norwegian leadership of the peacemaking process, resenting the increased internationalization of an issue in its own "backyard" (Philipson and Thangarajah 2005). However, since all external actors and conflicting parties recognized India's strategic interests in Sri Lanka, India was still consulted on regular basis (Rupesinghe 2006b, 339). A CPA report noted that, as a regional power, India was still the only external actor able to perform a high-profile intervention. However, its involvement was "conditioned by the 'once bitten twice shy' effect of the IPKF experience in the late 80s" (CPA 2007, 5). The CPA also highlighted a alteration in Indian interest in Sri Lanka: as economic interests increasingly take center stage, "high profile political or in the extreme case, military intervention, carries with it the risks of upsetting and even undermining the growing economic stake" (CPA 2007, 5).

The co-chair system

At the Tokyo Conference on Reconstruction and Development of Sri Lanka, which took place in June 2003 without the LTTE's participation, the donors collectively pledged foreign aid in the amount of approximately US$4.5 billion over the four-year period between 2003–2006 and closely linked the disbursement of the aid to progress in the peace talks (Shanmugaratnam and Stokke 2004). The policy of conditionality, intended to be a big carrot, soon become a big failure for the international community, as they were unable to incentivize the parties to return to the negotiating table. First of all, neither one of the conflicting parties was truly aid dependent. Second, the conference contributed to the LTTE's mounting dissatisfaction, prompted by the perception that it was not being treated as an equal party. Moreover, the impact of international fund raising on the LTTE was limited by the fact that the organization "did not have a legally constituted instrument under its control to receive the funds for reconstruction" (Shanmugaratnam and Stokke 2004, 16). Given the fact that LTTE was banned by several important donors, it remained unclear how the organization could possibly benefit from these incentives. The policy of conditionality lost its significance in the aftermath of the tsunami that struck Sri Lanka in December 2004. As Goodhand and Klem pointed out, "the threat of withholding aid in an 'over-aided' environment will have very little effect" (2005, 14). Overall, the donors relied on 'carrots' as long as they assumed that the process was headed in a positive direction, but once success appeared more elusive, they failed to substitute the carrot with the stick (Frerks and Klem 2006, 54).

The co-chairs maintained constructive and cooperative relations. Their statements reflected a common voice. Although the co-chair framework offered the possibility of a predictable division of labor, this division was still accidental and "based purely upon the policies of the home foreign ministry and aid ministry policies, not on the needs of the peace process in Sri Lanka" (Philipson and Thangarajah 2005, 48; ICG 2006a). More importantly, it appeared that the division of labor did not reflect the various types and degrees of leverage that each actor had at its disposal. For instance, the US' close relations with the government were never put to use in delivering the government to a mutually acceptable agreement. The lack of strategic interests prevented the US from using more meaningful carrots and sticks in its dealings with the government. At the same time, the US' reluctance to work directly with the LTTE reduced the likelihood of softening up the LTTE for the peace process. In previous instances, when it was instrumental for the advancement of its strategic interests, the US had not been reluctant to engage with specific terrorist organizations. In other words, as

Lunstead pointed out, the decision not to talk to the LTTE was a policy choice and not a legal requirement (Lunstead 2007). Evidently, the limited role of the US resulted from its limited strategic interests in the conflict.

The sticks applied in the process were limited to statements of condemnation. Numerous studies have pointed out the negative repercussions of third-party involvement that does not go beyond scolding (Uyangoda 2006, Bouffard and Carment 2006, Smith 2007, CPA 2007). The more the mediators' interests appeared limited in the eyes of the conflicting parties, as evidenced by their limited use of sticks, the more impotent their leverage became. According to the CPA report, once the Sri Lankan government became aware of the limited international interest in the conflict, it assumed a 'let's see what we can get away with' attitude vis-à-vis the external actors' involvement. At the same time, the government also realized that it could improve its bargaining position by forum shopping among other, non-Western international actors, such as Pakistan, Iran, China and Russia, which were willing to offer their assistance without any conditions (CPA 2007).[8]

Failure of the peace process

Following the US refusal to allow the LTTE to attend the conference in Washington in April 2003 and the subsequent LTTE decision to suspend all direct talks with the government (it also refused to attend the Tokyo conference in June 2003, at which donors had pledged US$4.5 billion to the peace process) based on the perception that it was not being treated as an equal party by the other participants, the peace process reached a deadlock. The government was also experiencing difficulties in maintaining its commitment to the process, especially due to the uneasy cohabitation with President Kumaratunga of the SLFP. The tension between the two political forces had lingered ever since the UNF government took office and, with international support, initiated the peace process. The President who was the commander in chief, head of state and head of the cabinet – with the power to call for elections at his or her own discretion once the government had been in office for a year – was largely excluded from the talks. A critical juncture was reached in November 2003 when the president managed to secure control over three key ministries. Soon after, the president dissolved the parliament and called for new elections, which were held in April 2004 and marked the end of the UNF government (Fernando 2006). Despite the changes in the Sri Lankan political landscape, the Norwegian-led mediation continued not only with the new government in place, but also after the newly elected president, with a nationalist and pro-military-solution platform, Mahinda Rajapaksa of the SLFP, came to power in 2005. In 2006, the situation on the ground had gradually deteriorated from sporadic skirmishes into full-fledged open warfare, particularly in the east. There were attempts to reignite the peace process, which had been stalled since April 2003, with two rounds of peace talks held in Geneva in February and October 2006. But these efforts also eventually failed.

In spite of such a promising start to the peace talks and the leadership of a strongly committed prime minister and experienced Norwegian mediators, there are a number of reasons why the process reached an impasse in 2003 and ultimately failed in 2006. First, the conflict in Sri Lanka has always had the capacity for intense re-escalation (Uyangoda 2007). Both sides accepted the initial cease-fire, at least in part, for devious reasons: as an opportunity to rearm and reorganize for the future and to seek international support and legitimization for their respective interests (Höglund and Svensson 2009). In other words, as the parties never really lost the appetite for a military solution, the situation was never really ripe for peaceful resolution (Smith 2007). Second, the relationship between the government and the LTTE was based entirely on the CFA, as they failed to sign an interim settlement agreement of any kind. Uyangoda points out that the basis for the negotiations and the CFA "was the preservation of the parties' strategic interests through a condition of no-war.... Consequently, the problem-solving and conflict transformation approach became entirely absent" (Uyangoda 2006, 4). Third, the peace process was focused exclusively on two parties: the government, led by Wickremesinghe, and the LTTE. President Kumaratunga and other southern political elites were largely excluded from the process and non-LTTE Tamil parties and Muslim parties had no role at all. As pointed out by the ICG, "much of the dynamic of this conflict is within ethnic communities, and the failure of the peace process to address this, made a lasting peace less likely" (ICG 2006a, i). In 2004, two significant developments changed the balance of power between the parties. The defection of the LTTE's eastern commander, Vinayagamoorthy Muralitharan, known as Colonel Karuna, and the losses suffered by the LTTE's naval wing in the tsunami of December 2004, led some sections of the government and armed forces to believe that the LTTE's offensive capacity was weakened and that a highly concentrated war against the LTTE, with the help of the breakaway faction, would be winnable (Uyangoda 2006).

In conclusion, all of the aforementioned developments induced the parties to start exploring their military options again and contributed to the subsequent failure of the talks. But without discounting the internal developments that contributed to the failure of the peace talks, it is important to understand the part that the international mediators and their self-interest played in the peace process. The third parties' interests in the conflict proved to be insufficiently strong to engage in a properly coordinated multiparty mediation process. Therefore, the evident lack of strategic interests within the co-chair system created an environment within which Norway was unable to successfully coordinate multi-party mediation efforts through the co-chair system. The leverage that the third parties possessed was never used to guide the disputants toward a mutually acceptable solution. Instead, the mediators, including the US or even the EU, blocked any possibility of reaching a solution through the peace process due to their reluctance to engage in direct talks with the LTTE. This 'defection' strategy created internal incoherence within the mediating coalition, which was a signal to the government (which had solid relations with the US and the EU) that a military solution could still be explored. This provides sufficient evidence of the existence of a causal mechanism indicating that in the event that mediators do not reach a convergence of interests, the conflicting sides will be induced to defect from negotiations, making it more likely that the peace process will fail. The fact that in the case of Sri Lanka the necessary strategic interests hampered the achievement of a convergence of interests between the third parties as the process was unfolding. Weak interests in the conflict induced the parties not to rethink their policies as the peace process hit the wall. Based on the theory presented here, it is hypothesized that in cases where the third parties realize that their ongoing strategies are not producing expected results, they will be induced to rethink their policies. However, due to a lack of interest in the conflict, the parties were also not sufficiently interested in altering their strategies. As the mediators were unable to reach a convergence of interests and instead maintained their initial positions regarding the conflict, the conflicting sides saw this as a signal of lack of commitment to the peace process and eventually resorted to violence once again.

Notes

1 This chapter is based on Groeneveld-Savisaar and Vuković (2011). I am greatly indebted to Maria Groeneveld-Savisaar whose meticulous research is at the foundations of this chapter.
2 There were many anti-government Tamil groups active in the beginning, only during the second phase of the civil war (after the Indian had been defeated) was LTTE the sole rebel group.
3 Svensson (2014) discusses and defines the Indo-Lanka Accord as a partial 'success.' Although this was not a peace agreement in a traditional sense, it is still a 'borderline case.'
4 Yet, there is also the alternative interpretation: that parties learn from previous lessons, or that even failure might create changes that move the parties closer to a solution.
5 On November 28, 2002 the LTTE's leader declared: "We can't ignore the realities of today's world. We have to realize this and adjust our path to freedom" (quote from Höglund and Svensson 2007, 107).
6 The eventual reescalation of violence transformed SLMM from a peace-monitoring mission to a war monitoring one. A further complication came in the summer of 2006 when the EU listed the LTTE as a terrorist organization, requesting its member states to freeze the existing and prohibit further direct or indirect provision of funds and other financial assets to LTTE (Council of the European Union 2006). The LTTE reacted by insisting that all EU countries leave the mission. The SLMM terminated its operations in January 2008, when the government of Sri Lanka abrogated the cease-fire agreement (SLMM 2008).
7 The US conveyed this message using various channels: formally through Norwegian delegation which was officially facilitating the talks, secretly through Tamil diaspora in the US, and even publically. In a speech delivered in February 2003, Armitage announced:

> If the LTTE can move beyond the terror tactics of the past and make a convincing case through its conduct and its actual actions that it is committed to a political solution and to peace, the United States will certainly consider removing the LTTE from the list of Foreign Terrorist Organizations.
>
> (Armitage quoted in Lunstead 2007, 16)

8 That prediction proved true. The new kid on the block, offering unconditional financial, military, and diplomatic support, has been, since early 2007, a player with straightforward – and certainly strategic – interests: China. After the March 2007 agreement that allowed China to build a US$1 billion port in southern Sri Lanka, allegedly to use as a refueling and docking station for its navy, Beijing appears to have significantly increased arms sales to Sri Lanka. China has also provided crucial diplomatic support in the UN Security Council, blocking efforts to put Sri Lanka on the agenda, and also boosted financial aid to Sri Lanka, even as Western countries have reduced their contributions. A spoiler has indeed emerged.

8 Discussion and lessons for practice

This research departed from the assumption that cooperation between mediators is not only beneficial to the multiparty mediation process but also to them as rational actors who are driven by self-interests. Even despite the inevitable costs of mediation coupled with costs of cooperating, cooperation still proves to be more beneficial than defecting strategies. As the five case studies illustrate, cooperation between mediators is by no means exogenous to the process. First of all, cooperation changes in intensity according to the dynamics of the conflict and of the conflict management process. When outside parties do not have converging interests on how the conflict should end they often resort to limited cooperation. Limited cooperation produces a limited result. When third parties are unwilling to use their full mediating potential – for instance, when a patron state is unwilling to use more directive strategies to move the partner party in conflict toward an agreement – this choice might send mixed signals to the conflicting parties which might produce lack of commitment to negotiate a settlement. In other words, lack of cooperation within the mediating coalition directly gets transposed into a lack of cooperation between the conflicting sides and third parties.

However when the situation on the ground changes and becomes unbearable to the outside actors they might decide to achieve full cooperation. Cooperating in these circumstances becomes more cost/benefit efficient and effective than previous strategies. Sometimes these changes do not induce all parties to engage in cooperative manner. As the case studies suggest, the party which has the strongest interest in resolving the conflict will most likely be the one that will try to encourage the other side to establish a more cooperative mutual relationship. Ultimately, it is worth noting that coordination might also be related to a much bigger framework of relations and strategic choices an outside party has and makes. As most (self) interests are interrelated into a network of strategic interests, developments on the regional and global level which might endanger these strategic interests have the potential to induce a third party to radically shift its outlook on the actual conflict. In these circumstances cooperation again proves to be more cost/benefit efficient and effective, which allows the third party to explore the option of cooperating in order to preserve its self-interests.

As parties manage to achieve convergence of interests and become able to work from a common script, this sends a strong signal to the parties in conflict that they should also be more inclined to cooperate and compromise both with mediators and with other conflicting sides. Overall, this signaling helps the mediating effort to move conflicting sides more smoothly toward an agreement.

Utility of cooperation

Reflecting back on the game-theoretical model presented in Chapter 2, the employment of cooperative strategies for external actors appears to be more beneficial than spoiling the process. In fact, even the cumulative costs of cooperating and mediating, complemented with potential benefits of acting as a spoiler, still do not manage to match the benefits generated by cooperative strategies. As the model shows, although the choice of non-cooperating at first might appear appealing to a third-party, spoiling the process might actually backfire. A third-party's decision not to cooperate while the multiparty endeavor under way – thus implying that other mediators are engaged in the mediation in a cooperative manner – undercuts its own potential to exercise influence (or leverage) in the mediation and loses the potential to create expected benefits for itself and its partner side in the conflict. As long as a biased mediator is outside the mediating coalition, the conflicting party it is supporting might still remain in the process. In such circumstances the chances that potential solutions will be tilted to its partner's advantage (i.e., conflicting side it supports) get reduced. Consequently, as a particular conflicting side is losing through mediation, so will its outside partners (i.e., biased mediators), even though they are officially not cooperating in the process. For instance, the international reputation of a third party might be undermined. At the same time their leverage to influence future developments in the process might be considerably undercut. Therefore, the model induces a conclusion that both the non-cooperative outside actor and its partner party to the conflict will face far smaller benefits than those who opt to cooperate and potentially (through constructive dialogue and exercising necessary leverage) move the proposed solution to their advantage.

In light of a lower payoff, it is expected that a rational mediator will chose to alter its strategy and start cooperating with the rest of the group. Although the process of cooperation implies certain costs, and as such produces smaller utility that in cases when no party cooperates (point (a) in the model), the choice of altering the strategy and starting to cooperate will undeniably generate bigger benefits compared to those attained if a mediator remains outside the mediating coalition. By being a part of the mediating coalition, each mediator is able to exercise a certain influence over the process, and potentially negotiate a solution that is in favor of the side in the conflict that they have special relations with. Thus, (biased) mediators attain important utility as the conflicting side that they support actually starts gaining important benefits through mediation. Despite the costs of mediating and cooperating, the second outside actor still manages to create greater benefits through coordinated activities than if it opted to spoil the process and stay outside of the coalition.[1] Therefore, the model prescribes a

dynamic that unequivocally remains in line with the initial statement and definition that cooperation implies the creation of new gains for each party that were
unavailable to them by unilateral action, albeit at some costs (Zartman and
Touval 2010).

If interpreted through classical game theory, cooperation represents a
dominant strategy in this model, and the Nash equilibrium is point (c) (2,2).
ToM also provides a similar interpretation, given that once the multiparty mediation starts, cooperative behavior produces higher payoffs than defection, and
the final state is also in point (c). Overall, cooperation can be identified as a
rational strategy that leads to nonmyopic equilibria. Once a party chooses to
cooperate, short-term goals which induced a party to defect are no longer a priority. Rather, for a rational outside party that has received low payoffs from a
defecting strategy, cooperation becomes a useful mechanism through which it is
possible to limit the other side's utility.

As cooperation proves to be decidedly beneficial not only to the overall
process but more importantly also to the parties themselves, it is also important
to understand what mechanisms can deter a party from defecting from the group.
Inducing a party to switch from defection to cooperative behavior is obviously
not a simple process, as it directly implies interference in another party's policy
objectives. It would be too simplistic to assume that just by reproving party's
non-cooperative behavior, or warning that such behavior is not constructive for
the overall process of mediation, would motivate a change in a defector's
strategy. This research departed from the rational choice assumption that in order
to change its stratagem and pursue cooperative strategies the defecting party
needs to realize the potential benefits of such a change. As third parties get
involved in managing a particular conflict, not only for altruistic and humanitarian reasons but also to gain something from it, the choice of cooperating also
needs to be in line with each party's self-interests.

In essence, a potential incompatibility of interests between mediators creates
a conflict in the mediating coalition that requires management. If not managed,
the mediators might start working at cross purposes by sending mixed signals to
the conflicting parties, which greatly reduces the chances of success for the
peacemaking process. Thus, prior to managing a particular conflict that brings
them together in a mediating coalition, third parties first need to manage the conflict of interests between themselves. Managing the conflict between mediators
depends on their ability to realize the inadequacy of unilateral action and recognize the utility of cooperation. Following the logic of ripeness theory (Zartman
1989a, Steadman 1991, Zartman 2001), this book has identified three distinct
mechanisms that have the potential to induce convergence of interests between
the third-parties and promote the spirit of cooperation within the mediating
coalition.

Exogenous geo-political shifts – significant developments on a systemic level
caused by pivotal political, social, economic and/or natural events – might encourage a party to rethink its guiding principles. This is because no policy objective is
ever self-motivated or independently strong enough to linger indefinitely; it should

rather be seen as a building block of a complex network of strategic choices developed by each actor in the international arena. Although such geo-political shifts are largely exogenous to the conflict that is being managed, they still have the potential to alter external actors' interests in mediating the dispute. In some instances, these shifts may lead third parties to the point where their interests in managing the conflict converge. As the case of Tajikistan shows, Taliban storming of Kabul induced Russia and Iran to rethink their policies in the region, to put more pressure on conflicting sides in Tajikistan and to drive them toward a commonly acceptable solution. In Cambodia, two events had a similar impact. As Hampson and Zartman indicate,

> Gorbachev's accession to power in the Soviet Union in the mid-1980s brought changes in the interests and positions of major outside parties. As a part of its overall effort to normalize relations with China, the Soviet Union began to step up its own efforts to resolve the conflict, by encouraging Vietnam to withdraw its army unit from Cambodia and threatening termination of its military and economic aid to Vietnam.
>
> (Hampson and Zartman 2011, 137)

In fact the secret warning that the USSR delivered to Vietnam, in which they indicated their intention to stop supporting Vietnam's military presence in Cambodia and confrontation with China, resulted in Vietnam's announcement of troop withdrawal (which initially did not produce the results needed to move the process toward an agreement) that on the long run contributed to Sino-Vietnamese rapprochement. In Namibia, the advent of Gorbachev to power also proved to be of crucial importance for the achievement of rapprochement between the USSR and the US, and their subsequent convergence of interests in managing the conflict by linking together the issues pertinent to the conflicts in Angola and Namibia. In the case of Kosovo, changes on the systemic level also had an effect, however this time negative. When Russia started restoring its global relevance in the late 90s, its policies shifted from implicit compliance to implicit confrontation with the West, especially with the US. For Levitin this "deterioration has to be understood in the context of more general and long standing trends in Russian foreign policy" (Levitin 2000, 138). Finally, in the case of Sri Lanka, the 9/11 terrorist attacks on Twin Towers in New York strongly affected US foreign policy. The war on terror doctrine reduced the possibilities for US diplomats to engage in direct talks with an organization such as the LTTE. This lack of flexibility had a dual impact: on the one side the US was unable to employ all of its leverage in the peacemaking process, which limited the effectives of the mediating coalition; on the other, the LTTE saw this as a signal that it was not treated fairy in the peace process, and as a consequence opted to walk away from the talks.

Changes in conflict dynamics might induce those outside actors that are directly involved in the conflict – for example by providing logistical and/or military support – to consider using mediation as a viable option for ending the conflict. While exogenous geo-political shifts create a trickle-down effect (i.e., the mediators' decision to re-evaluate their interests in the conflict is induced by factors that are external to it), the more the third parties expand their degree of involvement in the conflict, the more their interests become susceptible to the dynamics of the conflict. Even though formally they might act as mediators or external actors supporting the mediation process, these actors could still employ violence as an off-the-table tactic in the same way conflicting parties do. In cases where external actors provide logistical and/or military support to one of the conflicting parties, they may experience mounting costs and losses more directly. As the conflict dynamics on the ground start to take their toll, the desirability of continuing the conflict may start to wane. Consequently, as the confrontational strategies start yielding higher costs than expected benefits, the non-cooperative third party may opt to explore cooperative engagement with other external actors as a suitable way of achieving greater benefits. In the case of Tajikistan, each time the parties failed to come to an agreement, they would resort to violence. This was especially problematic for Russia that had stationed troops there. As such violent dynamics produce unwanted costs in lives and military equipment, Russia begun resorting to more active strategies in order to push the government to accommodate the opposition and find a commonly acceptable solution. In the case of Namibia, the achieved stalemate between Cuban and South African troops was an indication that a military victory in the conflict was unfeasible and that the existing non-cooperative strategy in the peace process was not producing any substantial results that would outweigh the military stalemate. In the case of Cambodia, the Soviet decision to stop financing the Vietnamese 'tug of war' with China and change the strategies toward Beijing induced a more cooperative strategy both between the Soviet Union and China, and between China and Vietnam. In the case of Kosovo, the new reality on the ground, created by UNMIK's presence, prompted Russia to agree with the rest of the Contact Group on independence as a viable solution to the problem. However, this convergence did not last for long, and chances of acting in concert faded. Finally, in the case of Sri Lanka, the conflict had a very limited impact on the mediators' strategic interests. As the external actors did not experience the pain (both material and non-material) of an escalating conflict, they had less reason to alter their policy preferences and act more assertively in managing the conflict.

Both exogenous geo-political shifts and changes of conflict dynamic imply that the defector will change their strategy through their own initiative. However, a third trigger of cooperation is also feasible – the initiative might come from the rest of the coalition, through *bargaining for cooperation*. In view of the fact that defection is often a direct expression of a party's self-interested goals, another way of encouraging change is to engage a defecting party in a bargaining process, where an alternative to their current behavior can be found by offering them sufficient incentives to make participation an attractive option. As the likelihood of negotiating a cooperative arrangement increases with the number of participants, a series of measures conducive to effective negotiation may be taken: the issues should be narrowed down to the most relevant ones; the negotiating process should be conducted by a selected group of actors that have a direct stake in those particular issues that are being discussed; and additional actors should be included only if they can contribute to the establishment of collective effort.

The choice to pursue a non-cooperative approach will not only have an impact on the mediating coalition, but also on the overall peacemaking process, as it might encourage at least one conflicting party to stop cooperating in peace talks. When cooperating with other mediators, biased mediators are useful insomuch as they can use their special relationship with one conflicting side to influence its behavior, positions and perceptions and consequently move it toward an agreement. However, when these actors decide not to cooperate with the rest of the group, the conflicting side that they have a special relationship with might suffer in the negotiation process. In such circumstances, the party to the conflict might find the agreement less attractive, and consequently refuse to accept it. At the same time, a conflicting party may understand their partner's non-cooperative attitude to be an acceptable and recommended form of behavior. Thus, by cementing their positions, non-cooperative external actors produce significant complications for the bargaining process and put mediation efforts at risk. As the case studies show, the transposition of non-cooperative behavior from an external actor onto a conflicting party may take different forms, and range from a mere stalling of the process, to the use of violence as a beyond-the-table tactic, to the complete abandonment of the peacemaking process.

At a certain point, the coalition members might pick up this signal, approach the defector and bargain for a new arrangement which will create new benefits for both. However, it is not always clear who should take responsibility for steering a party off a non-cooperative course. As experience shows in these situations, the responsibility for encouraging a mediator to develop a common idea about a final solution and opt for cooperative strategy might rest with others in the mediating coalition. In the case of Cambodia, the US managed to create momentum within the P5 and negotiate an acceptable solution for USSR and China which was crucial for the success of the peace process. Nonetheless, as noted by Solomon, "ultimately, the success came when the two major protagonists in the region's conflicts of the 1980s and 1990s – China and Vietnam made a secret, bilateral deal to reconcile their differences and support the United Nations peace plan for Cambodia" (Solomon 2000, 4). A similar dynamic was also tried in the case of Kosovo with the last attempt by the Troika, when the EU not only tried to find a solution to the conflict but also to mediate a solution acceptable to other mediators (the US and Russia). However, as this effort eventually failed, the process was driven to a deadlock.

In sum, although each of the three reasons to change policy objectives seems to work on their own, success is most guaranteed if they are combined. The case of Cambodia proves this point, as

the combined effects of a military stalemate among Cambodia's political factions, diplomatic efforts to construct a settlement during the preceding decade by a number of interested parties, and the desire of the major powers to disengage from Indochina's travails created a context for successful diplomacy.

(Solomon 2000, 4)

Achieving and implementing coordination

All five case studies also show that coordinated efforts between mediators are strongly related to their strategic interests in the conflict. The case of Sri Lanka indicates the significance of strategic interests for a coordinated endeavor between multiple mediators. As the co-chairs lacked strategic interests in the conflict, they were unwilling to employ their leverages to guide the parties in conflict toward an agreement, taking the Norway-led mediation efforts to a deadlock. Similarly, in case of Tajikistan, strategic relevance of the area for both Russia and Iran, especially in light of a perceived threat coming from Afghanistan and increasing costs of supporting the warfare for Russia which was not yielding expected results (i.e., victory through military means), allowed for a well-coordinated mediation activity under the UN leadership. The UN leadership was perceived as legitimate by both Russia and Iran as its involvement was not incompatible with their interests in the conflict. A somewhat different dynamic was observed in the case of Namibia, where the US – generally perceived as a powerful state – had a clear set of interests to promote in the conflict, and was certainly biased toward particular conflicting sides; it still managed to be an effective coordinator of mediation activities. First of all, its mediation activities were gradually accepted and publically stated by all conflicting sides as 'indispensable,' allowing the US to acquire the necessary degree of legitimacy. At the same time the US managed to generate converging interests with the USSR (a patron state of MPLA and Cuba) which in turn, allowed for a successfully coordinated multiparty mediation effort by a powerful (and biased) state. Similarly, in the case of Cambodia, the US managed to successfully coordinate mediation activities even though it was quite clear to all the parties involved that it had an agenda it was trying to promote. However, in this case the success was more related to the fact that the US was able to 'borrow' the needed degree of legitimacy from the UN, as it skillfully transferred the bargaining process between mediators (with incompatible interests) to the UN bodies. Again, just as in the case of Namibia, the US was able to take the leadership role once the powerful states managed to reach an agreement and reach a convergence of interests amongst themselves. Finally, in the case of Kosovo, the strategic interests of key patron states were not moving towards a convergence point (as was the case in Tajikistan, Cambodia and Namibia). In fact, every time the parties signaled readiness to work together and transfer the responsibility of coordination to a particular party, such as the UN, the conflicting sides were moving toward reaching an agreement. However, the necessary degree of legitimacy, that the UN initially enjoyed (most likely do to its reputation and credibility) was gradually challenged by those third parties (in this case Russia) who saw UN's agenda and proposals for conflict resolution as incompatible with their interests.

Lessons for practice

Reflecting on what was previously stated, for all case studies it could be concluded that a successfully coordinated multiparty mediation activity is directly dependent on the compatibility of interests between the party that coordinates and the third parties that have strong vested interests in the conflict and leverage to influence the behavior of the parties in conflict. Consequently, while coordinator's legitimacy is an important ingredient for a successfully coordinated effort, it cannot be put into effect before the third parties have reached the needed convergence of interest. This, in other words, supports the initial premise of this book: that the first step of a successful multiparty mediation effort is the achievement of third-parties' willingness to cooperate (convergence of interests), which opens the doors to the second stage of coordination where the parties split the task of leveraging the parties toward an agreement.

When designing a peace process it is not only important to know which parties in the conflict should participate in the negotiations, it is also crucial to know which external parties should be included as well. The choice to exclude an external actor that has the capacity to leverage one or more conflicting parties toward an agreement, just because that particular external actor has diverging interests with the rest of the mediating coalition, will have detrimental consequences for the peace process. On the one side, the mediating coalition will have limited capacity to incentivize the parties to negotiate a mutually acceptable solution. On the other, those parties in conflict that have established partnerships with the excluded external actors might also have less reason to compromise as they might fear that their interests are not well protected within the mediating coalition. Therefore, before starting a peace process (and if faced with an incompatibility of interests between external actors) it is essential that the external actors realize how important it is that they reach a convergence of interests in managing a conflict, speaking from a common script. Moreover, it is not only important to affirm the convergence of interests between likeminded actors, but to find ways to achieve this convergence with other international actors that have the capacity to improve the overall effectiveness of the peace process. Numerous cases, including the ones analyzed in this book, show that this convergence of interest is often a product of dynamics that are external to the conflict being managed. Thus, the ability to establish cooperative relations between rival international actors may not only contribute to the effectiveness of a particular conflict management process, but create multiplying effects by establishing pact-building relationships and a sense of shared decision making on the international level that can accelerate the achievement of cooperation in future conflict management processes.

Also, just as the parties in conflict may be inclined to explore negotiations and cooperation with their opponents once their unilateral confrontational strategies start yielding higher costs and lesser benefits, external actors that provide logistical and military support to one of the conflicting parties may have a similar reaction to the mounting costs and loses in an ongoing conflict. So, another possible way of achieving convergence of interests between relevant international actors is to increase the costs of supporting an ongoing conflict and promote the benefits of collaborative international efforts. This will send a strong signal to specific conflicting parties that they are losing an important source of sustenance for their belligerent activities, and induce them to seek gains through peaceful compromise with their rivals. Evidently, external actors should be aware that their attitudes have an extraordinary impact on the conflicting parties' behavior. If external actors maintain their confrontational relations, conflicting parties will pick up the signal that compromising and negotiating a peace deal is not in their interest. Therefore, the promotion of a spirit of cooperation and coordination among the relevant international actors will directly contribute to an equivalent tendency between conflicting parties, and as a consequence a more effective and expedient management of their conflict.

Note

1 This is true only if the assumption from ToM – that mutual defection is not an option any more – continues to hold.

Annex I

The model[1] prescribes two choices (X) for each actor involved: to cooperate (1) or not to cooperate (0). That is: X_A, X_B, X_1, X_2, $X_3 = 0$ or 1. All other values in the model also range from 0 to 1.

In case parties are unable to engage in mediation, payoffs of resolving the conflict through fighting are described through expected utility functions:

$$A : P_w^A U_f^A - C_f^A$$
$$B : P_w^B U_f^B - C_f^B$$
$$1 : U_{Aw}^1 P_w^A$$
$$2 : 0$$
$$3 : U_{Bw}^3 P_w^B$$

Where, P_w is the probability that a conflicting party will win by fighting; U_f is the utility of winning through fighting, which is supposed to be very high ($U_f \approx 1$) given the fact that through fighting a party can either win or lose; C_f represents the costs of fighting, which are supposed to be also high ($C_f \approx 1$) in order to make the option of fighting not appealing; finally, as third parties are not involved directly in the conflict their payoffs are related to the probability of winning by a side they support and the utility of that victory (U_{Aw}^1, U_{Bw}^3); obviously party 2 does not have any utility if the fighting continues.

If there is agreement to conduct mediation, each actor has a payoff. The payoffs are still described through an expected utility function which for each conflicting side is:

$$P_m^A U_{ag}^A - C_m + i_1^A X_1$$
$$P_m^B U_{ag}^B - C_m + i_3^B X_3$$

Where, P_m is the probability of winning through mediation for a conflicting side; U_{ag} represents the utility each conflicting side has from an agreement achieved through mediation ($U_{ag} < U_f$); C_m is the cost of mediation; i is the influence a biased mediator has on a conflicting side. This relationship represents a cost that biased mediators face in order to influence their partners in conflict – it should not be too high, otherwise mediation is not very attractive for outside actors.

P_m has a function:
$$P_m^A = (P_m^A)^{(0)} + Q_{m1}^A X_1 - Q_{m3}^B X_3$$
$$P_m^B = (P_m^B)^{(0)} + Q_{m3}^B X_3 - Q_{m1}^A X_1 ;$$

$(P_m)^{(0)}$ stands for a fixed probability of winning through mediation; Q_m indicates the influence an outside party has on the mediation process – it comes into play only if $X=1$; the probability has a negative Q_m of the opposing side since an outside player by increasing chances of winning for their partners also decreases the probability of winning for the other conflicting side.

The cost of mediation C_m has a function: $C_m = C_m^{(0)} + C_m^{(1)}(2 - X_1 - X_3)$; $C_m^{(0)}$ indicates the fixed costs of mediation; the other part of the formula stands for additional costs of mediation that A and B face each time an outside actor does not participate in mediation – this refers to biased mediators 1 and 3, as the model assumes that neutral mediator 2 will always be engaged in the mediation process.

The model prescribes that mediators also benefit from participating in the mediating process. Biased mediators have a utility from what their partner state in the conflict wins through a reached agreement (U_{Aag}^1, U_{Bag}^3) – multiplied by the probability of them winning – which comes at a cost of their influence/relation with the conflicting side (i). Thus the payoffs for biased mediators are:

$$U_{Aag}^1 P_m^A - i_1^A$$
$$U_{Bag}^3 P_m^B - i_1^B$$

Fighting occurs unless both conflicting sides agree to mediation. For mediation to occur, both of these inequalities must be satisfied:

$$P_m^A U_{Aag}^A - C_m + i_1^A X_1 > P_w^A U_f^A - C_f^A$$
$$P_m^B U_{Bag}^B - C_m + i_3^B X_3 > P_w^B U_f^B - C_f^B \qquad (1)$$

Case 1: Neither mediator cooperates

If neither mediator cooperates, the conditions for mediation (1) become:

$$(P_m^A)^{(0)} U_{Aag}^A - C_m > P_w^A U_f^A - C_f^A$$
$$(P_m^B)^{(0)} U_{Bag}^B - C_m > P_w^B U_f^B - C_f^B \qquad (2)$$

If conditions (2) fail, fighting continues. The mediators receive their expected payoffs:

$$P_w^A U_{Aw}^1 - C_f^1 \text{ and } P_w^B U_{Bw}^3 - C_f^3$$

If conditions (2) hold, mediation takes place under mediator 2, without cooperation from 1 and 3. The mediators receive their expected payoffs:

$$(P_m^A)^{(0)} U_{Aag}^1 \text{ and } (P_m^B)^{(0)} U_{Bag}^3$$

Case 2: One mediator cooperates

In the case where mediator 1 cooperates but mediator 3 does not, the conditions for mediation become:

$$((P_m^A)^{(0)} + Q_{m1}^A)U_{ag}^A - C_m + i_1^A > P_w^A U_f^A - C_f^A$$
$$((P_m^B)^{(0)} - Q_{m1}^A)U_{ag}^B - C_m > P_w^B U_f^B - C_f^B \tag{3}$$

If conditions (3) fail, fighting continues, and the mediators receive their expected payoffs:

$$P_w^A U_f^A - C_f^A \text{ and } P_w^B U_f^B - C_f^B$$

If conditions (3) hold, mediation takes place under mediators 1 and 2, without cooperation from 3. The mediators receive their expected payoffs:

$$((P_m^A)^{(0)} + Q_{m1}^A)U_{Aag}^1 - C_m - i_1^A \text{ and } ((P_m^B)^{(0)} - Q_{m1}^A)U_{Bag}^3 - C_m$$

The case where mediator 3 cooperates and mediator 1 does not is similar.

Case 3: Both mediators cooperate

If both mediators cooperate, conditions for mediation are:

$$((P_m^A)^{(0)} + Q_{m1}^A - Q_{m3}^B)U_{ag}^A - C_m + i_1^A > P_w^A U_f^A - C_f^A$$
$$((P_m^B)^{(0)} - Q_{m1}^A + Q_{m3}^B)U_{ag}^B - C_m + i_3^B > P_w^B U_f^B - C_f^B \tag{4}$$

If conditions (4) fail, fighting continues. The mediators receive their expected payoffs:

$$P_w^A U_f^A - C_f^A \text{ and } P_w^B U_f^B - C_f^B$$

If conditions (4) hold, mediation takes place under all mediators. The mediators receive their expected payoffs:

$$((P_m^A)^{(0)} + Q_{m1}^A - Q_{m3}^B)U_{Aag}^1 - C_m - i_1^A$$
$$((P_m^B)^{(0)} - Q_{m1}^A + Q_{m3}^B)U_{Bag}^3 - C_m - i_3^B$$

Finally, if both:

$$((P_m^A)^{(0)} - Q_{m3}^B)U_{Aag}^A - C_m > P_w^A U_f^A - C_f^A$$

$$((P_m^B)^{(0)} - Q_{m1}^A)U_{Bag}^B - C_m > P_w^B U_f^B - C_f^B$$

then mediation is so good that the parties agree to it no matter what. In this case, the actions of mediators are determined by weighing their costs of cooperating against the utility they gain from influencing the mediation.

Thus, mediator 1 will cooperate if

$$Q_{m1}^A U_{Aag}^A - i_1^A - C_m > 0$$

and mediator 3 will cooperate if

$$Q_{m3}^B U_{Bag}^B - i_3^B - C_m > 0$$

Note

1 This model was originally developed during the 2009 YSSP research at IIASA, Laxenburg, Austria, and further expanded to its current state together with Dr. Ben Allen (Harvard University).

Bibliography

A/RES/3111 (1973) *Question of Namibia*, UN General Assembly Resolution. Available online at: http://daccess-dds-ny.un.org/doc/RESOLUTION/GEN/NR0/281/83/IMG/NR028183.pdf?OpenElement (accessed December 7, 2014).

A/RES/31/146 (1976) *Situation in Namibia Resulting from the Illegal Occupation of the Territory by South Africa*, UN General Assembly Resolution. Available online at: http://daccess-dds-ny.un.org/doc/RESOLUTION/GEN/NR0/303/29/IMG/NR030329.pdf?OpenElement (accessed December 7, 2014).

A/66/811 (2012) *Strengthening the Role of Mediation in the Peaceful Settlement of disputes, Conflict Prevention and Resolution*, Report of the Secretary General. Available online at: http://peacemaker.un.org/sites/peacemaker.un.org/files/SGReport_Strengh teningtheRoleofMediation_A66811.pdf (accessed December 7, 2014).

Abdullaev, K. and Barnes, C. (2001) *Politics of Compromise: The Tajikistan Peace Process*, Conciliation Resources, London.

Abdullaev, R. and Babakhanov, U. (1998) "Thank the Taliban for the Tajik Peace Agreement." in Rutland, P. (ed.) *Annual Survey of Eastern Europe and the Former Soviet Union 1997: The Challenge of Integration*, M.E. Sharpe, New York, pp. 393–395.

Abdullo, R.G. (2001) "Implementation of the 1997 General Agreement: Successes, Dilemmas and Challenges", in Abdullaev, K. and Barnes, C. (eds) *Politics of Compromise: The Tajikistan Peace Process*, Conciliation Resources, London, pp. 48–56.

Ahtisaari, M. (2007) *President Ahtisaari at the LSE: "Every conflict can be resolved"*, Speech delivered at London School of Economics, October 29. Available online at: www.finemb.org.uk/public/?contentid=103695&contentlan=2&culture=en-GB (accessed December 15, 2014).

Akiner, S. and Barnes, C. (2001) "The Tajik Civil War: Causes and Dynamics", in Abdullaev, K. and Barnes, C. (eds) *Politics of Compromise: The Tajikistan Peace Process*, Conciliation Resources, London, pp. 16–22.

Anan, K. (1999) "Statement," NATO Headquarters, Brussels, January 28, 1999. www.nato.int/docu/speech/1999/s990128a.htm (accessed December 15, 2014).

Anderson, M.B. (1996a) *Do No Harm: Supporting Local Capacities for Peace Through Aid*, Collaborative for Development Action, Cambridge, MA.

Anderson, M.B. (1996b) "Humanitarian NGOs in Conflict Intervention", in Crocker, C.A., Hampson, F.O. and Aall, P. (eds) *Managing Global Chaos: Sources of and Responses to International Conflict*, United States Institute of Peace Press, Washington DC, pp. 343–354.

Antonenko, O. (2000) "Russia, NATO and European Security after Kosovo," *Survival*, Vol. 41, No. 4, pp. 124–144.

Antonenko, O. (2007) "Russia and the Deadlock over Kosovo," *Survival*, Vol. 49, No. 3, pp. 91–106.

Armitage, R.L. (2003) "Sri Lanka Prospects for Peace," *Defense Institute of Security Assistance Management Journal*, Vol. 25, No. 3, pp. 89–92.

Asian Tribune (2003) "Way Out of Ethnic Conflict Is through negotiations – US Envoy," *Asian Tribune*, April 26. Available online at: www.asiantribune.com/news/2003/04/26/way-out-ethnic-conflict-through-negotiations-us-envoy (accessed December 15, 2014).

Assefa, H. (1987) *Mediation of civil wars: Approaches and strategies – The Sudan conflict*, Westview Press, Boulder, CO.

Axelrod, R. (1984) *The Evolution of Cooperation*, Basic Books, New York.

Axelrod, R. and Keohane, R.O. (1985) "Achieving Cooperation Under Anarchy: Strategies and Institutions", *World Politics*, Vol. 38, No. 1, pp. 226–254.

B92 (2008) "Kako je Milošević pobedio NATO", *Report on Milošević's stand regarding NATO*. Belgrade www.youtube.com/watch?v=-rHd0Vi9aAY.

B92 Istražuje (2008) "Kosovo – Da li je Srbija imala strategiju?" *Documentary on Serbian strategy towards Kosovo*. Belgrade, www.youtube.com/watch?v=V5oaNZuwXP0.

Bakke, K., Cunningham, G.K. and Seymour, L.M. (2012) "A Plague of Initials: Fragmentation, Cohesion, and Infighting in Civil Wars," *Perspectives on Politics*, Vol. 10, No. 2, pp. 265–283.

Baldwin, D.A. (1993) *Neorealism and Neoliberalism: The Contemporary Debate*, Columbia University Press, New York.

Banac, I. (2001) *Raspad Jugoslavije*, Durieux, Zagreb.

Bandarage, A. (2009) *The Separatist Conflict in Sri Lanka: Terrorism, Ethnicity, Political Economy*, Routledge, New York.

Barnes, C. and Abdullaev, K. (2001) "Introduction: From War to Politics," in Abdullaev, K. and Barnes, C. (eds) *Politics of Compromise: The Tajikistan Peace Process*, Conciliation Resources, London, pp. 8–13.

Bastian, S. (2006) "How Development Undermined Peace," in Rupesinghe, K. (ed.) *Negotiating Peace in Sri Lanka: Efforts, Failures and Lessons*, 2nd ed., Vol. 1, Foundation for Co-Existence, Colombo.

Bastian, S. (2008) "Negotiations in a Globalized World," in Griffiths, A. and Barnes, C. (eds) *Powers of Persuasion: Incentives, Sanctions and Conditionality in Peacemaking*, Conciliation Resources, London, pp. 83–85.

BBC (2004) *Anti-Norway protests in Sri Lanka*, November 24, 2004. Available online at: http://news.bbc.co.uk/2/hi/south_asia/4039825.stm (Last accessed November 16, 2014).

Beach, D. and Pedersen, R.B. (2012) *Process Tracing Method – Foundation and Guidelines*, University of Michigan Press, Ann Arbor, MI, pp. 207–220.

Beardsley, C.K. (2009) "Intervention without Leverage: Explaining the Prevalence of Weak Mediators", *International Interactions*, Vol. 35, No. 3, pp. 272–297.

Beardsley, C.K. (2010) "Pain, Pressure and Political Cover: Explaining Mediation Incidence," *Journal of Peace Research*, Vol. 47, No. 4, pp. 395–406.

Beardsley, C.K. (2011) *The Mediation Dilemma*, Cornel University Press, Ithaca, NJ.

Beardsley, C.K., Quinn, D.M., Biswas, B. and Wilkenfeld, J. (2006) "Mediation Styles and Crisis Outcomes," *Journal of Conflict Resolution*, Vol. 50, No. 1, pp. 58–86.

Beber, B. (2010) "The (Non-)Efficacy of Multiparty Mediation in Wars Since 1990," NY University, Unpublished Manuscript.

Beber, B. (2012) "International Mediation, Selection Effects, and the Question of Bias", *Conflict Management and Peace Science*, Vol. 29, No. 4, pp. 397–424.

Bellamy, A.J. (2006) "Whither the Responsibility to Protect? Humanitarian Intervention and the 2005 World Summit," *Ethics & International Affairs*, Vol. 20, No. 2, pp. 143–169.

Bennett, A. (2010) "Process Tracing and Causal Interference," in Brady, H.E. and Collier, D. (eds) *Rethinking Social Inquiry: Diverse Tools Shared Standards*, Rowman and Littlefield, Boulder, CO.

Bercovitch, J. (1984) *Social Conflicts and Third Parties*, Westview Press, Boulder, CO.

Bercovitch, J. (1996) "The United Nations and the Mediation of International Disputes," in Thakur, R. (ed.) *The United Nations at Fifty: Retrospect and Prospect*, Otago University Press, Dunedin, NZ, pp. 73–87.

Bercovitch, J. (2002) *Studies in International Mediation*, Palgrave Macmillan, London.

Bercovitch, J. (2005) "Mediation in the Most Resistant Cases," in Crocker, C.A., Hampson, F.O. and Aall, P.R. (eds) *Grasping the Nettle: Analyzing Cases of Intractable Conflict*, United States Institute of Peace Press, Washington DC, pp. 99–121.

Bercovitch, J. (2006) "Mediation Success or Failure: A Search for the Elusive Criteria," *Cardozo Journal of Conflict Resolution*, Vol. 7, No. 2, pp. 289–302.

Bercovitch, J. (2009) "Mediation and Conflict Resolution," in Bercovitch, J., Kremenyuk, V. and Zartman, I.W. (eds) *The Sage Handbook of Conflict Resolution*, SAGE, London, pp. 340–357.

Bercovitch, J. and Gartner, S.S. (2006) "Is There Method in the Madness of Mediation? Some Lessons for Mediators from Quantitative Studies of Mediation," *International Interactions*, Vol. 32, No. 4, pp. 329–354.

Bercovitch, J. and Gartner, S.S. (2009) *International Conflict Management: New Approaches and Findings*, Routledge, London.

Bercovitch, J. and Houston, A. (1996) "The Study of International Mediation: Theoretical Issues and Empirical Evidence," in Bercovitch, J. (ed.) *Resolving International Conflicts: The Theory and Practice*, Lynne Reinner, Boulder, CO, pp. 11–36.

Bercovitch, J. and Jackson, R. (2001) "Negotiation or Mediation? An exploration of factors affecting the choice of conflict management in international conflict," *Negotiation Journal*, Vol. 17, No. 1, pp. 59–77.

Bercovitch, J. and Jackson, R. (2009) *Conflict Resolution in the Twenty First Century: Principles, Methods and Approaches*, Michigan University Press, Ann Arbor, MI.

Bercovitch, J. and Langley, J. (1993) "The Nature of the Dispute and the Effectiveness of International Mediation," *The Journal of Conflict Resolution*, Vol. 37, No. 4, pp. 670–691.

Bercovitch, J. and Schneider, G. (2000) "Who Mediates? The Political Economy of International Conflict Management," *Journal of Peace Research*, Vol. 37, No. 2, pp. 145–165.

Bercovitch, J., Anagnoson, T.J. and Wille, D.L. (1991) "Some Conceptual Issues and Empirical Trends in the Study of Successful Mediation in International Relations," *Journal of Peace Research*, Vol. 28, No. 1, pp. 7–17.

Bergquist, C. (1998) "Profiles: Contemporary Actors in the Peace Process," in Hendrickson, D. (ed.) *Safeguarding Peace: Cambodia's Constitutional Challenge*, Conciliation Resources, London.

Berridge, G.R. (1989) "Diplomacy and the Angola/Namibia Accords," *International Affairs*, Vol. 65, No. 3, pp. 463–479.

Bert, W. (1993) "Chinese Policies and U.S. Interests in Southeast Asia," *Asian Survey*, Vol. 33, No. 3, pp. 317–332.

Biswas, B. (2006) "The Challenges of Conflict Management: A Case Study of Sri Lanka," *Civil Wars*, Vol. 8, No. 1, pp. 46–65.

Black, I. (1999) "Interim deal on Kosovo," *Guardian*, February 24, 1999. Available online at: www.guardian.co.uk/world/1999/feb/24/balkans1 (accessed July 10, 2015).

Böhmelt, T. (2011) "Disaggregating Mediations: The Impact of Multiparty Mediation," *British Journal of Political Science*, Vol. 41, No. 4, pp. 859–881.

Böhmelt, T. (2012) "Why Many Cooks if They Can Spoil the Broth? The Determinants of Multiparty Mediation," *Journal of Peace Research*, Vol. 49, No. 5, pp. 701–715.

Bouffard, S. and Carment, D. (2006) "The Sri Lanka Peace Process: A Critical Review," *Journal of South Asian Development*, Vol. 1, No. 2, pp. 151–77.

Brams, S. (1994) *Theory of Moves*, Cambridge University Press, Cambridge: UK.

Bullion, A. (2001) "Norway and the Peace Process in Sri Lanka," *Civil Wars*, Vol. 4, No. 3, pp. 70–92.

Burg, S.L. (2005) "Intractability and Third Party Mediation in the Balkans," in Crocker, C.A., Hampson, F.O. and Aall, P. (eds) *Grasping the Nettle: Analyzing Cases of Intractable Conflict*, United States Institute of Peace Press, Washington DC pp. 183–207.

Burton, J. and Dukes, F. (1990) *Conflict: Practices, Settlement, and Resolution*, Macmillan: London, UK.

Butterworth, R.L. (1978) "Do Conflict Managers Matter? An Empirical Assessment of Interstate Security Disputes and Resolution Efforts," *International Studies Quarterly*, Vol. 22, No. 2, pp. 195–214.

Campbell, J.C. (1976) *Successful Negotiation, Trieste 1954: An Appraisal by the Five Participants*, Princeton University Press, Princeton, NJ.

Caplan, R. (1998) "International Diplomacy and the crisis in Kosovo," *International Affairs*, Vol. 74, No. 4, pp. 745–761.

Carnevale, P.J. (1986) "Strategic Choice in Mediation," *Negotiation Journal* Vol. 2, No. 1, pp. 41–56.

Carnevale, P.J. (2002) "Mediating from Strength," in Bercovitch, J. (ed.) *Studies in International Mediation*, Palgrave Macmillan, London, pp. 25–40.

Carnevale, P.J. and Arad, S. (1996) "Bias and Impartiality in International Mediation," in Bercovitch, J. (ed.) *Resolving International Conflicts: The Theory and Practice of Mediation*, Lynne Rienner, Boulder, CO, pp. 39–53.

Carnevale, P.J. and Pruitt, D.G. (1992) "Negotiation and mediation," *Annual Review of Psychology*, Vol. 43, No. 1, pp. 531–582.

Carnevale, P.J., Conlon, D.E., Hanisch, K.A. and Harris, K.L. (1989) "Experimental Research on the Strategic-Choice Model of Mediation," in Kressel, K. and Pruitt, D.G. (eds) *Mediation Research: The Process and Effectiveness of Third-Party Intervention*, Jossey-Bass, San Francisco.

Chairman's conclusions (1999) "Chairman's conclusions of the ministerial Contact Group in London," January 29. Available online at: www.ohr.int/other-doc/contact-g/default.asp?content_id=3558 (accessed December 15, 2014).

Chandler, D. (1998) "Historical Context: Cambodia's Historical Legacy," in *Safeguarding Peace: Cambodia's Constitutional Challenge*, Conciliation Resources, London, pp. 12–19.

Clayton, G. (2013) "Relative Rebel Strength and the Onset and Outcome of Civil War Mediation," *Journal of Peace Research*, Vol. 50, No. 5, pp. 609–622.

CNN (2008) *Former Finland leader accepts Nobel Peace Prize*, December 10. Available online at: www.youtube.com/watch?v=dlfrvL3z4x8 (accessed December 15, 2014).

Collier, D., Brady, H.E. and Seawright, J. (2004) "Critiques, Responses and Trade-Offs: Drawing Together the Debate," in Brady, H.E. and Collier, D. (eds) *Rethinking Social Inquiry: Diverse Tools Shared Standards*, Rowman and Littlefield, Boulder, CO, pp. 195–227.

Conciliation Resources (2008) *Learning from the Indonesia-Aceh peace process*, Policy brief, London. Available online at: www.c-r.org/sites/default/files/Accord%2020_Indonesia_policybrief_2008_ENG.pdf (accessed November 17, 2014).

Contact Group – Ten Guidelines principles (2005) "Guiding principles of the Contact Group for a settlement of the status of Kosovo," October 7. Available online at: www.unosek.org/docref/Contact%20Group%20-%20Ten%20Guiding%20principles%20for%20Ahtisaari.pdf (accessed December 15, 2014).

Contact Group Statement (1999) "Contact Group Statement: Rambouillet Accords: Co-Chairmen's Conclusions," February 23. Available online at: www.ohr.int/other-doc/contact-g/default.asp?content_id=3560 (accessed December 15, 2014).

Contact Group London Statement (2006) "Statement by The Contact Group on The Future of Kosovo," January 31, 2006. Available online at: www.unosek.org/docref/fevrier/STATEMENT%20BY%20THE%20CONTACT%20GROUP%20ON%20THE%20FUTURE%20OF%20KOSOVO%20-%20Eng.pdf (accessed December 15, 2014).

Contact Group New York Statement (2006) "Contact Group Ministerial Statement, 20 September 2006". Available online at: www.unosek.org/docref/2006-09-20_-_CG%20_Ministerial_Statement_New%20_York.pdf (accessed December 15, 2014).

CPA (2007) "War, Peace and Governance in Sri Lanka," Centre for Policy Alternatives, December 31. Available online at: www.reliefweb.int/rw/RWB.NSF/db900SID/AMMF-6ZPDGQ?OpenDocument&rc=3&cc=lka (accessed December 15, 2014).

Crawford, W.T. (2002) "Pivotal Deterrence and the Kosovo War: Why the Holbrooke Agreement Failed," *Political Science Quarterly*, Vol. 116, No. 4, pp. 499–526.

Crescenzi, M.J.C., Kadera K.M., McLaughlin Mitchell S. and Thyne C.L. (2011) "A Supply Side Theory of Mediation," *International Studies Quarterly*, Vol. 55, No. 4, pp. 1069–1094.

Crocker, C.A. (1993) *High Noon in Southern Africa: Making Peace in a Rough Neighborhood*, W. W. Norton & Co Inc., London and New York.

Crocker, C.A. (1999) "Peacemaking in Southern Africa: The Namibia–Angola Settlement of 1988," in Crocker, C.A., Hampson, F.O. and Aall, P.R. (eds) *Herding Cats: Multiparty Mediation in a Complex World*, United States Institute of Peace Press, Washington DC, pp. 207–244.

Crocker, C.A., Hampson, F.O. and Aall, P.R. (1999) *Herding Cats: Multiparty Mediation in a Complex World*, United States Institute of Peace Press, Washington DC.

Crocker, C.A., Hampson, F.O. and Aall, P.R. (2001) "Crowded Stage: Liabilities and benefits of Multiparty Mediation," *International Studies Perspectives*, Vol. 2, No. 1, pp. 51–67.

Crocker, C.A., Hampson, F.O. and Aall, P.R. (2003) "Two is Company but three is Crowd? Some Hypotheses about Multiparty Mediation," in Bercovitch, J. (ed.) *Studies in International Mediation*, Palgrave Macmillan, London, pp. 228–257.

Crocker, C.A., Hampson, F.O. and Aall, P.R. (2004) *Taming Intractable Conflicts: Mediating in the Most Resistant Cases*, United States Institute of Peace Press, Washington DC.

Crocker, C.A., Hampson, F.O. and Aall, P.R. (2005) *Grasping the Nettle: Analyzing the Cases of Intractable Conflicts*, United States Institute of Peace Press, Washington DC.

Council of the European Union (2006) *Declaration by the Presidency on Behalf of the European Union Concerning the Listing of the LTTE as a Terrorist Organization*, Council of the European Union, May 31. Available online at: www.consilium.europa.eu/uedocs/cms_Data/docs/pressdata/en/cfsp/89790.pdf (accessed December 15, 2014).

Cunningham, D.E. (2006) "Veto Players and Civil War Duration," *American Journal of Political Science*, Vol. 50, No. 4, pp. 875–892.

Cunningham, D.E. (2010) "Blocking Resolution: How External States Can Prolong Civil Wars," *Journal of Peace Resolution*, Vol. 47, No. 2, pp. 115–127.

Curran, D., Sebenius, J.K. and Watkins, M. (2004) "Two Paths to Peace: Contrasting George Mitchell in Northern Ireland with Richard Holbrooke in Bosnia–Herzegovina," *Negotiation Journal*, Vol. 20, No. 4, pp. 513–537.

D'Aspremont, J. (2007) "Regulating Statehood: The Kosovo Status Settlement," *Leiden Journal of International Law*, Vol. 20, No. 3, pp. 649–668.

Daily Mirror (2002) "LTTE Comes Two Steps Down," *Daily Mirror*, December 6.

Danilov, D. (1999) "Russia's Role," in Cohen, J. (ed.) *A Question of Sovereignty: The Georgia–Abkhazia Peace Process*, Conciliation Resources, London, pp. 42–49. Available online at: www.c-r.org/sites/default/files/Accord%2007_10Russia%27s%20role_1999_ENG.pdf (accessed November 21, 2014).

Davies, J.E. (2007) *Constructive Engagement? Chester Crocker & American Policy in South Africa, Namibia and Angola*, Ohio University Press, Athens, OH.

DeVotta, N. (2007) "Sinhalese Buddhist Nationalist Ideology: Implications for Politics and Conflict Resolution in Sri Lanka," *Policy Studies 40*, East-West Center. Available online at: www.eastwestcenter.org/fileadmin/stored/pdfs/ps040.pdf (accessed December 15, 2014).

Diehl, P.F. and Lepgold, J. (2003) *Regional Conflict Management*, Rowman and Littlefield Publishers, Boulder, CO.

Dixit, J.N. (2002) *India-Pakistan in War and Peace*, Routledge, New York.

Dixon, I.W. (1993) "Democracy and Management of International Conflict," *Journal of Conflict Resolution*, Vol. 37, No. 1, pp. 42–68.

Dobrynin, A. (1995) *In Confidence: Moscow's Ambassador to America's Six Cold War Presidents*, Times Books, New York.

Drašković, V. (2006) "Kosovu sve osim UN-a," *B92*, 30 March, Belgrade.

Druckman, D. (1997) "Negotiating in the International Context," in Zartman, I.W. and Rasmussen, J.L. (eds) *Peacemaking in International Conflict: Methods and Techniques*, United States Institute of Peace Press, Washington DC, pp. 81–124.

Dunn, L.A. and Kriesberg, L. (2002) "Mediating Intermediaries: Expanding Roles of Transnational Organizations," in Bercovitch, J. (ed.) *Studies in International Mediation*, Palgrave Macmillan, London, pp. 195–212.

Economist (2001) "Hitting the Tigers in Their Pockets," *The Economist*, March 8.

European Commission (2003) "Commissioner Patten Visits Sri Lanka on 25–26 November 2003," November 21. Available online at: http://eu-un.europa.eu/articles/en/article_3024_en.htm (accessed December 15, 2014).

European Commission (2010) "EU Temporarily Withdraws GSP+ Trade Benefits from Sri Lanka," February 15. Available online at: http://trade.ec.europa.eu/doclib/press/index.cfm?id=515 (accessed December 15, 2014).

Evans, G. (2008) "The Responsibility to Protect: An Idea Whose Time Has Come ... and Gone?," *International Relations*, Vol. 22, No. 3, pp. 283–298.

Favretto, K. (2009) "Should Peacemakers Take Sides: Major Power mediation, coercion, and bias," *American Political Science Review*, Vol. 103, No. 2, pp. 248–263.

Fearon, J.D. (1995) "Rationalist Explanation of War," *International Organization*, Vol. 49, No. 3, pp. 379–414.

Fearon, J.D. (1998) "Bargaining, Enforcement, and International Cooperation," *International Organization*, Vol. 52, No. 2, pp. 269–306.

Fernando, A. (2006) "The Peace Process and Security Issues," in Rupesinghe K. (ed.) *Negotiating Peace in Sri Lanka: Efforts, Failures and Lessons.* 2nd ed., Vol. 1, Foundation for Co-Existence, Colombo.

Financial Times (2006) *Russia and China "pledge not to block new Kosovo,"* March 14. Available online at: www.ft.com/cms/s/0/24b5d91e-b399-11da-89c7-0000779e2340. html#axzz3OcAPpLRZ (accessed December 15, 2014).

Fisher, R. (2006) "Coordination Between Track Two and Track One Diplomacy in Successful Cases of Prenegotiation," *International Negotiation*, Vol. 11, No. 1, pp. 65–89.

Fisher, R. and Keashly, L. (1991) "The Potential Complementarity of Mediation and Consultation Within a Contingency Model of Third Party Intervention," *Journal of Peace Research*, Vol. 28. No. 1, pp. 29–42.

Fortna, V.P. (2003) "Scraps of Paper? Agreements and the Durability of Peace," *International Organization*, Vol. 57, No. 2, pp. 337–372.

Fournier, D. (1999) "The Alfonsìn Administration and the Promotion of Democratic Values in the Southern Cone and the Andes," *Journal of Latin American Studies*, Vol. 31, No. 1, pp. 39–74.

Franck, T.M. (1990) *The Power of Legitimacy among Nations*, Oxford University Press, Oxford.

Frazier, D.V. and Dixon, W.J. (2006) "Third Party Intermediaries and Negotiated Settlements, 1946–2000," *International Interactions*, Vol. 32, No. 4, pp. 385–408.

French, J.R.P. and Raven, B. (1959) "The Bases of Social Power," in Cartwright, D. (ed.) *Studies in Social Power*, Institute for Social Research, Ann Arbor, MI, pp. 150–167.

Frerks, G. and Klem, B. (2006) "Conditioning Peace among Protagonists: A Study into the Use of Peace Conditionalities in the Sri Lankan Peace Process," Netherlands Institute of International Relations "Clingendael," June. Available online at: www.clingendael.nl/publications/2006/20060600_cru_frerks_klem.pdf (accessed December 15, 2014).

Fretter, Judith (2002) "International Organizations and Conflict Management: the United Nations and the Mediation of International Conflicts," in Bercovitch, J. (ed.) *Studies in International Mediation*, Palgrave Macmillan, London, pp. 98–126.

Galtung, J. (1969) "Violence, Peace, and Peace Research," *Journal of Peace Research*, Vol. 6, No. 3, pp. 167–191.

Galtung, J. (1990) "Cultural Violence," *Journal of Peace Research*, Vol. 27, No. 3, pp. 291–305.

Gartner, S.S. (2013) "Deceptive Results: Why Mediation Appears to Fail but Actually Succeeds," *Penn State Journal of Law and International Affairs*, Vol. 2, No. 1, pp. 27–37.

Gartner, S.S. and Segura, G.M. (1998) "War, Casualties and Public Opinion," *Journal of Conflict Resolution*, Vol. 42, No. 3, pp. 278–300.

Gartner, S.S. and Segura, G.M. (2000) "Race, Opinion and Causalities in the Vietnam War," *Journal of Politics*, Vol. 62, No. 1, pp. 115–146.

Gartner, S.S., Segura, G.M. and Barratt, B. (2004) "Causalities, Positions and State Elections in the Vietnam War," *Political Research Quarterly*, Vol. 53, No. 3, pp. 467–477.

Geldenhuys, J. (1995) *A General's Story: From an Era of War and Peace*, Jonathan Ball, Johannesburg.

Gent, S.M. and Shannon, M. (2011) "Bias and the Effectiveness of Third-Party Conflict Management Mechanisms," *Conflict Management and Peace Science*, Vol. 28, No. 2, pp. 124–144.

George, A.L. and Bennett, A. (2005) *Case Studies and Theory Development in the Social Sciences*, MIT Press, Cambridge, MA.

Gerring, J. (2005) Causation: A Unified Framework for the Social Sciences, *Journal of Theoretical Politics*, Vol. 17, No. 2, pp. 163–198.

Gerring, J. (2007) *Case Study Research*, Cambridge University Press, Cambridge.

Gleijeses, P. (2006) "Moscow's Proxy? Cuba and Africa 1975–1988," *Journal of Cold War Studies*, Vol. 8, No. 2, pp. 3–51.

Glennan, S.S. (1996) "Mechanisms and the Nature of Causation," *Erkenntins*, Vol. 44, No. 1, pp. 49–71.

Goodhand, J. (2006a) "Conditioning Peace? The Scope and Limitations of Peace Condition-alities in Afghanistan and Sri Lanka," Netherlands Institute of International Relations "Clingendael" June. Available online at: www.clingendael.nl/publications/2006/20060800_cru_goodhand.pdf (accessed December 15, 2014).

Goodhand, J. (2006b) "Internationalization of the Peace Process," Lecture held at the international seminar "Envisioning New Trajectories for Peace in Sri Lanka," Zurich, April 7–9.

Goodhand, J. and Bart, K. (2005) "Aid, Conflict and Peacebuilding in Sri Lanka 2000–2005," *Sri Lanka Strategic Conflict Assessment 2005*, Vol. 1, Asia Foundation. Available online at: http://asiafoundation.org/publications/pdf/208 (accessed December 15, 2014).

Goodhand, J. and Korf, B. (2011) "Caught in a Peace Trap? On the illiberal consequences of liberal peace in Sri Lanka," in Goodhand, J., Korf, B. and Spencer, J. (eds) *Conflict and Peacebuilding in Sri Lanka: Caught in a Peace Trap?*, Routledge, London, pp. 1–15.

Goodhand, J., Korf, B. and Spencer, J. (2011) *Conflict and Peacebuilding in Sri Lanka: Caught in a Peace Trap?* Routledge, London.

Gordon, B.K. (1986) "The Third Indochina Conflict," *Foreign Affairs*, Vol. 65, No. 1, pp. 66–85.

Goryayev, V. (2001) "Architecture of the International Involvement in the Tajik Peace Process," in Abdullaev, K. and Barnes, C. (2001) *Politics of Compromise: The Tajikistan Peace Process*, Conciliation Resources, London, pp. 32–37.

Greig, M.J. (2005) "Stepping into the Fray: When Do Mediators Mediate," *American Journal of Political Science*, Vol. 49, No. 2, pp. 249–266.

Greig, M.J. and Diehl, P. (2012) *International Mediation*, Polity, Cambridge, UK.

Gretsky, S. (1995) "Civil war in Tajikistan and its international repercussions," *Critique*, Vol. 4, No. 6, pp. 3–24.

Groeneveld-Savisaar, M. and Vuković, S. (2011) "Terror, Muscle and Mediation: Failure of Multiparty Mediation in Sri Lanka," in *Engaging Extremists: Trade-Offs, Timing and Diplomacy*, Zartman, I.W. and Faure, G.O. (eds) US Institute of Peace Press: Washington DC, pp. 165–198.

Hampson, F.O. (1995) *Multilateral Negotiations*, Johns Hopkins University Press, Baltimore, MD.

Hampson, F.O. (2010) "Deconstructing Multilateral Cooperation," in Zartman, I.W. and Touval, S. (eds) *Cooperation: The Extensions and Limits of International Multilateralism*. Cambridge University Press, New York, pp. 60–77.

Hampson, F.O. and Zartman, I.W. (2011) *The Global Power of Talk: Negotiating America's Interests*, Paradigm Publishers, Boulder, CO.

Hara, F. (1999) "Burundi: Case of Parallel Diplomacy," in Crocker C.A., Hampson, F.O. and Aall, P. (eds) *Herding Cats: Multiparty Mediation in a Complex World*, United States Institute of Peace, Washington DC, pp. 135–157.

Hay, E.R. (2001) "Methodology of the inter-Tajik negotiation process," in Abdullaev, K. and Barnes, C. (eds) *Politics of Compromise: The Tajikistan Peace Process*, Conciliation Resources, London, pp. 38–44.

Hedström, P. and Swedberg, R. (1998) *Social Mechanisms and Analytical Approach to Social Theory*, Cambridge University Press, Cambridge.

Heldt, B. (2013) "The Lack of Coordination in Diplomatic Peacemaking," *Penn State Journal of Law and International Affairs*, Vol. 2, No. 1, pp. 9–16.

Hendrickson, D. (1998) *Safeguarding Peace: Cambodia's Constitutional Challenge*, Conciliation Resources, London.

Herrberg, A. and Savaloainen, M. (2009) *What is a Good Mediator? Personal Insights on the Essentials of a Good Mediator: Martti Ahtisaari, Nobel Peace Prize Laureate 2008*, Initiative for Peacebuilding, Brussels. Available online at: www.initiativefor-peacebuilding.eu/pdf/WHAT_IS_A_GOOD_MEDIATOR.pdf (accessed December 15, 2014).

Hill, W. (2005) *Russia, the Near Abroad, and the West: Lessons from the Moldova-Transdniestria Conflict*, The Johns Hopkins University Press, Baltimore, MD.

Hiltrop, J.M. (1985) "Mediator Behavior and the Settlement of Collective Bargaining Disputes in Britain," *Journal of Social Issues*, Vol. 41, No. 2, pp. 83–99.

Hiltrop, J.M. (1989) "Factors Affected with Successful Labor Mediation," in Kressel, K. and Pruitt, D.G. (eds) *Mediation Research: The Process and Effectiveness of Third-Party Intervention*, Jossey-Bass, San Francisco, CA, pp. 241–262.

Hiro, D. (1995) "Tajikistan: Peace is elusive," *Middle East International*, 499: 14–15.

Hiro, D. (1996) "Tajikistan: A fractured country," *Middle East International*, 540: 14.

Hiro, D. (1998) "Politics in Central Asia: two contrasting cases," *Middle East International*, 571: 18–20.

Höglund, K. and Svensson, I. (2006) "'Sticking One's Neck Out': Reducing Mistrust in Sri Lanka's Peace Negotiations," *Negotiation Journal*, Vol. 22, No. 4, pp. 336–87.

Höglund, K. and Svensson, I. (2007) "The Peace Process in Sri Lanka," *Civil Wars*, Vol. 5, No. 4, pp. 103–118.

Höglund, K. and Svensson, I. (2009) "Mediating between Tigers and Lions: Norwegian Peace Diplomacy in Sri Lanka's Civil War," *Contemporary South Asia*, Vol. 17, No. 2, pp. 175–191.

Höglund, K. and Svensson, I. (2011) "Schizophrenic Soothers: The International Community and Contrast Strategies for Peace-Making in Sri Lanka," *Cooperation and Conflict*, Vol. 46, No. 2, pp. 166–184.

Holbrooke, R. (1998) *To End a War*, Random House, New York.

Holsti, K.J. (1966) "Resolving International Conflicts: A Taxonomy of Behaviour and Some Figures on Procedures," *Journal of Conflict Resolution*, Vol. 10, No. 3, pp. 272–296.

Holsti, K.J. (1991) *Peace and War: Armed Conflict and International Order*, Cambridge University Press, Cambridge.

Hood, L. (2006) "Missed Opportunities: The United Nations, Police Service and Defence Force Development in Timor-Leste, 1999–2004," *Civil Wars*, Vol. 8, No. 2, pp. 143–162.

Hopmann, P.T. (1996) *The Negotiation Process and the Resolution of International Conflicts*, University of South Carolina Press, Columbia, SC.

Hopmann, P.T. (2001) "Bargaining and Problem Solving: Two Perspectives on International Negotiation." in Crocker, C.A., Hampson, F.O. and Aall, P.R. (eds) *Turbulent Peace: The Challenges of Managing International Conflicts, United States Institute of Peace Press*, Washington DC, pp. 445–468.

Hopmann, P.T. (2010) "Synthesizing Rationalist and Constructivist Perspectives on Negotiated Cooperation," in Zartman, I.W. and Touval, S. (eds) *Cooperation: The Extensions and Limits of International Multilateralism*, Cambridge University Press, New York, pp. 95–110.

Horvat, B. (1988) *Kosovsko pitanje*, Globus, Zagreb.

Human Rights Watch (1995) *Sri Lanka: Stop Killing Civilians*, Human Rights Watch, July 1.

Hume, C. (1994) *Ending Mozambique's War: The role of mediation and good offices*, United States Institute of Peace Press, Washington DC

Hurd, I. (2002) "Legitimacy, Power, and the Symbolic Life of the UN Security Council," *Global Governance*, Vol. 8, No. 1, pp. 35–51.

Hyde Smith, P. (2005) *Moldova Matters: Why Progress is Still Possible on Ukraine's West Flank*, Atlantic Council: Washington DC

ICG (2006a) "Sri Lanka: The Failure of the Peace Process," International Crisis Group, November 28, 2006, Brussels.

ICG (2006b) "Kosovo: The Challenge of Transition," *International Crisis Group, Europe Report* No. 170, February 17, 2006, Brussels.

ICG (2006c) "Kosovo Status: Delay is Risky," *International Crisis Group, Europe Report* No. 177, November 10, 2006, Brussels.

ICG (2007a) "No Good Alternatives to the Ahtisaari Plan," *International Crisis Group, Europe Report* No. 182, May 14, 2007, Brussels.

ICG (2007b) "Kosovo Countdown: A Blueprint for Transition," *International Crisis Group, Europe Report* No. 188, December 6, 2007, Brussels.

Iji, T. (2001) "Multiparty Mediation in Tajikistan: The 1997 Peace Agreement," *International Negotiation*, Vol. 6, No. 3, pp. 357–385.

Iji, T. (2005) "Cooperation, Coordination and Complementarity in International Peacemaking: The Tajikistan Experience," *International Peacekeeping*, Vol. 12, No. 2, pp. 189–204.

Iji, T. (2011) "Contact Group Diplomacy: The Strategies of the Western Contact Group in Mediating Namibian Conflict," *Diplomacy & Statecraft*, Vol. 22, No. 4, pp. 634–650.

Inbar, E. (1991) "Great Power Mediation: The USA and the May 1983 Israeli-Lebanese Agreement," *Journal of Peace Research*, Vol. 28, No. 1, pp. 71–84.

IPS News (2006) *SRI LANKA: Sinhala Groups Tire of Norwegian Peace Brokers*, Colombo, March 24. Available online at: www.ipsnews.net/2006/03/sri-lanka-sinhala-groups-tire-of-norwegian-peace-brokers/ (accessed November 16, 2014).

Jackson, E. (1952) *Meeting of Minds, a Way to Peace through Mediation*, McGraw Hill: New York.

Jeremić, V. (2006) "Priznavanje nezavisnosti – političko samoubistvo," *B92*, April 14, 2006, Belgrade.

Joenniemi, P. (2014) "Peace Mediation and Conflict Resolution: The Policies Pursued by Four Nordic Countries," in Lehti, M. (ed.) *Nordic Approaches to Peace Mediation Research, Practices and Policies*, Tampere Peace Research Institute, TAPRI Studies in Peace and Conflict Research No. 101, pp. 93–144.

Jones, B.D. (2002) "Challenges of Strategic Coordination," in Stedman, S.J., Rothchild, D. and Cousens, E.M. (eds) *Ending Civil Wars: The Implementation of Peace Agreements*, Lynne Rienner, Boulder, CO, pp. 89–116.

Kelleher, A. (2006) "A Small State's Multiple-level Approach to Peace-making: Norway's Role in Achieving Sudan's Comprehensive Peace Agreement," *Civil Wars*, Vol. 8, No. 3–4, pp. 285–311.

Kelleher, A. and Taulbee, J.L. (2005) "Building Peace Norwegian Style: Studies in Track I½ Diplomacy," in Richmond, O.P. and Carey, H.F. (eds) *Subcontracting Peace: The Challenges of NGO Peacebuilding*, Ashgate, Aldershot, UK.

Keohane, R.O. (1984) *After Hegemony: Cooperation and Discord in the World Political Economy*, Princeton University Press, Princeton, NJ.

Keohane, R.O. and Nye, J.S (1977) *Power and Interdependence: World Politics in Transition*. Little Brown, Boston, MA.

Ker-Lindsay, J. (2009) *Kosovo: The Path to Contested Statehood in the Balkans*, I.B. Tauris, London.

Kiernan, B. (1985) *How Pol Pot Came to Power: A History of Communism in Kampuchea, 1930–1975*, Verso, London.

Kiernan, B. (2002) Introduction: Conflict in Cambodia, 1945–2002, *Critical Asian Studies*, Vol. 34, No. 4, pp. 483–495.

Ki-moon, B. (2008) *Secretary-General's Remarks at Security Council High-Level Debate on Mediation and the Settlement of Disputes*, New York. Available online at: www.un.org/sg/statements/?nid=3416 (accessed December 15, 2014).

Ki-moon, B. (2009) *Report of the Secretary General on Enhancing Mediation and its Support Activities*, New York. (United Nations Security Council Document S/2009/189) Available online at: www.un.org/en/ga/search/view_doc.asp?symbol=S/2009/189 (accessed December 15, 2014).

King, G., Keohane, R.O. and Verba, S. (1994) *Designing Social Inquiry: Scientific Inference in Qualitative Research*, Princeton University Press, Princeton.

Kissinger, H. (1999) *Years of Renewal*, Simon & Schuster, New York.

Kleiboer, M. (1994) "Ripeness of Conflict: A Fruitful Notion?," *Journal of Peace Research*, Vol. 31, No. 1, pp. 109–116.

Kissinger, H. (1996) "Understanding Success and Failure of International Mediation," *Journal of Conflict Resolution*, Vol. 40, No. 2, pp. 360–389.

Knoll, B. (2005) "From Benchmarking to Final Status? Kosovo and The Problem of an International Administration's Open-Ended Mandate," *The European Journal of International Law*, Vol. 16, No. 4, pp. 637–660.

Knoll, B. (2006) "Legitimacy through defiance: The UN and local institutions in Kosovo," *Helsinki Monitor*, No. 4, pp. 313–326.

Kolb, D. (1983) "Strategy and Tactics of Mediation," *Human Relations*, Vol. 36, No. 3, pp. 247–268.

Kreilkamp, J.S. (2003) "U.N. Postconflict Reconstruction," *New York University Journal of International Law and Politics*, Vol. 35, No. 3, pp. 619–670.

Kriesberg, L. (1991) "Formal and Quasi-Mediators in International Disputes: An Explanatory Analysis," *Journal of Peace Research*, Vol. 28, No. 1, pp. 19–27.

Kriesberg, L. (1996) "Coordinating Intermediary Peace Efforts," *Negotiation Journal*, Vol. 12, No. 4, pp. 341–352.

Kriesberg, L. (2003) *Constructive Conflicts: From Escalation to Resolution*, Rowman and Littlefield, Lanham, MD.

Kriesberg, L. (2005) "Nature, Dynamics, and Phases of Intractability," in Crocker, C.A., Hampson, F.O. and Aall, P.R. (eds) *Grasping the Nettle: Analyzing Cases of Intractable Conflict*, United States Institute of Peace Press, Washington DC, pp. 65–97.

Kronstadt, A. K. (2004) "India-U.S. Relations," in *CRS Issue Brief for Congress*, November 4. Congressional Research Service, Library of Congress. Available online at: http://fpc.state.gov/documents/organization/37996.pdf (accessed March 22, 2012).

Kumanovo Agreement (1999) "Military Technical Agreement Between the International Security Force ("KFOR") and the Governments of Federal Republic of Yugoslavia and the Republic of Serbia," June 9. Available online at: www.nato.int/kosovo/docu/a990609a.htm (accessed July 10, 2015).

Kydd, A. (2003) "Which Side Are You On? Bias, Credibility and Mediation," *American Journal of Political Science*, Vol. 47, No. 4, pp. 579–611.

Kydd, A. (2006) "When Can Mediators Build Trust?," *American Political Science Review*, Vol. 100, No. 3, pp. 449–462.

Large, S. and Aguswandi (2008) "Introduction: The Forging of Identity, the Imperative of Political Voice and Meeting Human Needs," in Aguswandi and Large, S. (eds) *Reconfiguring politics: the Indonesia – Aceh peace process*, Conciliation Resources, London, pp. 6–11.

Laurence, H. (2007) "Japan's Proactive Foreign Policy and the Rise of the BRICS," *Asian Perspective*, Vol. 31, No. 4, pp. 177–203.

Lax, D.A. and Sebenius J.K. (1991): "Thinking Coalitionally: Party Arithmetic, Process Opportunism, and Strategic Sequencing," in Young, H.P. (ed.) *Negotiation Analysis*, University of Michigan Press, Ann Arbor, MI, pp. 153–193.

Levitin, Oleg (2000) "Inside Moscow's Kosovo Muddle," *Survival*, Vol. 42, No. 1, pp. 130–140.

Lewicki, R.J., Gray, B. and Elliott, M. (2003) *Making Sense of Intractable Environmental Conflicts: Concepts and Cases*, Island Press, Washington DC.

Lund, M.S. (1996) *Preventing Violent Conflicts: A Strategy for Preventive Diplomacy*, United States Institute of Peace Press, Washington DC.

Lund, M.S. (2005) "Early Warning and Preventive Diplomacy," in Crocker, C.A., Hampson, F.O. and Aall, P. (eds) *Managing Global Chaos: Sources of and Responses to International Conflict*, United States Institute of Peace Press, Washington DC, pp. 379–402.

Lunstead, J. (2007) "The United States' Role in Sri Lanka's Peace Process 2002–2006," *Asia Foundation*. Available online at: http://asiafoundation.org/publications/pdf/209 (accessed December 15, 2014).

Maoz, Z. and Terris, L.G. (2006) "Credibility and Strategy in International Mediation," *International Interactions*, Vol. 32, No. 4, pp. 409–440.

Maoz, Z. and Terris, L.G. (2009) "Credibility and Strategy in International Mediation," in Bercovitch J. and Gartner, S.S. (eds) *International Conflict Management: New Approaches and Findings*, Routledge, London, pp. 69–95.

Martin, B.L. (1989) "American Policy Towards Southern Africa in the 1980s," *Journal of Modern African Studies*, Vol. 27, No. 1, pp. 23–46.

Martin, H. (2006) *Kings of Peace, Pawns of War: The Untold Story of Peace-making*, Continuum, London.

Maundi, M.O., Zartman, I.W., Khadiagala, G. and Nuamah, K. (2006) *Getting In: Mediators' Entry into the Settlement of African Conflicts*, United States Institute of Peace, Washington, DC.

McLaughlin Mitchell, S. (2002) "A Kanitan System? Democracy and Third-Party Conflict Resolution," *American Journal of Political Science*, Vol. 46, No. 4, pp. 749–759.

Meerts, P. (2004) "Entrapment in International Negotiations," in Zartman, I.W. and Faure, G.O. (eds) *Escalation and Negotiation in International Conflicts*, Cambridge University Press, Cambridge, pp. 111–140.

Meijer, G. (2004) *Accord: From Military Peace to Social Justice? The Angolan Peace Process*, Conciliation Resources, London.

Meijer, G. and Birmingham, D. (2004) "Angola from Past to Present," in Meijer, G. (ed.) *Accord: From Military Peace to Social Justice? The Angolan Peace Process*, Conciliation Resources, London, pp. 10–15.

Melin, M.M. (2013) "When States Mediate," *Penn State Journal of Law and International Affairs*, Vol. 2, No. 1, pp. 78–90.

Melin, M.M. and Svensson, I. (2009) "Incentives for Talking: Accepting Mediation in International and Civil Wars," *International Interactions*, Vol. 35, No. 3, pp. 249–271.

Melin, M.M., Gartner, S.S. and Bercovitch, J. (2013) "Fear of Rejection: The Puzzle of Unaccepted Mediation Offers in International Conflict," *Conflict Management and Peace Science*, Vol. 30, No. 4, pp. 354–368.

Mesbahi, M. (1997) "Tajikistan, Iran, and the international politics of the 'Islamic factor'," *Central Asian Survey*, Vol. 16, No. 2, pp. 141–158.

Meyer, G. (2004) From Military Peace to Social Justice: The Angolan Peace Process, Conciliation Resources, London.

Miall, H. (1992) *The Peacemakers: Peaceful Settlements of Disputes Since 1945*, Palgrave Macmillan, London.

Mišović, M. (1987) *Ko je tražio republiku: Kosovo 1945–1985*, Narodna Knjiga, Beograd.

Mitchell, C.R. (1981) *Peacemaking and the consultant's role*, Nicholas, New York.

Mitchell, C.R. (1993) "The process and stages of mediation: two Sudanese cases," in Smock, D.R. (ed.) *Making War and Waging Peace: Foreign Intervention in Africa*, United States Institute of Peace Press, Washington DC, pp. 139–159.

Mitchell, R.J. (1978) A New Brezhnev Doctrine: The Restructuring of International Relations, *World Politics*, Vol. 30, No. 3, pp. 366–390.

Mohan, C.R. (2006) "India and the Balance of Power," *Foreign Affairs*, Vol. 85, No. 4, pp. 17–32.

Moolakkattu, J. S. (2005) "Peace Facilitation by Small States: Norway in Sri Lanka," *Cooperation and Conflict*, Vol. 40, No. 4, pp. 385–402.

Moore, C.W. (1986) *The Mediation Process*, Jossey-Bass, San Francisco, CA.

Mueller, J. (1973) *War, Presidents and Public Opinion*, Wiley, New York.

Nan, S.A. and Strimling, A. (2006) "Coordination in Conflict Prevention, Conflict Resolution and Peacebuilding," *International Negotiation*, Vol. 11, No. 1, pp. 1–6.

Nguyen, H.P. (1993) "Russia and China: The Genesis of an Eastern Rapallo," *Asian Survey*, Vol. 33, No. 3, pp. 285–301.

Nizich, I. (1992) "Human rights abuses in Kosovo, 1990–1992," *Human Rights Watch*, Helsinki Watch, New York.

Noyahr, K. (2006) "The Role of the International Community," in Rupesinghe, K. (ed.) *Negotiating Peace in Sri Lanka: Efforts, Failures and Lessons.* 2nd ed., Vol. 1, Foundation for Co-Existence, Colombo.

NY Times, (2009) *Moscow Set To Back UN Resolution On Kosovo*, June 3. Available online at: www.nytimes.com/1999/06/03/news/03iht-nato.2.t_1.html (accessed December 15, 2014).

Nye, J.S. (2004) *Soft Power: The Means to Success in World Politics*, Public Affairs: New York.

Nye, J.S. (2008) "Public Diplomacy and Soft Power," *The ANNALS of the American Academy of Political and Social Science*, Vol. 616, pp. 94–109.

Nye, J.S. (2011) *The Future of Power*, Public Affairs: New York.

Olusoga, D. and Erichsen, C.W. (2010) *The Kaiser's Holocaust: Germany's Forgotten Genocide and the Colonial Roots of Nazism*, Faber and Faber, London.

Ott, M. (1972) "Mediation as a Method of Conflict Resolution: Two Cases," *International Organization*, Vol. 26, No. 4, pp. 595–618.

Oye, K.A., Lieber, J.L. and Rothchild, D. (1987) *Eagle Resurgent? The Regan Era in American Foreign Policy*, Little Brown & Co., Boston.

Page, J. (2009) "Chinese Billions in Sri Lanka Fund Battle against Tamil Tigers," *Times* (London), May 2.

Perritt Jr, H.H. (2005) "Final Status for Kosovo," *Chicago-Kent Law Review*, Vol. 80, No. 3, pp. 3–27.

Pevehouse, J.C. (2002) "With a Little Help From My Friends? Regional Organizations and the Consolidation of Democracy," *American Journal of Political Science*, Vol. 46, No. 3, pp. 611–626.

Philipson, L. and Thangarajah, Y. (2005) "The Politics of the North-East," *Sri Lanka Strategic Conflict Assessment 2005*, Vol. 4. Asia Foundation. Available online at: http://asiafoundation.org/publications/pdf/212 (accessed March 22, 2012).

Phillips, D.L. (2012) *Liberating Kosovo: Coercive Diplomacy and U.S. Intervention*, MIT Press, Cambridge, MA.

Pinfari, M. (2013) "Interregionalism and Multiparty Mediation," *International Journal of Peace Studies*, Vol. 18, No. 1, pp. 83–101.

Posen, R.B. (2000) "The War for Kosovo: Serbia's Political-Military Strategy," *International Security*, Vol. 24, No. 4, pp. 39–84.

Powell, R. (2002) "Bargaining Theory and International Conflict," *Annual Review of Political Science*, Vol. 5, pp. 1–30.

Prantl, J. (2005) "Informal Groups of States and the UN Security Council," *International Organization*, Vol. 59, No. 3, pp. 559–592.

Prantl, J. (2006) *The UN Security Council and Informal Groups of States*, Oxford University Press, Oxford.

Princen, T. (1992) *International Intermediaries in Conflict*, Princeton University Press, Princeton, NJ.

Pruitt, D.G. (2002) "Mediator Behavior and Success in Mediation," in Bercovitch, J. (ed.) *Studies in International Mediation*, Palgrave Macmillan, London, pp. 41–54.

Pycroft, C. (1994) "Angola – 'The Forgotten Tragedy'," *Journal of Southern African Studies*, Vol. 20, No. 2, pp. 241–262.

Ram, N. (2001) "I Can Confirm that the Peace Process Is Moving," Interview with Lakshman Kadirgamar, *Frontline* Vol. 18, No. 8, pp. 124–127. Available online at: www.hinduonnet.com/fline/fl1808/18081230.htm (accessed December 15, 2014).

Ramet, S.P. (1992) *Nationalism and Federalism in Yugoslavia 1962–1991*, Indiana University Press, Bloomington and Indianapolis.

Rao, P.V. (1988) "Ethnic Conflict in Sri Lanka: India's Role and Perception," *Asian Survey*, Vol. 28, No. 4, pp. 419–436.

Ratner, S.R. (1993) "The Cambodia Settlement Agreements," *The American Journal of International Law*, Vol. 87, No. 1, pp. 1–41.

Raymond, G. and Kegley, C. (1985) "Third Party Mediation and International Norms: A Test of Two Models," *Conflict Management and Peace Science*, Vol. 9, No. 1, pp. 33–52.

Regulation 2001/9, Constitutional Framework for Self-Government www.unmikonline.org/regulations/2001/reg09-01.htm.

Richmond, O. (1998) "Devious Objectives and the Disputants' View of International Mediation: A Theoretical Framework," *Journal of Peace Research*, Vol. 35, No. 6, pp. 707–722.

Rohan, A. (2005) "Press Briefing by UN Deputy Special Envoy for the Future Status Process for Kosovo Albert Rohan," December 14, 2005, Priština. Available online at: www.unosek.org/docref/fevrier/2005-12-14-Albert_Rohan_press_conference.pdf (accessed July 10, 2015).

Ross, R.S. (2006) "Comparative Deterrence: The Taiwan Strait and the Korean Peninsula," in Johnston, A.I. and Ross, R.S. (eds) *New Directions in the Study of China's Foreign Policy*, Stanford University Press, Stanford, CA, pp. 13–49.

Rotberg, R.I. (1999) "Sri Lanka's Civil War: From Mayhem toward Diplomatic Resolution," in Rotberg, R.I. (ed.) *Creating Peace in Sri Lanka: Civil War and Reconciliation*, Brookings Institution Press, Washington DC

Roy, O. (2001) "Inter-Regional Dynamics of War," in Abdullaev, K. and Barnes, C. (eds) *Politics of Compromise: The Tajikistan Peace Process*, Conciliation Resources, London, pp. 23–24.

Rubin, B.R. (1998) Introduction: The Tajikistan Peace Agreement. Available online at: www.eurasianet.org/resource/regional/rubinintro.html (accessed May 11, 2011).

Rubin, J.Z. (1980) "Experimental Research on Third-Party Intervention in Conflict," *Psychological Bulletin*, Vol. 87, No. 2, pp. 379–391.

Rubin, J.Z. (1992) "Conclusion: International Mediation in Context," in Bercovitch, J. and Rubin, J.Z. (eds) *Mediation in International Relations: Multiple Approaches to Conflict Management*, St. Martins' Press, New York.

Ruffert, M. (2001) "The Administration of Kosovo and East-Timor by the International Community," *International and Comparative Law Quarterly*, Vol. 50, No. 3, pp. 613–631.

Ruggie, J.G. (1993) *Multilateralism Matters: The Theory and Praxis of an Institutional Form*, Columbia University Press, New York.

Rupesinghe, Kumar (2006a) *Negotiating Peace in Sri Lanka: Efforts, Failures and Lessons*. 2nd ed., Vol. 1, Foundation for Co-Existence, Colombo.

Rupesinghe, Kumar (2006b) "Interview with Erik Solheim, Minister of International Development," in Rupesinghe, K. (ed.) *Negotiating Peace in Sri Lanka: Efforts, Failures and Lessons*, 2nd ed., Vol. 1, Foundation for Co-Existence, Colombo.

Rupesinghe, Kumar (2006c) "Introduction," in Rupesinghe, K. (ed.) *Negotiating Peace in Sri Lanka: Efforts, Failures and Lessons*, 2nd ed., Vol. 1, Foundation for Co-Existence, Colombo.

S/1999/648 (1999) Rambouillet Accords, February 23, 1999. Available online at: http://peacemaker.un.org/kosovo-rambouilletagreement99 (accessed July 10, 2015).

S/1999/1250 (1999) Report of the Secretary General on the United Nations Interim Administration Mission in Kosovo, December 23, 1999. Available online at: www.un.org/en/ga/search/view_doc.asp?symbol=S/1999/1250 (accessed July 10, 2015).

S/PRST/2005/51 (2005) "Statement by the President of the Security Council," October 24, 2005. Available online at: www.unosek.org/docref/s-prst-2005-51%20-%2024-10-2005%20-%20launch%20of%20the%20Status%20discussions%20in%20kosovo.pdf (accessed July 10, 2015).

S/RES/1160 (1998) United Nations Security Council Resolution 1160, March 31, 1998. Available online at: www.sipri.org/databases/embargoes/un_arms_embargoes/yugoslavia/yugoslavia-1998/1160 (accessed July 10, 2015).

S/RES/1199 (1998) United Nations Security Council Resolution 1199, September 23, 1998. Available online at: www.un.org/en/ga/search/view_doc.asp?symbol=S/RES/1199(1998) (accessed July 10, 2015).

S/RES/1244 (1999) United Nations Security Council Resolution1244, June 10, 1999. Available online at: http://daccess-dds-ny.un.org/doc/UNDOC/GEN/N99/172/89/PDF/N9917289.pdf?OpenElement (accessed July 10, 2015).

Samaranayake, G. (2006) "Of Phases and Paces," in Raman, B., Sathiya, M.N. and Chittaranjan, K. (eds) *Sri Lanka: Peace without Process*, Vijitha Yapa, Colombo.

Sambandan, V.S. (2002) "Our Options Limited in Sri Lanka: Sibal," *Hindu*, December 9.

Saravanamuttu, P. (2003) "Sri Lanka: The Best and Last Chance for Peace?," *Conflict, Security and Development*, Vol. 3, No. 1, pp. 129–138.

Saunders, H. (1996) "Prenegotiation and Circum-negotiation: Arenas of the Peace Process," in Crocker, C.A., Hampson, F.O. and Aall, P.R. (eds) *Managing Global Chaos: Sources of and Responses to International Conflict*, United States Institute of Peace Press, Washington, DC pp. 419–432.

Saunders, H. (1999) "The Multilevel Peace Process in Tajikistan," in Crocker, C.A., Hampson, F.O. and Aall, P. (eds) *Herding Cats: Multiparty Mediation in a Complex World*, United States Institute of Peace, Washington DC, pp. 159–181.

Seymour, L. (2014) "Let's Bullshit! Arguing, Bargaining and Dissembling over Darfur," *European Journal of International Relations*, Vol. 20, No. 3, pp. 571–595.

Shanmugaratnam, N. and Stokke, K. (2004) "Development as a Precursor to Conflict Resolution: A Critical Review of the Fifth Peace Process in Sri Lanka," in Shanmugaratnam, N. (ed.) *Between War and Peace*, James Currey, Oxford.

Shearman, P. (1987) "Gorbachev and the Third World: An Era of Reform?," *Third World Quarterly*, Vol. 9, No. 4, pp. 1083–1117.

Sick, G. (1985) "The Partial Negotiator: Algeria and the U.S. Hostages in Iran," in Touval, S. and Zartman, I.W. (eds) *International Mediation in Theory and Practice*, Westview, Boulder, CO.

Simić, P. (1995) "Dynamics of the Yugoslav Crisis," *Security Dialogue*, Vol. 26, No. 2, pp. 153–172.

Sisk, T. (2009) *International Mediation in Civil Wars: Bargaining with Bullets*, Routledge, London.

Slim, R. and Saunders, H. (2001) "The Inter-Tajik Dialogue: From Civil War Towards Civil Society," in Abdullaev, K. and Barnes, C. (eds) *Politics of Compromise: The Tajikistan Peace Process*, Conciliation Resources, London, pp. 44–47.

Smith, A.M. and Plater-Zyberk (1999) "Kosovo: Russia's Response," *Defence Academy of the United Kingdom*, www.da.mod.uk/colleges/csrc/archive/eastern-europe/KOSOVO% 20%20RUSSIAS%20RESPONSE.pdf.

Smith, C. (2007) "The Eelam Endgame?," *International Affairs*, Vol. 83, No. 1, pp. 69–86.

Smith, J.D.D. (1994) "Mediator Impartiality: Banishing the Chimera," *Journal of Peace Research*, Vol. 31, No. 4, pp. 445–450.

SLMM (2008) Sri Lankan Monitoring Mission. Available online at: www.slmm-history. info/ (accessed December 15, 2014).

Solomon, H.R. (1999) "Bringing Peace to Cambodia," in Chester, C.A., Hampson, F.O. and Aall, P. (eds) *Herding Cats: Multiparty Mediation in a Complex World*, United States Institute of Peace, Washington DC, pp. 275–325.

Solomon, H.R. (2000) *Exiting Indochina: U.S. Leadership of the Cambodia Settlement and Normalization with Vietnam*, United States Institute of Peace, Washington DC

Spiegel (2014) "Colombian President Santos: 'Waging War Is More Popular than Negotiating'," May 21. Available online at: www.spiegel.de/international/world/spiegel-interview-with-colombian-president-juan-manuel-santos-a-970308.html (accessed December 15, 2014).

Stahn, C. (2001a) "Constitution Without a State? Kosovo Under the United Nations Constitutional Framework for Self-Government," *Leiden Journal of International Law*, Vol. 14, No. 3, pp. 531–561.

Stahn, C. (2001b) "The United Nations Transitional Administrations in Kosovo and East Timor: a First Analysis," in *Max Planck Yearbook of United Nations Law*, Vol. 5, pp. 105–183.

Stein, J.G. (1989) "Getting to the Table: The Triggers, Stages, Functions, and Consequences of Prenegotiation," in Stein, J.G. (ed.) *Getting to the Table: The Process of International Prenegotiation*, The Johns Hopkins University Press, Baltimore, MD, pp. 239–268.

Stedman, S.J. (1991) *Peacemaking in Civil War: International Mediation in Zimbabwe, 1974–1980*, Lynne Rienner, Boulder, CO.

Stedman, S.J. (1997) "Spoiler Problems in Peace Processes," *International Security*, Vol. 22, No. 2, pp. 5–53.

Stewart, F. (2002) "Horizontal Inequalities: A Neglected Dimension of Development," *QEH Working Paper Series*, University of Oxford.

Strimling, A. (2006) "Stepping Out of the Tracks: Cooperation Between Official Diplomats and Private Facilitators," *International Negotiation*, Vol. 11, No. 1, pp. 91–127.

Surroi, V. (1996) "The Albanian National Question: The Post Dayton Pay-Off," *War Report*, No. 4, May.

Svensson, I. (2007) "Mediation with Muscles or Minds? Exploring Power Mediators and Pure Mediators in Civil Wars," *International Negotiation*, Vol. 12, No. 2, pp. 229–248.

Svensson, I. (2014) *International Mediation Bias and Peacemaking: Taking Sides in Civil Wars*, Routledge, London.

Svensson, I. and Wallensteen, P. (2010) *The Go-Between: Jan Eliasson and the Styles of Mediation*, United States Institute of Peace Press, Washington DC

Tago, A. (2005) "Determinants of Multilateralism in US Use of Force: State of Economy, Election Cycle, and Divided Government," *Journal of Peace Research*, Vol. 42, No. 5, pp. 585–604.

Themnér, L. and Wallensteen, P. (2014) "Armed Conflicts, 1946–2013," *Journal of Peace Research*, Vol. 51, No. 4, pp. 541–554.

Themnér, L. and Wallensteen, P. (2013) "Armed Conflicts, 1946–2012," *Journal of Peace Research*, Vol. 50, No. 4, pp. 509–521.

Thornton, T.P. (1985) "The Indo-Pakistan Conflict: Soviet Mediation at Tashkent 1966," in Touval, S. and Zartman, I.W. (eds) *International Mediation in Theory and Practice*, Westview, Boulder, CO.

Touval, S. (1975) "Biased Intermediaries: Theoretical and Historical Considerations," *Jerusalem Journal of International Affairs*, Vol. 1, No. 1, pp. 51–69.

Touval, S. (1992) "The Superpowers as Mediators" in Bercovitch, J. and Rubin, J.Z. (eds) *Mediation in International Relations*, St Martin's Press, New York, pp. 232–248.

Touval, S. (1994) "Why the UN Fails," *Foreign Affairs*, Vol. 73, No. 5, pp. 44–57.

Touval, S. (1996) "Lessons of Preventive Diplomacy in Yugoslavia," in Crocker, C.A., Hampson, F.O. and Aall, P. (eds) *Managing Global Chaos: Sources of and Responses to International Conflict*, United States Institute of Peace Press, Washington DC, pp. 403–417.

Touval, S. (2002) *Mediating the Yugoslav Wars: The Critical Years 1990–95*, Palgrave, New York.

Touval, S. (2010) "Negotiated Cooperation and its Alternatives," in Zartman, I.W. and Touval S. (eds) *Cooperation: The Extensions and Limits of International Multilateralism*, Cambridge University Press, New York, pp. 78–91.

Touval, S. and Zartman I.W. (1985) "International mediation: Conflict resolution and power politics," *Journal of Social Issues*, Vol. 41, No. 2, pp. 27–45.

Touval, S. and Zartman I.W. (1989) "Mediation in International Conflicts," in Kressel, K. and Pruitt, D.G. (eds) *Mediation Research: The Process and Effectiveness of Third Party Intervention*, Jossey-Bass, San Francisco, CA, pp. 115–137.

Touval, S. and Zartman I.W. (2006) "International Mediation in the Post-Cold War Era," in Crocker, C.A., Hampson, F.O. and Aall, P.R. (eds) *Turbulent Peace: The Challenges of Managing International Conflicts, United States Institute of Peace Press*, Washington DC, pp. 427–443.

Troebst, S. (1998) "Conflict in Kosovo: Failure of Prevention? An Analytical Documentation, 1992–1998," *ECMI Working Paper #1*, European Centre for Minority Issues, Flensburg.

Troika Proposal (2007) Troika Assessment of Negotiations: Principal Conclusions. Available online at: www.securitycouncilreport.org/atf/cf/%7B65BFCF9B-6D27-4E9C-8CD3-CF6E4FF96FF9%7D/Kosovo%20S2007%20723.pdf (accessed July 10, 2015).

UN Report on Sri Lanka (2012) *Report of the Secretary-General's International Review Panel on United Nations Action in Sri Lanka*, November, New York. Available online at: www.un.org/News/dh/infocus/Sri_Lanka/The_Internal_Review_Panel_report_on_Sri_Lanka.pdf (accessed December 15, 2014).

UN Charter (1945) *The Charter of the United Nations*. Available online at: www.un.org/en/documents/charter/index.shtml (accessed July 10, 2015).

USAID (2000) "USAID/Sri Lanka Country Strategy Paper 2001–2005". Available online at: http://pdf.usaid.gov/pdf_docs/PDABT334.pdf (accessed December 15, 2014).

Uyangoda, J. (2006) "Sri Lanka's Crisis: The Peace Process Wears Thin," *Polity,* Vol. 3, (1–2).

Uyangoda, J. (2007) "Ethnic Conflict in Sri Lanka: Changing Dynamics," *Policy Studies 32,* East-West Center. Available online at: www.eastwestcenter.org/fileadmin/stored/pdfs/PS032.pdf (accessed December 15, 2014).

Vesti (2012) *Nisam kriv što su Srbi izgubili Kosovo,* Interview with Maarti Ahtisaari, September 16. Available online at: www.vesti-online.com/Vesti/Srbija/254646/Nisam-ja-kriv-sto-su-Srbi-izgubili-Kosovo (accessed December 15, 2014).

Vuković, S. (2011) "Strategies and Bias in International Mediation," *Cooperation and Conflict,* Vol. 46, No. 1, pp. 113–119.

Vuković, S. (2012) "Coping with Complexity: Analysis of Cooperation and Coordination in Multiparty Mediation Processes," *International Negotiation,* Vol. 17. No. 2, pp. 265–293.

Vuković, S. (2014a) "International Mediation as a Distinct Form of Conflict Management," *International Journal of Conflict Management,* Vol. 25, No. 1, pp. 61–98.

Vuković, S. (2014b) "Three Degrees of Success in International Mediation," *Millennium Journal of International Studies,* Vol. 42, No. 3, pp. 966–976.

Walter, B.F. (1997) "The Critical Barrier to Civil War Settlement," *International Organization,* Vol. 51, No. 3, pp. 335–364.

Walter, B.F. (2004) "Does Conflict Beget Conflict? Explaining Recurring Civil War," *Journal of Peace Research,* Vol. 41, No. 3, pp. 371–388.

Weller, M. (1999) "The Rambouillet conference on Kosovo," *International Affairs,* Vol. 75, No. 2, pp. 211–251.

Werner, S. and Yuen, A. (2005) "Making and Keeping Peace," *International Organization,* Vol. 59, No. 2, pp. 261–292.

Whitefield, T. (2007) *Friends Indeed? The United Nations, Groups of Friends, and the Resolution of Conflict,* United States Institute of Peace Press: Washington DC

Whitefield, T. (2010) *External Actors in Mediation: Dilemmas and Options for Mediators,* Centre for Humanitarian Dialogue, Geneva, Switzerland.

Wilkenfeld, J., Young, K., Quinn, D. and Asal, V. (2005) *Mediating International Crises,* Routledge, New York.

Willigen, N. van (2009) *Building Sustainable Institutions? The Results of International Administration in Bosnia & Hezegovina and Kosovo,* Doctoral Dissertation, Leiden University.

Wood, B. (1991) "Preventing the vacuum: determinants of the Namibia settlement," *Journal of Southern African Studies,* Vol. 17, No. 4, pp. 742–769.

Wu, X. (2006) *Taipingyang shang bu Taiping (Turbulent Water: U.S. Asia-Pacific Security Strategy in the Post–Cold War),* Fudan University Press, Shanghai.

Yin, R.K. (2003) *Case Study Research: Design and Methods*, SAGE, London.

Young, O.R. (1972a) *The Intermediaries: Third Parties in International Crises*, Princeton University Press, Princeton, NJ.

Young, O.R. (1972b) "Intermediaries: Additional Thoughts on Third Parties," *Journal of Conflict Resolution*, Vol. 16, pp. 51–65.

Zartman, I.W. (1989a) *Ripe for Resolution: Conflict and Intervention in Africa*, Oxford University Press, New York.

Zartman, I.W. (1989b) "Prenegotiation: Phases and Functions," in Stein, J.G. (ed.) *Getting to the Table: The Process of International Prenegotiation*, The Johns Hopkins University Press, Baltimore, MD, pp. 1–17.

Zartman, I.W. (1995) "Negotiations in South Africa," in Zartman, I.W. (ed.) *Elusive Peace: Negotiating an End to Civil Wars*, Brookings Institute, Washington DC, pp. 147–174.

Zartman, I.W. (2001) "The Timing of Peace Initiatives: Hurting Stalemates and Ripe Moments," *The Global Review of Ethnopolitics*, Vol. 1, No. 1, pp. 8–18.

Zartman, I.W. (2008) "Introduction: Bias, Prenegotiation and Leverage in Mediation," *International Negotiation*, Vol. 13, No. 3, pp. 305–310.

Zartman, I.W. (2009) "Interest, Leverage and Public Opinion in Mediation," *International Negotiation*, Vol. 14, No. 1, pp. 1–5.

Zartman, I.W. (2010) "Cooperation and Conflict Management," in Zartman, I.W. and Touval, S. (eds) *Cooperation: The Extensions and Limits of International Multilateralism*, Cambridge University Press, New York, pp. 213–237.

Zartman, I.W. and Berman M.R. (1982) *The Practical Negotiator*, Yale University Press, New Haven, CT.

Zartman, I.W. and de Soto, A. (2010) *Timing Mediation Initiatives*, United States Institute of Peace Press, Washington DC

Zartman, I. W. and Touval S. (1996) "International Mediation in the Post-Cold War Era," in Crocker, C.A., Hampson, F.O. and Aall, P. (eds) *Managing Global Chaos: Sources of and Responses to International Conflict*, United States Institute of Peace Press, Washington DC, pp. 445–461.

Zartman, I. W. and Touval S. (2010) *Cooperation: The Extensions and Limits of International Multilateralism*, Cambridge University Press, New York.

Zimmermann, W. (1995) "The Last Ambassador: A Memoire of the Collapse of Yugoslavia", *Foreign Affairs*, Vol. 74, No. 2, pp. 2–20.

Index

For Product Safety Concerns and Information please contact our
EU representative GPSR@taylorandfrancis.com Taylor & Francis
Verlag GmbH, Kaufingerstraße 24, 80331 München, Germany